SUMMER HOLIDAYS: The paddle-steamer *Jeanie Deans*, in L.N.E.R. colours, approaching Dunoon Pier from the west. Note the bull's-eye signalling apparatus on the tower.

THE
FIRTH OF CLYDE

By

GEORGE BLAKE

COLLINS
ST JAMES'S PLACE, LONDON

FIRST IMPRESSION   JULY, 1952
SECOND IMPRESSION   JANUARY, 1954

PRINTED IN GREAT BRITAIN
COLLINS CLEAR-TYPE PRESS: LONDON AND GLASGOW

To the Memory
of the Boys of Form Senior V
Greenock Academy, 1909-1910
most of whom were killed
in the First War, 1914-1918

Forsitan et haec
olim meminisse juvabit

CONTENTS

Contents

ILLUSTRATIONS

Illustrations

Illustrations

Author's Note

PERHAPS a writer of novels, who has derived so much of his material and background (and his modicum of inspiration) from the scenery and activity of the Firth of Clyde, may be allowed to describe this work, however sentimentally, as a labour of love.

It is not the work of a duly qualified scientist nor that of a trained historian. It is not even the sort of writing that can serve as a guide-book for the tourist from day to day. I would rather think of it as something which the intelligent adventurer in Scotland might profitably read in advance of his visit ; perhaps better after the visit as a stimulus of emotion recollected in tranquillity. (It is my own experience of travel that the guide-book becomes rather more comprehensible after than before the exploration.) The special hope is that the general reader may find herein something worth reading at any time.

The Firth of Clyde is a very large expanse of water, and it quite fantastically indents the mainland of south-western Scotland. The gentle reader is therefore begged to keep an eye on the map as he reads, lest he misses one of those topographical subtleties that it is quite beyond the power of the pen to convey.

Being merely a writer, I have had recourse to the advice of specialists in scientific fields. Thus the concluding chapters on the Natural History of the Firth were contributed by several members of the staff of the Marine Station at Millport on the larger Isle of Cumbrae. The contributions of Dr. R. H.

Author's Note

Millar, Dr. David T. Gauld and Mr. H. T. Powell—only slightly revised to fit into the literary pattern—are duly acknowledged in the chapters for which they are so largely responsible.

In the important matter of the Clyde River Steamers I have enjoyed the unique and passionate advice of the Rev. William C. Galbraith of St. George's-in-the-Fields, Glasgow. The comparative tables of the costs of yacht-building and yacht-maintenance over the past 50 years or so are the work of an old friend, Mr. John A. Bain of the motor-yacht building firm of Silver's at Rosneath : a shrewd and informed observer of the estuarine scene.

None of these collaborators is in any way responsible for the opinions and generalisations so lavishly aired in the following pages.

GEORGE BLAKE.

Rhapsody by way
of Introduction to the Firth

THE train, suddenly gathering speed, began to race downhill from the uplands about Kilmacolm to sea level, a drop of some 350 feet in five miles or so. The line was precariously cut into the side of the hills that rose nearly sheer from a water's edge studded with the uprights and gantries of ship-yards, and it seemed to those who saw the carriages swaying down the incline and also to those who travelled in them that the 9.35 a.m. out of St. Enoch's must, like a spent rocket, hurtle at length into the sea : so vertiginous is the drop in that section of the old Glasgow and South-Western Railway system.

In one of the carriages of this train in a hurry two twelve-year-old boys, twins in fact, were so excited by the delirious passage downhill that, forgetting their mother's cautions, they rose from their seats and fought for pride of place at the window, rather rudely trampling the toes of their older sister, who sat demurely in the corner, reading one of her school prizes.

" Now, be careful, boys," Mama issued another warning, but tolerantly.

" They'll be all right," said Papa, who sat opposite his daughter. However, he tested the firmness of the door's lock and held the strap tightly.

The boys saw the sea below them. At their feet, as it seemed, a range of sandbanks stretched to the farther shore, and on the golden ridges lay the hulls of snub-nosed lighters, puffing steam mightily from their bulbous sides as the winches hauled in great buckets of sand ; and Papa explained that these comic craft would float on the next tide and, laden almost to the gunwales, puff away to the wharves of building contractors in half a dozen small harbours. The hills were low and green beyond the sandbanks, but then, twisting their necks to peer ahead, the Twins saw the stretch of deep-water anchorage men call the Tail of the Bank. They saw big ships at anchor there—a covey of tramp steamers and two liners : one with three black funnels and a black hull, the other with a single funnel painted red, with a white strip below a black top. Again Papa explained that the first was an Anchor liner —would it be the *Columbia* ?—bound for New York ; the other an Allan liner for the St. Lawrence and Canada.

" Too many people emigrating these days, unfortunately," he observed across the carriage to Mama. " And the best of our stock, too."

Mama agreed that this was a pity, but for the Twins it was remote and grown-up talk ; and they had discerned the small and graceful shape of a paddle-steamer, her funnel painted like that of the Allan liner, a plume of churned water behind her, crossing the upper Firth as if to meet their train's arrival.

" Oh, there's our boat, Papa ! " cried one, and the other added more cautiously : " Is that our boat, Papa ? "

Papa said No, but patiently. That was only the old *Lucy Ashton* on her forenoon ferry run from the North British terminal at Craigendoran to Greenock and then round the Gareloch piers. He added more impatiently :

" Better get back to your seats, boys. There will be plenty to see before the day's over. We're going into the tunnels now. Mama, you had better get your parcels ready."

The train crashed into the sulphurous mouth of the first of the tunnels so laboriously and expensively bored by Irish

OLD STAGER: The *Mercury* of the Glasgow and South Western Railway fleet heading eastwards for Princes Pier, Greenock, *circa* 1907: the entrance to Loch Long in the background.

SMALL CRAFT: Yachts of the Dragon class racing north-eastwards across the Tail of the Bank off Greenock towards Helensburgh.

COASTWISE LIGHT: The Cloch, innermost lighthouse of the Firth of Clyde: Strone Hill and the Holy Loch behind.

THE INNER FIRTH: The view eastwards from Castle Hill, Dunoon, towards Gourock: a modern turbine vessel, *Duchess of Hamilton*, at the pier.

navvies through the hard, igneous rock on which the upper, precipitous parts of the town of Greenock are built. It slowed down and then disappointingly stopped while tickets were collected at a small, dull station in a surprising break between tunnels. The Twins fidgeted but were silent, knowing that Papa's temper could be sharp and sudden when he was absorbed in the business of getting the family to the Coast.

The engine-whistle screamed at length, and the train jangled cautiously into the last of the series of tunnels. The sulphurous smoke imprisoned within that burrow seeped through the joints of the carriage windows and started up Mama's cough. Their sister held a fine handkerchief to her nose, the female gesture implying both disdain and disgust. The Twins, however, thought this passage through the bowels of the earth a novel, heroic and wholly delightful experience. It was a rising towards climax, and their eyes blinked when at length the 9.35 from St. Enoch's ran out between the engine-sheds to give them a brief glimpse of the shining Firth, within a stone's throw now and smelling weedily, and then slipped under the gables of the terminal station.

It was a bright Saturday morning of July, 1908, and the long train voided hundreds of people heading for three-score destinations up and down the long, indented coasts of the Firth of Clyde and its ramifying sea-lochs. The Twins, restless and adventurous, were momentarily engulfed in the torrent of adult humanity making urgently for the pier and the steamers. They were jostled ; they felt very small, and they were glad to see Papa shouldering his way through the tide to their rescue. He was angry.

" Will you two stop this nonsense and stay beside your mother and sister, or do you want your ears boxed ? Now, stay there till I go back and see about the luggage. There's plenty of time," he relented a little, suddenly remembering his own boyhood. " There's no need to get excited."

The Firth of Clyde

The Twins could discern that Papa was quite as excited as they were themselves, but they obeyed Papa, whose hand could be sudden and heavy. They fidgeted, but they did not move far from Mama's side and the little pile of personal baggage about her feet, and they wondered that their sister could, in such a glorious moment, still stand and read her rotten prize. Girls were asses. But Papa came striding down the platform, in good temper again, and said :

" That's all right. Yes, everything's there. Don't worry. Boys, take as much of that stuff as you can carry. Come along."

The young family of five moved in the tail of the procession making along the station platform for the steamers, and so down the ramp leading to the level of Princes Pier. The marine buildings were in a sort of Bavarian style, with deep eaves and tiled roofs and a clock on each of twin towers in brick ; they were smart in a carnival blend of cream and lime-green paints. To the twin boys from the city, however, these delicacies of maintenance could make no appeal. They were suddenly out in the salty open after a long autumn, winter and spring in Town. They were too young to record and catalogue the facts, but they felt in their nostrils the fresh, salty odours blown up-stream by a mild sou'-westerly breeze. They were aware of the bustle and colour and special character that inform all of mankind's dealings in tidal waters. It was all fresh, new and enchanting.

It seemed to those small boys of 1908 that a fleet of steamers lay against the pier. Your first sight was of a forest of gleaming, varnished masts and red-and-black funnels, with coloured pennants and flags fluttering against the northern sky. Then you were lost amid high mounds of luggage—pyramids made up of wicker baskets, tin trunks and the portmanteaux in which the decent people of the period packed the paraphernalia of a family's month-long holiday at the Coast—and you were frightened for a moment lest the boat go off without you ; and then there was Papa appearing round a corner of the pyramid of luggage and urging you towards the gangway.

" Plenty of time. Don't get excited. There's a long day before you."

It profoundly impressed his sons that Papa appeared to be the complete master of the intricate processes of embarkation and settling-down in a steamer. His first step was to secure three deck-chairs, with the arms of the railway company woven into the carpet seats, and these he arranged in a pleasant position in the lee of a deck-house. Having settled Mama and their daughter in these with their rugs, their reading matter and the paraphernalia of female travel, he led the boys to the forward sponson where, down a slide of broad and heavy planks, railway porters and deck-hands were loading luggage and perishable supplies for shopkeepers in the coastal townships. This deck cargo included even a very young Ayrshire calf, lambent-eyed and sewn up to the neck in a sack, but apparently resigned to a very strange fate.

The Twins were proud again when the ship's mate, supervising these operations, turned at the sound of Papa's greeting, smiled and raised a huge, work-worn hand to the peak of his cap.

" It's yourself again, mister ? " he said in his Highland way. " You've got a grand day for it. And these will be your boys ? Aye, your stuff iss all safe abaft the funnel. I saw it coming on and knew the way you liked it. But if you will excuse me . . ."

" Thank you, Mr. Maclachlan. I know you're busy."

Papa ushered the boys aft along the raised saloon deck. They had to thread their way down passages between rows of benches that were also unsinkable rafts, these passages sufficiently cluttered with deck-chairs and children who, just as excited but less carefully obedient than the Twins, must run

up and down, up and down, in the ecstasy of their release from
the urban streets into this paradise of free and open sea. Father
and sons leant over the rails above the after mooring-platform,
and the children were entranced to see the name of their ship,
P.S. *Mercury*, painted on a lifebelt lashed to the rails down
there : even more by the spectacle of a monstrous sea-gull,
milk-blue, perched on the gilt top of the jackstaff. Their
greatest wonder was that Papa could answer all the questions
about those river steamers that were the most absorbing
elements of this hour in their young lives.

This *Mercury* of theirs was a fine ship, built by Napier,
Shanks & Bell in 1892, Papa assured them. (They would see
for themselves the builder's plate below the ship's bell under
the bridge.) Yes, she was fast : probably capable of more than
17 knots. The smaller vessel lying astern was the *Glen Rosa*,
about to set off on the ferry service round the piers of the Holy
Loch run. She had done it once already that morning ; she
would do it three or four times before the setting of this bright
morning's sun. The steamer behind that again was the *Mars*,
and the Twins gathered that her high, built-up bows would
cleave the waters of Loch Long and take her passengers almost
into the heart of the West Highlands at Arrochar. But this
was only the 11 o'clock run. Already at nine the *Jupiter* had
set off for the Kyles of Bute and Arran, accompanied by the
Neptune for the open Firth and the port of Ayr, the latter
being the stout sister-ship of the *Mercury*. There would be
another big run outwards at three o'clock, another at five
o'clock ; and then there would be the late Saturday night run
at eight o'clock.

The Twins listened eagerly, nearly ecstatically, but it was
all very confusing : so many steamers making so many long
runs in the course of one summer's day, as if all the world were
bent on sailing on this northern waterway. They felt replete
with a richness of information and impressions ; they had

the feeling of having arrived in a world it would take them long to understand. As it chanced, their near-boredom with Papa's copious enthusiasms was broken by the approach downstream of still another passenger vessel that, paddling with a sort of halting gait, elaborately insinuated herself into the last available berth between the stern of the *Mars* and the sharp bow of the *Lucy Ashton*, lying far back in the North British berth.

" There's a funny old tub," observed the older by twenty minutes of the Twins.

She had enormously high paddle-boxes. Her funnel was rather like the *Lucy Ashton's*, except that the white band was subdivided by a thin ridge of black. She was so crowded with passengers that, as she approached the pier, the weight of their rush to the landward side gave her an alarming list to port. The noise of melodeons and rough singing from her foredeck drifted down to the ears of the more expensive travellers in the smarter railway steamers.

" The old *Edinburgh Castle* for Lochgoilhead. She leaves Glasgow about eight. Of course," Papa explained aloofly, " she's only an excursion steamer. Cheap fares and rather a rough crowd. But look at the time ! "

The thick hands of the clocks on the Bavarian towers of the marine station pointed to within a minute of the quarter before 11 o'clock.

" Come, boys, and we'll watch the engines starting."

So much was there to see, so many things were happening at once, a boy's mind was a welter of emotions, impressions and delights. These Twins were perhaps fortunate in being guided about this fascinating world by a patient and knowledgeable Papa. They could not know that sharper minds might see him as a limited, smug and complacent man of a privileged order of society ; still less easily could they have understood the more generous view of him as a man seeking to relive his boyhood in the enchantment of his sons. And here were the Engines, gleaming and smelling of oil !

Their brightness was entrancing, from the sheen on the great diagonals of polished steel to the glint on the burnished brass of grease-boxes. The darkness of the pit in which they were embedded, shot with red fire now and again as a furnace door was opened, fed and shut, was delightfully ominous. A battery of dials set into a board before the control-platform hinted at fascinating and complex mysteries of power. The younger twin, sensitive, wondered that an engineer in white overalls could sit smoking his pipe on a bench, his eyes only lazily watching the flicker of the needles.

The bells of the telegraph from the bridge suddenly rang out the warning call to Stand by Engines, and the hands on the largest dial swiftly traversed the arc from STOP to FULL SPEED AHEAD and back again. The engineer in white thrust the bowl of his pipe into a pocket of his overalls and rose to grasp two shining levers, one large and one small.

" That's us off now," said Papa.

The bells rang again. The hand on the dial swung into another arc. The engineer pulled back the large lever and ever so gently moved the smaller a notch or two forward. The great, smooth shoulders of the diagonals began to turn. The boys could hear the first slow churning of paddles and the drain of water between the floats.

" That's to get her nose canted out from the pier," Papa explained, " and to give the sailors time to get the hawsers inboard."

The bell rang again, and now it was STOP, and the younger twin had the sudden, awful feeling that the expedition was already ending in calamity and failure. Soon enough, however, the bright note rang through the engine-room once more, and the pointer moved to SLOW AHEAD. The heavy shoulders of the cranks started to turn again deliberately ; and then another clang suggested HALF SPEED AHEAD; and then, gaily, the bell rang and the hand on the dial simultaneously announced FULL SPEED AHEAD.

You could not take your eyes off those pounding shoulders of the diagonals, nor off the subtle movements of the timing-rods ; least of all off the solidly churning movements of the eccentrics. Then there was the little, separate engine that Papa described as the power unit of the steam steering-gear. It flew backwards and forwards in funny, spasmodic bursts of activity. Cascades of water roared and sluiced within the awful mystery of the paddle-boxes.

" Now," said Papa, " I think . . ."

But the Twins must now run to the mooring recess behind the port paddle-box and watch the water churned by the steamer's passage. There they were vaguely aware of Princes Pier slipping into the background, of the esplanade of Greenock unrolling like a strip of cinematograph film, but the boil of water from under the paddles almost wholly fascinated them. The older twin said it was lemonade and the younger, more justly, said it was ginger beer with that cream of froth upon it. They were in a fair way to quarrel, when Papa said firmly :

" That'll do, you two ! You're going to miss everything. Come with me, or I'll send you up to sit with Mama."

Somewhat impatiently, their father led the small boys forward along the port alleyway and over the hump of curved plating above the paddle-shaft, but he had to wait again while the children halted to consider another new-found wonder. This was the galley in which the cook with his high white hat, and in a hot and richly odorous atmosphere, a rag about his neck, worked angrily with his pots, pans and ovens. It was almost equally fascinating that, in an alcove opposite the galley door, a pale youth sat peeling enough potatoes to fill a large tub. The Twins goggled at these remarkable sights, and they were greatly stirred when the sweating cook turned to catch sight of their peering faces and winked broadly, asking :

" Does yer mither ken you're oot ? "

This trope in the *patois* of Clydeside they only vaguely comprehended, and it was much more serious to hear Papa's voice, the edge of anger in it now.

" Are you two never coming ? You're going to miss the best of it."

Yet something of that brief passage below deck-level was to remain with them for the rest of their lives as memorable. It was perhaps just that this one small ship on a northern estuary had its own *smell*. Such a little thing, but so immemorially redolent !

It had affected them as they came on board. It was at first a curious conflict of tarry odours from ropes and the seams of the shining decks with the sulphurous whiff of bunker coal from the funnel, but with undertones of richer flavours in it. Now, as they followed Papa up the forward companionway to the fore-deck, they knew, and as if it were really important, that the odours of hot oil from the engine-room and of boiling soup and simmering joints from the galley, with salty essences from the bilges and the scudding seas overside, contributed to the unique symphony. This was the smell of the *Mercury* : a variant of the smell of every passenger vessel that ever ploughed the seas.

Their emergence from the gloom of the lower deck had at first a blinding effect, so bright the July sun, so full of glancing colour the scenery and traffic of the Firth. They saw that the small fleet which had lain so quietly at Princes Pier, red-and-black funnels above french-grey hulls, had dispersed and was now racing in single numbers towards various points North of West. As the *Mercury* came abreast of Gourock Pier three lithe ships with yellow funnels detached themselves from that whale-like length of wharf and joined in the race. Over against the green peninsula of Rosneath, red, white and black funnels of the North British steamers scudded urgently. You had the notion of three separate flights of arrows speeding towards three targets.

" It's like a race ! " cried the younger Twin.

" It often is," said Papa, smiling out of superior knowledge. "Just watch the *Mars* and the *Talisman* racing for Kilcreggan. And there's the *Duchess of Fife* coming up behind us. There'll be a nice scramble for first place at Kirn."

" I'll bet we'll beat that old Caley tub," asserted the older Twin brashly.

" I wouldn't say that," Papa demurred. " Those Caledonian boats are very smart. There's nothing in it between the *Mercury* and the *Fife*. But look now, boys . . ."

The ship had already made so far across the upper estuary as to have opened up the view down the Firth proper. The ragged frieze of the Cowal hills towards which they were heading was splendid enough, but the prospect south-westwards towards the open sea had in it the luminous and foreshortened quality of a dream. When the younger Twin, the sensitive one, was older and had taken to reading poetry, this coloured picture seen in childhood slipped like a lantern slide across the screen of inner vision as he read or remembered the lines about the magic casements and the perilous seas in faery lands forlorn.

The picture was framed as it were between the white pillars of the Cloch lighthouse on the southern shore and of Toward farther down on the northern. A barrier of low islands, the two Cumbraes and Bute, lay like a breakwater between Inner and Outer Firth, but the vast and tempestuous extent of the latter was explicitly suggested by the seeming remoteness of Arran's leonine peaks. If that were not enough to suggest the vastness of this inland sea, the volcanic cone of Ailsa Craig, fully 40 miles away, loomed blue through the slight haze of the July morning.

The Firth of Clyde

While the little ships of the pleasure fleet held to the northern shores of the estuary the main shipping lane over towards the Renfrewshire coast carried its quota of deep-water traffic. Papa identified for his boys one of Sloan's coasting vessels coming in from the Bristol Channel, a lighter puffing outwards with a load of coal for one of the Inner Hebrides, a red hopper-barge of the fleet that endlessly carries the sludge endlessly dredged from the Ship-Channel of the Clyde out to be dumped in deep water by the Garroch Heads, a destroyer on trials from one of the up-river yards, and a large cargo vessel inward-bound that Papa thought—though he wouldn't like to be sure—was a Lamport & Holt ship from South American ports. The Twins, however, were specially entranced to see that the expanse of waters was dotted with the white sails over frail hulls of coveys of racing yachts.

" The Clyde Fortnight, of course," Papa explained, as if his sons should have known. " Come over to this side and you'll see something worth seeing. The big chaps should be starting about now."

Many of their fellow-passengers were already crowded in the bay before the forward paddle-box, but Papa's address and the tenderness of a British crowd for children allowed the Twins to clamber to a point of vantage almost under the bridge-ladder. They were faintly alarmed up there, for the ship was tipping over with the weight of passengers on one side, and then she slackened speed and almost stopped.

" That's quite all right, boys," Papa assured them. " A ship under power must always give way to a ship under sail, and you'd never find a Clyde skipper spoiling a good race. Look ! Here they come."

The Twins were confused by this admonition, but their willing eyes followed the mass inclination of the crowd about them ; and they had a sudden glimpse of beauty in vivid action. The *Mercury's* skipper had deftly turned his ship's head to port, and there surged past the grey hull, racing neck-and-neck, two great yachts making on the starboard tack for the mark-buoy off Inverkip on the Renfrewshire shore. The shadows cast by their pyramidal canvas darkened the paddle-steamer's decks for a space, but the younger Twin observed that the light filtered through those bellowing sheets was the colour of a ripe peach. The older Twin saw how the crews of these great racing-machines lay face-down like so many corpses on the decks, heads towards the weather rails, but understood the dynamics of the technique. Both heard the surging noises of great yachts crashing through brisk seas ; both saw the sparkling perfection of their fittings, the blonde sheen of holystoned decks, the loveliness of a cutter's lines—some 90 feet along the water-line, Papa told them afterwards.

It had been a glimpse of a special sort of splendour, and his sons were slightly bored when Papa said, with his faint air of patronage and as the *Mercury* started up to take her turn at Kirn pier :

" Well, that was something worth seeing, wasn't it ? The green boat was *Shamrock*—Sir Thomas Lipton's, you know ; the white one was *White Heather*. That's the *Erin* lying off Hunter's Quay—Tommy Lipton's steam-yacht."

The Twins dutifully considered that lovely white shape : fiddle-bowed, yellow-funnelled, sitting the water like a swan.

" There'll be a crew of nearly thirty men in that ship," said Papa thoughtfully. " It must cost a mint of money. But here we are at Kirn."

The *Mercury* was featly laid alongside the wooden pier and quickly warped against it by the power of her own steam-capstan aft. A number of their fellow-passengers disembarked, the womenfolk among them waving ecstatically as they crossed the gangway to equally ecstatic female relatives on the landing-stage : so happy did most people seem to be on this day of popular holiday and escape. A dim traveller in fancy goods, stooping with the weight of the cases he carried, and the call wrapped up to the neck in the sugar bag, seemed alone in a faint, bewildered melancholy. Of Kirn the Twins took only a dim general impression—of a parish church in red sandstone, of an esplanade very much like any other esplanade—sandstone villas and painted boarding-houses in a riparian ribbon, with many other villas among trees covering the steep slopes behind. The eye of childhood is microscopic rather than comprehensive. These two children retained on the whole only the general impression that its pier buildings oddly echoed in miniature the Bavarian *motif* of Princes Pier. They were more interested in the lick of waves over the smooth rocks under these buildings —fangs of green breaking into white over an evangelical exhortation painted upon them in large, crude letters. This told those little boys that

CHRIST
DIED FOR YOUR
SINS

The bells rang below. The paddles started to splash. The ship moved forward.

" Now for Dunoon," said Papa, as if he were announcing the approach of a special grandeur.

In that very moment the Twins heard for the first time the blast of gay and brassy music, an agreeable noise issuing from somewhere near where Mama and their sister were sitting with their books and newspapers. They sped aft to see what new marvel had come into their lives, and they hardly heeded Papa's bland explanation :

" Ah ! The German Band."

Eight men stood in a circle, playing a somewhat sluggish version of the *El Capitan* march on various brass and woodwind instruments, and a sensitive ear might have likened the general effect to that of a braying of asses. Three of the group were men of middle-age or more, thickly bespectacled, and the rest, who might have been their sons or nephews, were fair and lumpish youths of serious mien. These were clearly harmless and earnest men, and it was the enchanting rumour of the period that they were good creatures escaping the horrors of conscription under that Kaiser of theirs. They were, in fact, Saxons so lacking in purchasing power at home that they found in the four months' tour of duty on the Clyde steamers the best part of their annual income. Probably the younger among them were good German soldiers ; probably they all died dutifully on the Western Front in due course. They could not even now shed the Teutonic fondness for a quasi-military uniform.

The Twins stood and stared, enchanted. This music of the German Band was what they liked. They were fascinated to see how quickly one of the cornet-players, a tiny man with a squint behind one of his convex lenses, peeled off from the ring and, his instrument under his arm, cruised round the saloon deck, chinking a money-bag in black velvet. It was gratifying to the boys that Papa, though with a faintly ostentatious gesture of tolerant contempt, dropped a sixpennybit into it and received a sonorous *Danke schon, mein Herr*, from the collector.

The *Mercury* came in against the long length of Dunoon Pier, and still the German Band played away, splendidly advertising the ship's importance. Papa would have the Twins look at Dunoon from the sea and observe the Castle Gardens and Highland Mary's Monument on the Castle Hill, but his sons saw not much more than a statuette on an eminence near the pier and, amid the dark gardens, the grey shape of a dull mansion in the Victorian Gothic style. They did see that the pier and the broad promenade ashore were cluttered with human beings whom Papa, quite innocently and in the idiom of his period, described as " rather common people, I'm afraid. This is a wonderful change for them." The Twins remained more fascinated by the German Band and by the fact that the *Mercury*, leaving Dunoon, must circumvent a reef of rocks surmounted by a navigation light on a slender white pillar. It was all the more interesting when Papa described this sea-mark as The Gantocks—a name that seemed almost to smell of the sea and the sea-birds that barked and cackled endlessly above the spines of rock.

The bells rang below. The paddles began to turn. The German Band struck up the blameless air of *Sobre les Olas*. The *Mercury* swung to round The Gantocks, the high, black nose of the *Duchess of Fife* cutting through her frothy track less than fifty yards astern.

" There may be a race in it for Innellan," said Papa. " But just look at those idiots ! "

His contemptuous arm indicated the clutter of hired rowing-boats on the waters of the West Bay of Dunoon. Here, indeed, a comic regatta seemed to be in progress. Even the young boys could see that few in these varnished skiffs had a glimmering of how a tiny craft should be handled by oar. The merrymakers in that fortunate sheet of sheltered water committed in mass every conceivable sin of boat-management. The catching of crabs was the least of it. The oarsmen would not look where they were going. If there were girls in the sternsheets, all the wilder the efforts of the young men on the thwarts : the eternal male effort to be funny for the girls' sake. Pairs of rowers, wildly skying their oars, brought them down in a syncopation that wasted more than half the joint effort. Boats collided to a chorus of guffaws. Boats were rowed hard on to the hard outliers of The Gantocks. One adventurous craft in charge of two loutish youths, and down by the bows, was saved from destruction by the skill of the *Mercury's* captain ; the edge of the starboard paddle-box missed it by a yard, and it corkscrewed helplessly along the ship's side and in its speeding wake.

" Clumsy louts ! " cried Papa. " Wonder more of them aren't drowned."

Now, however, the ship came abreast of The Gantocks, and the Twins were held for a space by that mystery which seems to brood over all small islands, even in the fairway of a busy steamer track. This reef of rocks was so alone, so aloof ; it belonged, not to humanity, but to the tides and the gulls. The younger boy at least would have looked back on it long enough, but Papa was now pointing out a landmark—the gleaming face of a quarry that had been cut and blasted into the face of the steep hill a mile or two west of Dunoon. On the steep, sheer face of the disused workings was painted in enormous white letters the legend

DUNN'S
SAUSAGES ARE THE
BEST

The Twins rocked with laughter to see this trope, and Papa was very well pleased with his own powers as a guide.

" Everybody laughs at that. Pretty smart bit of advertising, eh ? " he observed, adding carefully, " but rather vulgar, perhaps."

The Twins failed to take this point. They still thought the sausage advertisement was jolly funny, and they stared at the large letters entranced until a drumming of paddles sounded loud on the other side and Papa cried :

" Look, boys ! There's the *Fife* coming up. It's what I said—a race."

The bow of the yellow-funnelled ship had crept up until it was abreast of the *Mercury's* red funnel and threatened to shoot beyond it. Heat from eagerly-stoked furnaces was turning the yellow wash to an angry orange. The Twins were sad to see their own ship outstripped.

" She's going to beat us," wailed the older boy, and his brother knew that this observation might have come on a sob.

" No, she's not," Papa assured them grandly. " You'll see us putting on speed in a tick. There she goes. Feel the vibration ? There's hardly a yard in it in a mile between these two. Besides, we've got the inside berth."

In their desperate and partisan concern the boys did not take the meaning of this technicality. They hung over the port rails, watching that ominously sharp bow of their rival ; the black hull with the green bottom slipped all too easily through the seas. It did not fall behind ; and if it did not gain, it could not be shaken off. While the lovely Cowal shore streaked past on the other side, a shore dotted with the fantastic villas of the rich, the Twins had their eyes fixed on this damnable and menacing enemy. They ceased to listen to Papa's comments on the struggle. Their ears were filled with the thunder of competing paddles.

" Come on out of there, sonnies," urged a rough voice from behind. " Go and stand amidships."

It was the voice of the first mate who, assisted by a grizzled deck-hand, was clearing the sponsons on that port side of the *Mercury* and rigging ropes to confine the curious passengers to the inner area of the deck. A touch of Papa's fingers on their shoulders brought the Twins unhappily from their position by the rails.

" They're trimming the ship," he explained. " You see, if everybody runs over to that side to watch the *Fife*, our ship goes over on her beam-ends and loses speed. The port paddle digs too deep, and the other is only half-hitting the water."

Papa was now saying something of vital and immediate

THE GARELOCH: Motor yachts at moorings off Rosneath. In the distance, Loch Long intervening, the peaks of the " Duke of Argyll's Bowling Green " in Cowal.

THE GARELOCH: Another yacht anchorage at Rhu, looking south-east towards industrial Greenock on the Renfrewshire shore.

Loch Long: The view towards The Cobbler, 2891 feet, from the road along the eastern shore below Arrochar.

Through The Narrows: The Kyles of Bute from above Colintraive. A paddle-steamer heads towards Tighnabruaich and so down the western arm of the straits, between the Island of Bute, left, and the mainland.

interest ; and a returning wave of respect for his wisdom and knowledge came over his sons. Kindly adult hands helped them to a position of vantage on the funnel casing, and Papa smiled in his proprietorial pride of parenthood, pleased that his little boys in their Sunday kilts of Robertson tartan and their neat tweed jackets should be so agreeably favoured. The Twins, meanwhile, could not keep their eyes off that beastly *Duchess of Fife*, and the younger one thought to see her falling behind.

" We're winning, Papa ! " he cried. " Look ! She's away behind us now."

The middle-aged women about the child smiled tolerantly, all of them in love with the innocence of young boyhood, and Papa smiled with something of the smugness of one who produces a successful act by performing seals.

" I told you we were bound to win," he declared, and a little for the benefit of those who admired the boys. " We've got the inside berth. Just watch the signals on the pier."

The young eyes concentrated on three black discs, like bull's-eyes on targets, that were set into the wall of a sort of penthouse on top of the shed at the pier's seaward end. They saw the piermaster move to the base of this erection, consider the advance of the approaching steamers, and pull at a chain. They saw the innermost of the three bull's-eyes turn to white —as if the whole apparatus possessed a sub-human consciousness of its own.

" So we get in first," observed Papa with some self-satisfaction. " That's what I meant by the advantage of the inside berth."

" But I don't understand, Papa," protested the younger, intelligent Twin.

" Silly ass ! " cried his brother, but Papa went on patiently.

" Surely you can see for yourself. The *Fife* was always a little behind us. If she had got the signal to go in first, she'd

have had to cross our bows. We should have had to go Full
Speed Astern to let her in. There might have been a collision.
Surely that's obvious."

" Yes, Papa," agreed the younger boy, but without
conviction.

" And this is Innellan," said Papa.

The Twins got the impression of a township much smaller
and more widely dispersed than the quite solid community
made up by Kirn and Dunoon together. Here were no
esplanade, no Castle Gardens, no bandstands. There were
many solid villas along the road by the shore, and all sorts of
smaller villas in sandstone clung to the steep slopes above the
pier, but it was as if Innellan were a rather unhappy outpost
of Lowland industrialism in a Highland setting ; as if, on that
short stretch of coast between Dunoon and Innellan, Waddell's
Sausages intervening, a subtle boundary between two cultures
had insinuated itself.

Another batch of passengers got off at Innellan Pier,
awkwardly handling their personal luggage, effusively greeted
as visitants from another world by settled friends ashore.
Obviously English and mainly female, fantastically arrayed as
to outer garments against the legendary rigours of Scottish
weather, a smaller batch of people boarded the *Mercury*, bound
on some tour neatly arranged by a travel agency. The bells
rang again in the engine-room below. The paddles clawed at
the green waters of the Firth. The *Mercury* moved ahead
towards the slim pillar of the Toward lighthouse, the knobbly
outlines of Bute and the Cumbraes and, beyond these mild
silhouettes, the splendid frenzy of the Arran peaks.

" We're not going quite so far as that," allowed Papa in
answer to his younger son's ecstatic question. " We go round
the corner by the Toward Light there, into Rothesay Bay, and
then up the Kyles. Look at the map . . . That'll do you,
now ; that's quite enough ! . . . Come, and we'll get Mama

34

down to dinner. Of course," he added, " I booked our places
for the First Service."

He was a remarkable Papa. In contrast, Mama and their
sister seemed to the Twins astonishingly impervious to the
excitements of their own day. The sister still sat in her deck-
chair, frowning over her rotten prize ; the *Mercury* had beaten
the *Fife* in vain so far as she was concerned. Mama, the
Glasgow Herald over her knees, slept amid the clamour of the
steamer's progress and traffic ; and the young boys could not
take into the balance of affairs the fact that a woman in the
middle years of life, after packing until one in the morning,
had been up again at five to get them all off to the Coast.
Then, of course, Mama and her daughter must make a great
business of folding their wraps and so disposing their goods
that they could at once call the deck-chairs their own to the
end of the voyage and still leave nothing of real value to
establish the claim.

" Well, when you're ready, whenever that may be . . ."
Papa was impatient.

" We're hurrying as fast as we can," retorted Mama with
some asperity.

Papa led his family down the after companionway to the
level of the engine-room, and then Mama was taken with what
seemed to her sons an irrelevant and irritating notion.

" I think we'll . . ." she said on behalf of herself and her
daughter and pointed to a sign that said LADIES' TOILET.

" Well, don't be all day about it," remarked Papa. " We're
late enough as it is."

The Twins were quite happy to roam the levels of the
engine-room, dodging into the mooring platforms behind the
paddle-boxes to see, on one side, the far green hills of Renfrewshire and Ayrshire and, on the other, the peaks of Argyll
behind the white pillar of the Toward Light. A chap could
always go and, hanging over the rails of burnished steel, watch

the diagonals and eccentrics perform their countless revolutions. At length, however, they were sharply summoned by Papa to follow him and Mama to the Dining Saloon.

The family made its way down still another companionway into the very bowels of the ship. The Twins were entranced to see that the churned waters from underneath the paddles flicked and spat along the line of scuttles that, as they sat down to table, were high above their young heads. They were going to eat under water-level. They were, as it were, in a submarine.

The Chief Steward, in a sort of Eton jacket but with a dirty shirt-front, waved Papa to the head of one of the long tables.

" Kept it special for you, sir," he explained with a sort of greasy anxiety, " but "—and here he winked to the Twins— " better late than never. Now, what's it to be. There's the Scotch Broth. These bairns'll be needin' the broth. Sticks to yer ribs, eh ? " And again he winked to the bewildered Twins. " Then there's a rare gigot of Canterbury lamb—or would the Missus like a slice or two of cold boiled ham with salad and pickles an' that ? "

The Twins thought that Papa dealt with this familiar person both tolerantly and firmly. He made up the family order and transmitted it to the Chief Steward with a nice air of aloofness.

" Quite a character, Macrae," Papa allowed, when the Chief Steward had departed with the order. " Takes a few liberties, perhaps, but he's been on this run ever since I can remember."

" I wish," said Mama sharply, " that he wouldn't breathe beer down my neck."

" Ah, that's the real old Clyde hand, I'm afraid," demurred Papa blandly. " And that reminds me. What would you all like to drink ? "

Introduction to the Firth

What would they have to drink ! The Twins discerned that, even for Papa, the occasion was far out of the ordinary ; it was to be convivial, the familiar disciplines quite relaxed. The older Twin plumped like his sister for ginger beer, but the younger, a romantic, chose kola. Mama thought she would have a small bottle of cider, and when the Chief Steward came with the steaming plates of soup, Papa blandly conveyed the family order, saying that for himself he would have a nip of whisky to begin with—" The special, Macrae, of course "— and, to go with the meal, a bottle of Bass's beer. The soup breathed the odours of mutton bones, diced vegetables, green peas and onion—that flavour so much richer than the stench of engine oils it had competed with in the port alleyway.

" Tuck in, my dears, tuck in," Papa exhorted them.

Then there were the thick slices of Canterbury lamb for four, with boiled new potatoes fresh from the red fields of Ayrshire and white new turnip with a white sauce. The Twins wondered that Papa should choose from a long list called Cold Table a plate of ham and tongue with, at the Chief Steward's suggestion, a morsel of cold roast pork " to give it a bit gamey flavour, like." It was even more remarkable to these small boys that Papa should reject Queen of Puddings and Tapioca and Stewed Plums in favour of Biscuits and Cheese.

The *Mercury* had in the meantime slowed down and stopped at a pier, and the Twins fidgeted to be on their feet and run up on deck and see what was happening now.

" Sit down, you two ! " Papa commanded them quite angrily. " This is only Craigmore. A cup of coffee with me, Mama ? "

They had to sit as still as possible on the swivel chairs much too large for them and be good boys ; there was no escape with Papa in this munificent mood. Within just a few minutes after the departure from Craigmore the bell in the

37

engine-room rang again and again in a series of orders from the bridge, and the ship came to halt once more. The boys could hear the gangways run out and the tramp of departing feet on the maindeck above ; they also heard the ringing of a bell on the quay and a voice plangently declaiming irregular but powerful couplets of rude verse, such as

> *Ere ye again see Edinburgh Rock*
> *Ye'll buy a sprig from Heather Jock.*

Or

> *Where'er ye sail, where'er ye walk,*
> *Ye'll still buy a bunch from Heather Jock.*

A mighty confusion of voices on a busy pier, a great backing of horses and the objurgations of their tenders, the ring of bells from other steamers, a burst of communal song and its sequence of catcalls, the faint strains of a brass band playing in some distant bandstand on shore—the alluring welter of noise above had the Twins fidgeting again.

"Rothesay," announced Papa, picking a cigar from one box of four held before him by the Chief Steward and rolling it at his ear to hear the crackle of the leaf. "Heather Jock and the Pointing Porters. But you'll see plenty of Rothesay before the holidays are over. Rather a rough place just now. Greenock Fair, you know."

He did not understand, this self-possessed, slow-moving Papa of theirs. They had eaten ; the coloured world outside and above was going to waste.

The bells rang again in the engine-room. The *Mercury* stirred to the dig of her paddles. Papa called for the bill, and the younger Twin saw when it came that the meal and the refreshments for five had cost the huge sum of sixteen shillings and three pence. It was all the more staggering to see Papa slip a florin into the Chief Steward's palm. He must be a very rich man, thought his younger son.

Before the boys reached the freedom and light of the deck again the *Mercury* had stopped at and departed from still another pier—" Port Bannatyne," explained Papa dismissively —and was running out of a small brother, as it were, of Rothesay Bay, close inshore to a reach of rather bleak farming land and towards a point, on which stood the gaunt sheds of a slipdock.

They saw that the scene was dramatically changing in character, becoming wilder and lonelier. Far over on the other side opposite Rothesay the hillsides seemed fair and wooded, but to the westward of that stretch of the lands of Toward there loomed the mouths of lochs, somehow dark and portentous even on this bright July day. It was like arriving in Norway. The *Mercury* began to turn into the nearest opening among the hills.

" Ardmaleish," said Papa curtly, indicating the point on which stood the bald sheds. " Quite a place for yacht-building and so on. That's the mouth of Loch Striven over there, ahead. A gloomy sort of place ; nobody goes near it nowadays. But now, boys," he announced as the *Mercury* swung round the point of Ardmaleish, and as if he were producing a rabbit out of a hat, " there are the Kyles of Bute ! "

With the literalism of childhood the Twins looked about them for objects that could be identified as belonging to this curiously-named order of things. They thought it might be a number of rocks in the sea, even if they had known the phrase from infancy ; or a range of high and strange pillars on shore, or a horde of monstrous animals. They saw themselves looking forwards up a strait, the green, low hills of the island of Bute on one side and the high, furrowed hills of the Argyllshire mainland on the other, with less than a mile of tidal water between them. It seemed to the younger Twin that they were running into a blind alley, so firmly did this channel appear to be blocked by the rise of sheer mountains at the farther end. He said so, and Papa explained.

" No, no ! Don't you see ? The Kyles are simply the two channels between the mainland and Bute. It's like a canal between the two. The topmost end of Bute pokes its nose into the mainland. We're running up this arm of the Kyles a little North of due West. Soon we'll be running down the other almost due South. Look at the map. People," added Papa grandly, " travel a long way to see the Kyles of Bute."

The Twins were quite sure that Papa was all-wise in these matters, but they did not trouble to follow the niceties of his grown-up discourse. Past a little, lone kirk on the shore of this fjord, under mountainy farms perched high on the mainland hillsides, the *Mercury* was speeding towards a wooden pier which, beyond a short range of sandstone villas that looked decidedly lost in this sub-Highland setting, jutted out from an unexpected patch of sandy shore. They saw a white farmhouse perched on the hillside, as it were on a terrace of its own, directly above this pier. They were vaguely aware that another blob of white buildings among trees to the right might be a country hotel. They were more interested to perceive, however dimly, that they had passed from the civilised expanses of the Firth proper into quite another, and that a foreign sort of province.

Here above the narrow kyle the hills were steep and high, the skyline as seen from sea-level serrated ominously with the V-shaped channels of mountain streams. At the same time, the lower slopes of this West Highland countryside had a cosiness of their own, with thickets of hazel and scrub oak hanging over the bald rocks above high-water mark itself. On the westward side of the pier the shore took a sweet, short curve to form a little bay, and in this pleasant harbour under the hills lay a fleet of yachts at moorings. The younger Twin, at least, his chin on the rail before the *Mercury's* starboard sponson, doted on the loveliness of those floating shapes : the adorably curved bows, the painted hulls, the high, varnished masts of the small craft. His brother noted how many youngish men in yachting caps, reefer jackets, grey flannel trousers and rubber-soled shoes crossed the gangway on to the pier and so down the sandy road towards the hamlet.

" Colintraive," announced Papa. " A very nice place. See all these yachts in the bay ? Dozens of city men keep them down here ; lets them get farther afield at the week-end. But they can still get the seven o'clock steamer on Monday morning and be back in town in time for business by nine. Wonderful service ! "

The bells rang once more in the bowels of the *Mercury*. The bow-rope was cast off, and the ship canted on the fulcrum of the stern-rope to point her sharp nose outwards from the creaking timbers of the pier. Anon she sped forwards, her wash rocking the lovely yachts, towards a range of low-lying reefs that seemed to block the channel. The younger Twin, despairing, thought himself to be in danger of shipwreck.

" Now, look out, you two ! " said Papa. " We're going through the Narrows. This is quite a sight."

The ship was making, as it seemed, to pass between two light-pillars, so closely marking a narrow channel between islands that they might have been the goalposts in a game of football. The younger Twin, the sensitive one, thought (and hoped) that the captain on the bridge would tug at the brass handle of the engine-room telegraph and go cautiously through this hazard. But the *Mercury* blazed on. The green tide, luminous in aeration, swirled about the sea-marks ; there were so few feet to spare on either side that the taking of the hazard was almost sickening. And then, *presto* ! the little ship was through the needle's eye and, in a wide and easy arc, turning through some forty points of the compass to swing South of West down the outermost arm of the Kyles : broader and somehow kindlier than the shorter arm behind the Burnt Islands. She ran into the eye of the sun, its light gentle on hillsides, islands, peaks and all the wonder of the Firth beyond.

Now the hills above the fjord appeared to be higher, steeper, rougher and balder than they had been on the other side of the Burnt Islands. At the same time the setting was of that sort of enclosed, gothic prettiness you might more readily expect to find in Switzerland or even Italy ; somehow, it was at once rough and cosy, gnarled and pretty.

Above another gaunt pier in the dark roots of the hills stood, rather like a fortalice, an hotel with a battlemented terrace above the tides.

" Ormidale," said Papa dismissively. " This little loch is Loch Riddon. Not much of it, as you can see, and it dries out quite a bit at low tides. I really can't think it pays to call here."

In fact, two persons and a few parcels of groceries were put ashore before the *Mercury* swept in a tight circle about the head of the small loch and made back towards the Kyles proper. The Twins were fascinated to see, on their right as they came out of Loch Riddon, a wooded and rocky islet standing out from the point to starboard. It formed against the mainland a snug and lovely little harbour in which lay a motor-yacht, no doubt attached to the mansionhouse under the mainland hills. For the younger Twin again this scene held a quality of romance in the Italian mode, but Papa could always explain everything away.

" Glen Caladh. A very fine property. Belongs to the Clarks. Not the Paisley thread family. Big people in paint and varnishes, actually. Now, boys, look out for the Maids of Bute ! "

The gaze of these two young boys was thus directed towards

the steep and rugged shores of the Island of Bute that, on their left, formed the eastern bank of the western kyle. It was a harsh hillside, falling steeply from a considerable peak to the sea in terraces of heather and fallen rocks. Among the latter, conically up-ended on an otherwise dull hillside, were two twin rocks that somebody had once seen fit to paint crudely in the semblance of the traditional Welsh peasant woman— black conical hat, white petticoat, red gown.

" Now there," said Papa with pride, " are the Maids of Bute ! "

The younger Twin was grievously disappointed in the reality of a legend. In his subtle young eyes the Maids lacked life and even the verisimilitude of art. The child dimly perceived that the Maids of Bute were without the provenance of historical relics and were no doubt the sports of a bucolic joke, endlessly sustained. He tried to say as much, but Papa was brusque, declaring sharply :

" That's quite enough of that. The Maids have been there as long as I can remember. Now, run away to your mother and be ready to help her with the small pieces. We'll be at Tighnabruaich in a few minutes."

Tighnabruaich. The House on the Brow of the Hill. It lay under the scarp on the northern side of the western kyle, still taking its meed of the light and warmth of the westering sun. The young boys saw it vaguely as another loose aggregation of white cottages and stone-built villas in the crook of a shallow bay that harboured yachts, but they were promptly overwhelmed in the business of disembarkation. Sharing the burden of Mama's numerous small parcels, they watched Papa masterfully organise the heavy luggage from ship to pier and supervise its loading on to a horse-drawn lorry that waited there. Their male parent returned to his family at length with a satisfied smile.

" Well, that's that," he announced. " MacCallum promises

to have the heavy stuff up in twenty minutes. Got everything, boys ? *Don't* trail that mackintosh in the dust, Ian ! Come."

The middle-class family of 1908 marched up the spine of the pier. Papa paid the proper dues at the turnstile and the young boys stood at length on the soil of Argyllshire—and it might have been that of Brittany, so far from home did they now feel. They all walked along a sandy and rutted shore road to the furnished villa that was to be their home for a month—and it might have been for a year. The landlady, who was to retire for the season into a tarred hut at the back, had a kettle boiling and tea about to be infused ; on the deal table in the kitchen lay the stores Mama had instructed her to order in advance. The lorry came up the gravelled drive at length, the heavy luggage was carried into the hall, and Papa handed out tips to the driver and his mate. Soon enough the Twins were changed out of their Sunday kilts into knicker-bockers and sandshoes and told to go and play on the rocks by the shore.

" Look out for those bicycles on the road, dears," Mama pleaded anxiously, " and don't get your feet wet."

" No larking now, boys," Papa enjoined less tolerantly. " And don't get caught in the wash of the steamers. The waves they throw up are a good deal bigger than you would expect."

They were free. They were suddenly at liberty to play on a foreign shore, and they could not understand why their sister chose to carry a deck-cháir on to the lawn and lose herself again in her rotten book. There were pools on the rocks, translucent and strangely inhabited by small crabs, strangely decorated with weeds and sea-anemones like blobs of red currant jelly. They discovered and collected flat corks that had broken adrift from fishing nets and bright stones they thought must be precious. Anon the young boys dallied along the quiet shore road to the pier and wished they had pennies to spend on ice-cream advertised in a booth at the landward end of it. Nobody seemed to worry about pier dues now and, indeed, a kindly, wrinkled man on the landing-stage asked them if they were down for the month, and where they would be staying, and did they see that the *Columba* was even now coming up the kyle from the distant point of Ardlamont?

They had heard from their father enough to know that this, the most famous and long-lived of the paddle-steamers to ply on the Firth of Clyde, belonged to history. Had not Queen Victoria herself given her a sort of title? Was she not the essential link in Macbrayne's Royal Route—sharp away from the Broomielaw of Glasgow 7.11 each morning, as faithful as the clock in all her stops and starts. "A beautiful model," Papa had so often said, " and a lovely set of engines —oscillating and surface-condensing, of course. Nearest thing to a steam yacht ; goes like a sewing-machine."

The Twins appreciated the truth behind this conventional boast as the *Columba* came up to Tighnabruaich pier. She sat low on the water and had the curved bow of a racing yacht. Her two funnels were red with black tops like the *Mercury's*, but they had a sharper rake aft, and the hull was black. Her paddles, within small black boxes elaborately gilded, turned with the swift grace of a ballerina's toes, purposefully but without fuss. Into the pier she carried with her an air of consequence, and the young boys observed with particularity the human air of consequence worn by the bearded captain and the purser on the extension of the bridge over the paddle-box : such an authoritative pride as you might find in the officers of a crack Atlantic liner. The varnish of her deck-houses gleamed freshly in the afternoon sun.

She was no sooner gone, swinging out of sight through the Narrows, than up the kyle came a ship quite different. She came like an arrow, fast and lithe and smooth, and through the waters in the stillness of that summer afternoon there came to the boys' ears the drum of propellers turning at high speed. Her twin funnels, set closely together, were white with black tops.

The wrinkled man jerked the wet stem of his pipe towards this interesting craft, saying :

" There's a fine, new one for ye, lads ! One of Williamson's turbines, the *King Edward*, from Inveraray. You'll soon be seein' the old *Lord of the Isles* skelpin' up behind her, but I doubt the turbine's taken her trade away . . . Aye, there she is comin' round Ardlamont ; see the smoke."

The wet stem of the pipe pointed down that western arm of the kyle, and the old man chuckled.

" They're fairly slashin' the coal into the furnaces to keep up wi' the turbine, but I doubt it's a bit late in the day."

The implications of this remark escaped the Twins, and they were much more interested to observe the shape of the ship which emerged out of that cloud of brown smoke in the entrance to the strait. She emerged as a sizeable vessel with two funnels, widely-spaced and coloured in the combination of red, white and black they had seen on that of the *Edinburgh Castle* at Princes Pier. There was an air of urgency, of almost desperate purpose, about her. The boys were delighted to hear a German band on her after-deck play *El Relicario* with a matching desperation of pace and effort.

She came and went, slipping round that enchanting elbow of the Kyles by the Burnt Islands.

" That's all ye'll see for a while, lads," said the old man, heaving himself up and off a firkin of butter. " I'll away home for my tea now."

The twin boys of a successful business man of the Edwardian period were sent early to bed that night, Mama insisting with truth as well as the asperity of a weary housekeeping woman at the end of a long and eventful day that they must be dog-tired. So they were, but as a drunken man is at the end of his physical tether and yet eager in his mind for more and more experience of colour, song and conflict. Novelty and delight had bemused these little boys, so rich was this inland sea in colour and the variety of small shipping that served its coastal ports. They were too young to have formulated the conception of beauty, though they knew in the dim way of boyhood that a unique loveliness of gnarled hill, thickets of small oak and hazel and moving tides in small arms of the sea lay about them.

As he was dying of a bubbling wound in the lungs after Beaumont Hamel in 1917, the younger Twin, perhaps groping in his sense of doom to envisage the nature of Heaven, had in his mind's eye that old photograph of the Kyles and, in the very core of his understanding as an individual, the sense of magic in the light of the evening that had laid cloth of gold on distant hillsides and still but moving waters.

That first of the German Wars was to rob the Firth of Clyde of some of its familiar little ships, mined and shattered in shallow seas. The second, and the political and economic effects of both, was to reduce the fleets of small pleasure steamers, for better or worse, to one small self-coloured group of vessels, running to timetables devised by civil servants in distant places. The new order directed much of the traffic on to the roads, into the buses, and therefore away from the steamers. The little riparian townships decayed, their piers rotted ; and the diversity of life on the Firth as created by competition was dispersed and ironed out. The pretty yachts became as dying swans in the blizzard of mid-20th Century economics. Only the loveliness of the Firth remained intact.

The Twins were put to bed at length ; but as soon as they were sure that Mama had forgotten them, they flung back the sheets of the double-bed they shared in a front room and knelt at the window in their nightshirts. It was still bright day, as they saw it, and the yellow of the sun already set behind the hills of Tighnabruaich still gleamed on the tops of the Bute hills. Over there on the island side these hills fell nearly sheer to the water's edge, with great lumps of fallen rocks lying amid the heather that was ripening towards bloom. There was no beach at all on that other side : only recessed faces of grey-green rock, licked by small, smooth waves. All over the kyle was a glassy smoothness on this sultry summer night, but the water was always in movement, its undulations throwing up long gleams of sepia, sage and silver.

The smells of salt and weed mingled with the drift of scent from stock in the front-plot below. It was queer to hear so clearly the bark of a dog on a farm perhaps four miles away down on the island coast. With it seemed to come across the water the almost intolerably lovely scents of bog myrtle and briar blended.

It was for the small boys a stillness with the quality of miracle in it. On Monday evening, Papa had promised at supper, he would take them in a boat to troll for lythe and mackerel up against that rocky shore on the other side.

Into their delight in silence and beauty and prospect, however, there broke the sounds of dipping paddles. They leaned out of the window to see the *Mercury* swing through the Narrows again on the evening run. It was wonderful to know she would lie at Kames until early on the Monday morning and take such as Papa back in good time for business in the city.

" Wonderful service ! " Papa often said in his proprietorial way. " Nothing like it in the world."

Over in the shelter of Blackfarland Bay a small fleet of cruising yachts had anchored for the night : a pleasant journey's end for amateur mariners. Their sails were housed trimly, and, with the setting of the sun, only their club burgees drooped from the mastheads. Dinghies of absurdly small size and with but a few inches of freeboard were crossing the strait, carrying the week-end sailors towards the convivial amenities of mainland hotels. Suddenly a gramophone began to play from the deck of one of the small craft over there, the sentimental air of *In the Valley Where the Bluebirds Sing* ringing plangently over the calm waters between the high hills.

The Twins listened entranced ; and then Mama and Papa came out on the rough lawn below, and the boys raced back to bed, feverishly pulling the sheets about their ears. They were sound asleep at length, even before the last cadences of the trivial song, borrowing something of a forlorn beauty from its own echoes, had died away.

CHAPTER I

The Sea Area

TRAVELLING men will endlessly debate the relative splendours
of the world's great harbours. It is deep in mankind,
especially of the seafaring sorts, this instinct to recall with
passionate delight the glories of the fabled ports. It is produced, one may think, by much the same sense of wonder as
moves even the mere holidaymaker to remember throughout
a lifetime the exquisite sensations on making a first foreign
landfall—the lift of the white cliffs above Dieppe or the tall
dolls' houses on the dunes around Ostend, the enormous
precipices of Portugal, or the swinging of the Ambrose Light-
ship on the approaches to Sandy Hook and New York. It
comes of wonder, and its proper expression is poetry.

The finest harbours are always estuaries or the innermost
corners of archipelagos. Any British naval dockyard is no
doubt a remarkable and admirable work of engineering, but
its other than military interest rests entirely on natural
circumstances. Thus Devonport has a character—one had
almost said charms—completely lacking in Chatham and
Rosyth, for the first is rooted in the warmth of Devon scenery
and Devon tradition while the other two have been built more
arbitrarily on dull shores that happen to face the countries of
the King's traditional enemies. A harbour is great, and it
lives in the affections of men, in proportion to the splendour
and beauty of the natural scene and the interest of the life
that has developed along its shores.

Fine harbours inspire deep sentiments and even profound

loyalties. Anger and contempt may darken the atmosphere when an American debates with an Australian the relative splendours of the Golden Gate and Sydney. Ships' officers thump the café tables as they compare Valetta with Vigo or speak of Gibraltar, with the Rock so magnificently dominating the entrance to the Middle Sea, and then of Table Bay, the cloth of cloud almost always hanging mysteriously over the flat-topped mountain. A certain Norwegian fjord may have rested in the mind of one man, an anchorage within an atoll of coral in that of another. The preferences rest largely on first impacts and early associations and, to repeat the word, on man's not always obvious loyalties, but usually to loyalties acquired in youth.

Here we set out to discover, like those Twins of yesterday, the character of one of the most typical of the northern estuaries, the Firth of Clyde. It will not be suggested that it rivals the Golden Gate or Sydney Harbour in extent, importance or sub-tropical magnificence. It will, however, be maintained that the Firth of Clyde is far and away the most splendid of the greater natural harbours of Great Britain. It is scenically unique in Britain. It has many unique associations with the developments of British shipping and shipbuilding : the true cradle of steam shipping in particular and, at the other end of the scale of social expression, a favourite playground of generations of yachtsmen. Its coastal development has reflected in the most fascinating way the urges of an urban population about the bridgehead of the River Clyde proper. Its waters are very deep and very wide ; and they can be very wild. It serves the bulk of the population in the hinterland and services, both for imports and exports, one of the heaviest industrial concentrations in the world ; and it provides the people thereof with space for their recreation.

One airport on its shores is a main British base on the shortest air-route between Europe and North America.

The Firth of Clyde

Throughout a long and bitter period during the Second World War it was the very gullet of embattled Britain : the only free and freely working port on an island bombed incessantly and encircled by submarines. It has its own bird-life ; its own fish-life ; its own botany ; its own system of lights and navigational rules ; its own fleet of pleasure steamers. It encloses a cluster of islands, each with its own character and its own, often strange, history. It forms, finally, the basin within which two warring cultures, the Celtic from the northern shore and the Lowland from the other side, have contended and ultimately fused in picturesque variations.

All these matters will be attended to in due course. Here it is merely desirable and convenient to define the terms of reference. The dictionaries agree in defining " firth " as an " Arm of the sea, estuary," and then " estuary " as the " Tidal mouth of river." This is very well and agrees with the general understanding of most of us, but the definitions fail to meet the special case of the River Clyde and its extensions into salt water. A glance at the map shows that the town of Greenock, the uppermost point of deep-water anchorage, most obviously marks the upper limits of the Firth, but the tides continue to flow past Greenock and more than 20 miles beyond into the heart of Glasgow : into the very heart, indeed, of industrial Scotland. This is a circumstance which must be understood at the outset.

The Clyde proper is in the first place the result of the confluence of several pleasant little streams—burns, we prefer to call them in Scotland—rising out of green patches on the moorlands of the high sheep-farming country on the borders of Lanarkshire and Dumfriesshire. It flows northwards in the first place, oddly enough, and a gracious little river it is : an angling river well-stocked with trout and grayling. It follows at first an easy, winding course among the austerely charming uplands, under some ancient and beautiful bridges and past at least one historic meal-mill, and it receives several substantial tributaries as it goes along towards the county town of Lanark. There it receives its first check, passing from the pastoral to the tempestuous over high sills of rock at Corra Linn and Bonnington Falls. Hereabouts, the shadow of the shape of things to come, a power station, makes use of its momentum to generate electricity.

Below the Falls, however, the Clyde has still some miles of agreeable travel before it. It washes the orchards of a region surprisingly fertile and, in the season, flowery at such a relatively high altitude ; it borders and graces the " policies " of many a landed family's once splendid estate. But a thickening haze of smoke, carried on the prevailing south-westerly wind, intimates its ultimate fate. It begins to move into Black Country, flowing between pit-bings and rolling mills, and though the river has still many surprising and charming moments before it loses its identity in the great city, it must begin to carry sewage, however hygienically treated, chemical effluents and the inevitable quota of dead cats and dogs. In the heart of Glasgow, a bedraggled slattern by now, it spills over a weir into salt water.

Two hundred years ago the Clyde at Glasgow rippled through a lovely little city and then started a shallow flow over sandbanks, or hairsts, until it encountered real deep water at Greenock, 23 miles below Glasgow Bridge. Old prints show it to have been a pleasant stream, with women washing clothes, carters watering their horses, and children paddling where now there is berthage for ships of considerable draught. The ocean tides did flow into the confines of the city, but they were so dispersed over those hairsts that clotted the inner estuary between Greenock and Glasgow, no shipping of any substantial tonnage could reach the community which was, nevertheless, the natural *entrepôt* of Scottish trade. Greenock at the highest point of deep-water anchorage virtually controlled shipping into and out of the port. Between Greenock and Glasgow only a small and mainly passenger trade by water was carried on by what were called fly-boats, wherries or smacks that might spend hours between tides on one of those innumerable sandbanks separating the communities.

Scottish trade had benefited greatly by the terms of the Act of Union with England, 1707 (whatever the soul of Scotland may have gained or lost thereby), and the merchants of Glasgow became almost desperate in their efforts to circumvent the privilege of Greenock and bring their goods direct by ship to their own warehouses. They sought to do so by establishing or subsidising fore-ports on the outer estuary, and then by the deliberate and artificial creation of a port of their own on the very boundaries of Greenock. They remained determined that, somehow, the troublesome hairsts of sand between their warehouses and the last anchorage at Greenock could be so handled, so engineered and dominated, that ships of heavy burden might by-pass Greenock in its sentinel position and come to the heart of the natural distributing and manufacturing centre of industrial Scotland.

They succeeded at length, and it remains one of the most astonishing successes of foresight and energy in the history of private enterprise. Advised by a series of engineers so distinguished in their day as Rennie, Smeaton and Telford, but most effectively by John Golborne of Chester, they so dealt with the rambling tidal Clyde below the city that in 1806 the brig *Harmony* of Liverpool, 120 tons, made her way past Greenock to Glasgow on the spring tide. Exactly 130 years later this channel could carry the *Queen Mary* and then the *Queen Elizabeth* from the builders' fitting-out basin to anchorage off Greenock, some 18 miles downstream.

The details of the achievement are of fascinating interest, but they belong only indirectly to the history of the Clyde estuary. We note here merely that the merchants of Glasgow

54

created between the River Clyde proper and the Firth of Clyde proper a hermaphroditic phase, so to speak, like a metal tube inserted into the digestive system of a human being.

It is difficult to find even the right word to suggest the nature of that strange passage of the Clyde between Greenock and Glasgow. A canal it is not, for it is freely tidal. At the same time, its maintenance and use require an elaborate service of dredging and a continual carrying of the dredged material out to deep water by a fleet of hopper-barges ; strict regulations of pilotage ; a complicated system of buoying and lighting, and the constant attention of a covey of tug-boats. Glasgow's maritime economy rests gingerly, to say the least of it, in a complex of inter-related but often overlapping responsibilities ; the miracle being that it works. The shipping route between Greenock and Glasgow is perhaps best described as the Clyde Ship-Channel, and so it will be termed hereafter.

The definition is necessary, for the creation of this Ship-Channel subtly but profoundly affected the Firth, its economy, its social structure and the intimate lives of the folk up and down its shores. It had the effect of shifting the centre of industrial gravity in Scotland a distance of some 25 miles, and that is a long distance in terms of Scottish geography. When the *Harmony* of Liverpool sailed past Greenock in 1806 the Firth lost its commercial dominance to the city at the bridgehead upstream. The town of Greenock, which had shaped so long to be Scotland's first port on the North-Western Approaches, was bound in the long run to lose its sovereignty, and duly it did. Its fight for survival as a port has been bitter ever since the power passed to Glasgow. In a sense, the creation of the Ship-Channel of the Clyde was rather an extension of the Firth upwards than an extension of the River downwards.

Greenock remains by far the largest town on the Firth proper : a real seaside town, whereas thousands of the population of Glasgow have never even seen the narrow waterway below the bridges. Greenock is unmistakably a maritime community, and Glasgow is an inland city that became a great port by the will of man rather than by the dictate of nature. Nevertheless, the ultimate influence of Glasgow at the landward end of the Ship-Channel was ultimately to be much greater than that of Greenock at the seaward end : that is, on the development of the Firth as it is to-day.

On the banks of the Ship-Channel, and not long after its creation, one of the most significant scenes of the Industrial Revolution was staged. This was the establishment of the great shipbuilding and engineering industry of Clydeside, still the most productive group of its sort in all the wide world. It is not too much of a simplification to say that the ships built and engined along the shores of the artificial Ship-Channel had almost everything to do with the making and shaping and influencing of the Firth as it is to-day.

The influences overlap, but it is still possible to suggest the line of a frontier between the free Firth and the man-made, man-maintained Ship-Channel. Below the sands of the Great Bank, which dries out in yellow nullity opposite Greenock, is this Tail of the Bank, the uppermost point of anchorage for ships of size. Here begins the Firth as most men understand it.

Our concern hereafter is almost entirely with the spread of fresh, tidal waters below this line : that is, towards the Atlantic. Our business is with a sort of inland sea, occupying some 1100 square miles of the earth's surface : ramifying, often tempestuous, studded with islands, ringed by high hills, strangely and evanescently lighted by the continuous interplay of sunlight and rain, but always a social and geographical entity in its own right—the most splendid, the most fantastic estuary of Britain in its beauty and interest.

The specialist in oceanography is unwilling to speak and

write of the Firth of Clyde, for him an unscientific and
" popular " phrase. He considers only the Clyde Sea Area.
He has a nomenclature of his own for its various phases as a
sheet of water : speaking, for instance, rather contemptuously
of " the Estuary," by which he means that short and relatively
shallow stretch from the Tail of the Bank opposite Greenock
to an imaginary line between Gourock and Kilcreggan piers.
He then turns more happily to the deep lochs, and he is happiest
of all in the profound waters round Arran and out towards
the Irish Sea.

Our scientist can even be contemptuous of " popular "
notions as to where this sea-loch or that begins and ends. One
of the best authorities on the subject, the late Dr. Hugh R.
Mill, wrote in 1901 :

> " In the infinite irregularity and variety of bare
> mountain slopes and deep valley trenches, the uniform
> level of the smooth surface of the sea-lochs and the broader
> reaches of the sea area suggests a uniformity which does
> not really exist. Could one remove the veil of water, the
> hollows it covers would appear in their true character
> scarcely less varied in outline than the land, forming
> ridges, hollows, mountainous islands and shoals, sometimes
> of surprising steepness, and broad gently-sloping plains.
> The featureless monotony of the water is merely a mask, but
> it has caused names to be applied to different portions of
> the surface which do not correspond with the natural
> regions outlined by the hidden features whose influence on
> the *regime* of the water and its inhabitants is paramount."

This somewhat breathless assertion confesses the geographer's instinct to regard the Firth of Clyde as a branch of
the ocean rather than as a piece of water largely surrounded
by land, of which the inhabitants, swayed by economic and

historical and social pressures, have conferred upon it an identity distinct from that of, say, the Bristol Channel. To adopt Dr. Mill's terminology would be to confuse the lay reader working with conventional maps and charts. We remain grateful to him for those researches that allow us to understand something of what lies below the shining or stormy surface of this huge expanse of water.

The general pattern of these underwater configurations is quite easily grasped, and perhaps a short description would ease our understanding of them.

In the first place, in his beloved outer reaches of the Firth · southwards of Arran, the oceanographer discovers what he calls the Great Plateau, stretching from the Mull of Kintyre across a distance of 30 miles to the shallow sandy coast of Ayrshire. The relative shallowness of these seas, and it is no more than relative, seems to delight the specialist. " An upheaval of 150 feet," wrote Dr. Mill, " would entirely exclude the sea and convert the Clyde Sea Area into one great freshwater lake and half a dozen small ones." Both the layman and the seaman, however, can rest with reasonable security in the knowledge that the depth of water over the Great Plateau runs up to 25 fathoms.

It seems more remarkable that very deep waters are discovered on both sides of the Isle of Arran and inwards, or northwards, towards the Argyllshire mainland from these relative shallows. The oceanographer calls this the Arran Basin.

Within its western limb, in the Kilbrennan Sound between Arran and the peninsula of Kintyre, the maximum depth is not less than 84 fathoms. The eastern limb, lying fairly close to Arran in its first phase, sweeps round the northern end of that island to join the other, whereupon both run across towards the southern tip of Bute and so up the outer basin of Loch Fyne, almost to where that loch is nearly blocked by an outlying spit of sand called the Otter. At places the depths in this dark valley of the sea run up to 80 fathoms. The deepest, darkest point of all the Clyde Sea Area is well within the arms of outer Loch Fyne where, in a hole of only a few hundred yards in diameter near Skate Island, the lead descends to a depth of 107 fathoms.

This Arran Basin has two minor offshoots that run up the western arm of the Kyles of Bute and between the Bute and Cumbrae islands respectively, but the oceanographer is next most interested in what he calls the Dunoon Basin. This trough, or series of troughs, of deep water runs north-eastwards off the Isle of Bute, along the Cowal coast and up Loch Long, even into Loch Long's sombre offshot, Loch Goil. Opposite Dunoon itself the soundings go down to 56 fathoms. Even at the entrance to Loch Goil they are 55 fathoms by the mark.

Our authorities tend to think poorly of the Estuary, wherein the average depth of water is just about five fathoms. Being more concerned with what is below water level than with what is above it, they fail to observe that this brief stretch of water, in the lee of the Renfrewshire hills, forms a notably safe and notoriously picturesque anchorage for the largest vessels afloat. The humanist may incline to see that what the oceanographer most usefully demonstrates is the fitness of the Firth of Clyde as one of the world's great harbours, so deep up the fairway, so sheltered in its upper reaches, that the queens of all the seas can come up from the ocean at speed and without pilotage to the very heart of Scotland.

The lochs that fill the sea valleys of the Clyde Area mostly run roughly NW-SE as they were gouged out by the glaciers of prehistoric times. The exceptions are the splendid stretch of Loch Fyne and the upper reaches of Loch Long which tend to run on the NE-SW axis as the ice changed course about the obstacles thrown up by earlier volcanic action. All these lochs cut into the northern shores of the Firth, creating the fabulously rugged district of Cowal between Loch Fyne and Loch Long. It will be noted that a long fresh-water lake, Loch Eck, just fails to make of Cowal an island. There are no lochs to indent the southern shores of the Firth until, in the extreme outer reaches of the area, we come on the gentle, shallow basin of Loch Ryan.

The innermost arm of the Firth is the Gareloch which, as it were, turns abruptly backwards from the line of up-river approach opposite Greenock. It is in terms of scenery the suavest of the Clyde lochs. The slopes of land about it are relatively gentle and well-wooded, the hills immediately to the North neither notably high nor rugged. This character is reflected in the sea bed, which fails to impress the oceanographer in any notable degree. The greatest depth of water is " only 22 fathoms," while, in the Narrows through which it used to be entered between a long spit running out from the hamlet of Rhu to near the Rosneath peninsula, the depth was " no more than five fathoms . . ." The past tense has to be used since, during the Second World War, military necessity demanded the development of the Gareloch as a base of overseas operations, one of the imperatives being the widening and deepening of the Narrows. The results, however, were not so sensational as might have been expected. These workings did little to reduce the speed of the tidal race from $3\frac{1}{2}$ knots at ordinary spring tides.

Under her own steam the old *Aquitania*, a monstrous lump of a ship, proceeded safely through these Narrows in 1950 without even the hint of a mishap, and thus towards the knacker's yard.

By virtue of its geographical position, within easy access of Glasgow by a main road and then by rail, the Gareloch came within the suburban system as early as the 18th Century. As we shall see, the pleasant town of Helensburgh at its mouth was the outcome of a deliberate planning development by the local landowner. The merchant princes gradually extended their building of country or seaside houses in clusters right round the perimeter of the loch from Helensburgh to Gare-lochhead and from that hamlet down the southern shore to Clynder and Rosneath. This was a vast concentration of wealth and influence. Perhaps nowhere else on the Firth of Clyde, and in few other places in the wide world, did so much money decree a pleasure dome so solid if so peaceful. The mob hardly dared to invade this sweet enclave, along which the wealthy built high walls about the long gardens that sloped to the waters on which their lovely yachts lay moored by the score.

This nearness to the industrial hinterland and to the point where the Ship-Channel emerges from amid sandbanks into the estuary was to be the undoing of the Gareloch as an agreeable fragment of natural beauty. At any time in periods of economic depression it was apt to become a temporary cemetery of laid-up and rusting ships, riding high and empty on its quiet waters.

During the First World War the Admiralty used it as a testing place for submarines. During the Second several Services, British and American, stormed the loch and left it, scenically and even socially, a shambles. Great sheds and workshops were built at Rhu for the aircraft of Coastal Command. The Army, *not* the Navy, took a section of the northern shore—including the quiet little bay of Faslane, in which honest men used to troll quietly for sea trout on the outer edge of the line of golden seaweed—and made of it a series of deep-water berths with gantries and railway sidings all complete. From these were duly loaded and unloaded innumerable big ships engaged in the North African and D-Day landings and the provisioning of the Forces.

It was no doubt a useful imperative of war, but it created an abominable ugliness where beauty had once rested. Even towards the end of 1950, the dock-site leased to a shipbreaking concern, it did not seem that the grace of the Gareloch could ever again be what it once had been. If that were not enough, the Admiralty used this arm of the sea as a mortuary for all those strange and ugly craft that, brilliantly designed for the assault on Europe, had had their brief and useful day and were now so much junk. At the same time, the soldiery and the sailors had befouled the slopes and raised beaches with their hutments. The Americans had used Rosneath Castle and the wooded point beyond as headquarters and a testing ground for exercises in Combined Operations. Even by the turn of the mid-Century it seemed almost as if the Gareloch had been incorporated beyond hope into the industrial system of the larger Clyde Basin.

It is only reasonable to observe that the Gareloch never quite belonged by its special nature to the system of wilder fjords that claw into the province of Cowal. It was always rather suburban in the sense already suggested. One of the startling paradoxes of travel in that region is to be encountered merely by driving a car out of the mild Gareloch basin for a mile or two uphill and then to find oneself, at Whistlefield, staring westwards across the gloomy cleft of Loch Long, into the mysteries of Loch Goil, and into an angry sunset over a range of crowded and eccentric peaks. It is like having gone to sleep as the train passed among the mild hills of northern Lancashire and being wakened up amid the dark tangles of the Southern Uplands about Beattock. But let the oceanographer have his say meanwhile.

He inclines to dismiss the outer portion of Loch Long as belonging truly to the Dunoon Basin, but notes with quiet approval that it reaches a depth of 55 fathoms near the Dog Rock, at the entrance to Loch Goil, which, as the map shows, is a branch of Loch Long. Upper Loch Long, he says, is "simply the upper end of the Dunoon Basin," and he adds that its maximum depth is 35 fathoms. He is nearer the layman's point of view in allowing that Loch Long narrows in its upper reaches to only about one-half of a mile wide, and that it is " walled " by very steep mountain slopes. The scientist's true delight, however, is in the subsidiary Loch Goil which, over a bar with only seven fathoms of water on it, has the satisfactory maximum depth of 47 fathoms. " This depth, combined with the small area and shallow entrance, isolates the water of Loch Goil more completely than that in any other part of the Area."

That is one way of putting it. Loch Goil forms a charming corner of the Firth when the sun shines, but it has its forbidding aspects. The hills about it are hard, knobbly and high, running up to the 2000-feet level and beyond, and forming such a fantastical and delightful view from various distances as to be known facetiously as " the Duke of Argyll's Bowling Green." On a stormy evening the loch wears a most forbidding air of the romantic kind described in different mediums by Landseer and Scott.

The inner arm of Loch Long is also, while sometimes enchanting, often forbidding. The sheer slopes above the water give room for few human habitations until we arrive at the pleasant village of Arrochar at the loch-head and under the 2891-feet peak of The Cobbler, but our oceanographer is not, of course, interested in the fact that the West Highland railway line was cut high into the eastern slopes in a bold piece of enterprise that took a line across the soggy wastes of the Moor of Rannoch, over a high pass of the Grampians, and so to Fort William. It is always surprising to see a train puffing along a narrow shelf cut into a slope that lies at 45 degrees to the horizontal, and the spectacle fortifies the impression that this Loch Long is the most Norwegian-like of the Clyde fjords.

The yachtsman under honest sail has always distrusted this Loch Long for the ferocious eccentricities of its wind-eddies

and blistering rain-squalls that " take the top off the water."
Its narrowness leaves him at any time, except in a small craft,
little room for manœuvre ; and now he must, moreover, pay
the price of Admiralty. Even in the early years of the 20th
Century the naval authorities established here a testing range
for torpedoes turned out in a factory at Greenock. At Arrochar
they built the appropriate group of unhappily " functional "
buildings, and across one-half of the fairway down the loch
they moored platforms from which the movements of their
robots could be observed.

The Admiralty's interest in the Clyde estuary actually
increased after the Second World War, and the entrance of
pleasure vessels to Loch Goil, for instance, became severely
restricted. Clearly, the authorities were justified in using these
splendidly deep waters in close proximity to a unique aggregation of shipbuilding power, but the conflict between the
requirements of Defence and the traditional rights of the
People makes, at least, the subject of a nice study in priorities.
Innumerable writers of Letters to the Editor appeared to
think, or feel, that it was rather like wiring off the beach at
Blackpool for experiments in the subtler uses of landmines.

The Holy Loch is a pleasant interlude between the mouth
of Loch Long and the main stretch of the Firth proper, where
that channel turns out of the estuary and swings in a direction
only a little West of due South. Why Holy, no man seems to
know with certainty ; there is only a choice between two
agreeably romantic theories. Either this short arm of the sea
was so named because St Mun founded an early Christian
church at what is now Kilmun, or because a ship with a cargo
of soil from the Holy Land, intended for the foundations of
Glasgow Cathedral, was wrecked hereabouts. In its social
aspects the Holy Loch to-day is, like the Gareloch, very much
a product of the 19th and 20th Centuries, the subtle differences
lying in the fact that, while the Gareloch always enjoyed easy

land communications with Glasgow, the Holy Loch was built-up and peopled on a subtly lower level by the simplicity of its steamboat connections with the mainland, so to speak, through Greenock and, latterly, Gourock.

For the scientist the Holy Loch is " only a deep bay opening into the Dunoon Basin " and of rather special interest as " occupying the mouth of the valley of the fresh Loch Eck, and receiving its extensive drainage." He observes that its average depth is only about 9 fathoms and points out that it is shoal for a considerable distance below its head, where it takes in the considerable discharges of the River Echaig out of Loch Eck. It is hardly his business to point out that this short loch has its own scenic nobility, especially in the steep and well-planted slopes on its northern side and in the thrust of Strone Point, an arrogant Roman nose of rough land lunging into the Firth to mark its northerly entrance. The peculiar social developments along these pleasant shores, especially in relation to yachting, will be noted later on.

We pass in the meantime out of the Estuary through the deeps of Dunoon Basin and along the agreeable southern shore of the Cowal peninsula to where the island of Bute pushes its rocky, northern nose into the mainland with only a few hundred yards of tidal water intervening. Before the entrance to the fabulous Kyles of Bute, however, there intervenes the mouth of Loch Striven that runs nine miles into the Cowal mainland.

This is a strange, forlorn arm of the sea. Its hillsides, steep and sparsely inhabited especially along the western shore, create an effect of monotony without the charm of the sinister. Two steamboat piers once served the sparse loch-side communities but have long been out of action. This fjord has never been included in the regular steamer routes, and only now and again does a cruising turbine vessel turn in and, in a wide circle, turn out again. It is another of the Navy's playgrounds, set apart for research in noisy methods of destruction, but it is significant that public protest against the Admiralty's prohibitions in this area were never so indignant as the outcries against the closing of Loch Goil.

The Navy's addiction to Loch Striven is no doubt explained by the oceanographer's note to the effect that it has a satisfactory minimum depth of 42 fathoms. In the middle years of the 20th Century this forgotten loch took another forward step in the march of progress by the initiation of hydro-electrical works at its head. On the whole, however, we have to see Striven as a fjord that by nature lacked the beauties and amenities which give the rest of the Firth of Clyde a peculiar social flavour, so to speak, and that, as a *cul de sac*, suffered in competition with the more obvious charms of the Kyles of Bute.

These are powerful. Any narrow stretch of tidal water seems to have the peculiar quality of exciting human interest. The Kyles are unique in that their waters ebb and flow between the high and rugged land-masses of Cowal on the one hand and the gentler slopes of the island of Bute, always knobbly and picturesque but never " grand " in the guide-book sense, on the other. There are plenty of woodland and other forms of picturesque greenery. On any fine day these straits wear an enchanting air of open freshness in contrast to the relative gloom of such as Loch Striven : this agreeable effect, or illusion, being obviously created by the fact that the hills of Bute are comparatively low and thus leave the whole Kyles area open to the summer sun from dawn till near sunset.

The second factor behind their powers of attraction is the existence of the low reefs known as the Burnt Islands at that point where the vessel, having cruised happily up the eastern arm, must turn in a circle to traverse the western arm. Men experienced in the navigation of Clyde steamers tell of a curious moment of tidal crisis when, somewhere near Colintraive on the eastern arm, the competing tides up the two arms of the Kyles meet and an eerie period of stasis in dead water ensues.

Otherwise, the tides rip merrily about the Burnt Islands. Against the Bute shore a buoyed channel provides easy if tortuous passage, but it is an exciting moment when the pleasure steamer must barge through the rip between the painted beacons that mark the Narrows against the Cowal coast, the green, clean waters swirling in the mysterious strength of pure nature about the bases of these seamarks. There is a lot of good rough sport to be had hereabouts, especially with the help of an outboard motor on a rowing-boat. The fish may be only the coarse saithe, but there are mackerel to be had in these exciting waters, and lythe or pollack, all easily tempted by a penny fly.

Where eastern and western kyle meet beyond these Burnt Islands a short loch of great charm runs northwards from the elbow, so to speak, to end in the shallows created by the material brought down by the River Ruel. This is Loch Riddon. Even the oceanographer admits it to be "very picturesque." The western shore of this brief fjord is steep and thickly wooded, that of the Cowal mainland on the other side agreeably and roughly varied, while the arms of the Glendaruel valley most charmingly frame the picture.

Two islets within the mouth of the loch contribute a scenic touch in the tradition of Germanic romance. Eilean Dearg against the eastern shore is in fact not much more than a large rock with grass and a tree or two upon it, but it borrows a quaint sort of charm from history, having been fortified by the then Earl of Argyll in support of Monmouth's rebellion. What strategical or even tactical purpose this measure was supposed to serve it is now rather difficult to discern, but it took an English fleet to reduce the place and have the Earl beheaded in Edinburgh in 1685. This queer little monument to the vanity of human wishes is pleasantly matched, lower down, by Eilean Dubh, a thickly wooded islet that enchantingly protects the natural harbour before the mansionhouse of Glen Caladh : surely one of the most happily placed residences in all Britain.

The western arm of the Kyles of Bute follows a dog-legged course and might be considered by most people the more charming of the two. It is longer and more open than its eastern twin. The Bute shore softens to an opening-up of prosperous farmlands, while the brows above the mainland coast, while beetling for a space, have a wooded and toylike charm. At length the shores on both sides fall back in reasonable fertility from the sea, and there is opened up the immense vista of the outer Firth. The stranger's attention will no doubt be called to the Maids of Bute, two painted stones on the steep and heathery hillside just round the corner from the Burnt Islands.

These are twin chunks of rock on which somebody once exercised a crude art, painting them in black, white and red roughly to resemble two Welsh peasants in traditional dress. Why it should have been done at all nobody seems to know, but it was certainly done a great many years ago, and no doubt it helps the tourist trade. Much more interesting in the human sense are the associations of Ardlamont, the estate which shares its name with the frequently stormy point round which the long-distance steamers turn out of the Kyles of Bute into the expanses of Loch Fyne : the last, largest and perhaps loveliest of the lochs within the Sea Area. Hereabouts, in remoteness, was enacted the melodrama that in 1893 led to the appearance in the High Court of Justiciary in Edinburgh of A. J. Monson, charged with the murder of his pupil, Windsor Dudley Cecil Hambrough : two English strangers so fantastically involved in terror in such an improbable place.

The Sea Area

The oceanographer is inclined to dismiss the Kyles of Bute as having an average depth of only 12½ fathoms. He admits, however, that the maximum depth is 23 fathoms, the average axial depth—that is, along the bed of the sea-valley—being 21 fathoms : quite enough water to float a ship or drown a man. But it is with the scientist's delight that he turns into Loch Fyne with all its oddities and enchantments.

This is in truth a splendid arm of the sea and the veritable pattern of fine sub-Highland scenery. As we have seen, the scientist discovers in its outer reaches, near the Skate Island, a depth of water up to 107 fathoms. We follow him in his stricture to the effect that these outer reaches are really a sort of extension of the Kilbrennan Sound, between the island of Arran and the peninsula of Kintyre, and in fact the traveller does not discover much intimacy in the scene at the mouth of Fyne until the loch begins to narrow near the entrance to its offshoot, Loch Gilp, where a spit of sand called the Otter runs out from the Cowal shore, almost to overlap the opposite point on the western shore, to reduce the fairway to a breadth of three-quarters of a mile at low tide, and effectively to divide what is loosely called Loch Fyne into two distinct parts—with still another sub-division of the upper waters to come.

Within the Otter spit Loch Fyne is indeed a most beautiful arm of the sea, its great length and considerable breadth allowing for a startling variety of prospects. Here is the charm of the Kyles of Bute set in the grand scale. The mountains on both shores of the loch run high, well beyond the 1000-foot level in each case, but their descent to the beaches is fairly gentle in the main, and the lands on the shores are most agreeably wooded. This fjord has its twists and turns, so that the eye is continually and happily engaged in appreciating a new vista : all the vegetation so virginally green, and for a brief space so purple with the bloom of heather ; the natural history of the region so obviously rich and varied.

The Firth of Clyde

One is almost tempted to declare that any man who has sailed from Greenock or Gourock through the Kyles of Bute and up Loch Fyne to the lovely old ducal capital of Inveraray knows all that need be known of the quality of the Firth's beauty. It is nearly true, but it must be recorded that the picture can only be completed by a crossing between Arran and Ardrossan on a bright day when, seeing the Firth from the outside, as it were, the Highland hills soar, while still swooning in the ecstatic blue beauty of distance, above the nearer, greener, milder curves of the inner islands and more closely-gathered coasts.

Of Loch Fyne it has still to be observed, however, that only a few miles above the Otter spit the fairway is again obstructed and split by a pleasant group of islands at another elbow shaped by a point on the western shore below Minard Castle. The oceanographer observes that, between Otter and Minard, the axial depth of water is 31 fathoms, and then he regretfully records that the Minard islands split the loch into two channels of only 12 and 18 fathoms deep respectively. Beyond Minard, however, the prospect cheers him, for hereabouts the bed of this splendid loch begins to fall so far below sea level that it is at a depth of 40 fathoms off Furnace and then deepens to an average 60 fathoms, until the maximum depth is some 75 fathoms off Pennymore Point, just over the way from the pleasant settlement of Strachur.

This remarkably deep channel runs up the loch beyond Inveraray and beyond that past Dunderave Castle, of which the ruins, though now restored and made habitable, inspired Neil Munro with the idea of his excellent novel, *Doom Castle*. There Loch Fyne narrows and darkens to its appointed end amid high, rocky, remorseless hills. These upper reaches of the loch were much used during the Second World War for training in amphibious operations.

Several small lochs so-called run off Loch Fyne into its

70

western shore, but some of them, such as Loch Shira above Inveraray and Loch Gilp on the other side from the Otter spit, are little more than shallow bays. Between these two arms the little Loch Gair has a charm of its own, with a square tower at one point of entrance and a pleasant hamlet amid trees at its head, but it serves as little more than a convenient anchorage for an occasional yacht. The tiny inlet known as East Loch Tarbert is just a small natural harbour, but a most attractive one. Here, in the great days of the Loch Fyne herring fisheries, was the base of a numerous and picturesque fleet, but the centre of the industry's gravity has tended to move to the ports of the outer Firth. The village of Tarbert remains reasonably prosperous and certainly delightful, its villas and cottages piled high and in nearly a full circle about the bay. The effect in bright sunlight has the startling quality of a Mediterranean or at least a Cornish scene, woodlands and rocky islets contributing their notes of charm.

Near the outermost boundary of the Firth, a mile or two inwards from the Mull of Kintyre, is Campbeltown Loch, its entrance guarded by the mass of Davaar Island. Just as Campbeltown is Tarbert on a larger, industrial scale, its loch is austere and adequate rather than delightful. As we shall discover in detail later on the town of Campbeltown is, in its given situation, a surprising outpost of industrialism, with fishing, coal-mining and distilling as its staples. The navigation of the Loch is tricky, requiring a considerable system of sea-marks, but it is safe enough to be one of the standard submarine bases of the Royal Navy.

The strict geographer might not allow the inclusion of Loch Ryan within the Clyde Sea Area. This short arm of the sea opens its mouth northwards to the outer Firth and assists to form the hammer-headed peninsula known as the Rhinns of Galloway, the town of Stranraer at its head, a terminus of the short sea-route to Northern Ireland. This is, or was, a pretty little loch, a bowl within tracts of gentle and fertile farmlands.

It was destined, however, to become still another victim of exigency during the Second World War. It was always a seaplane or flying-boat base of importance in relation to its position on the North-Western Approaches, and one redoubtable aircraft type in this class got its name from Stranraer itself. It was later fated to suffer much the same sea-change as the Gareloch, when the Ordnance authorities built a large series of not notably beautiful harbour-works about the once delightful riparian village of Cairnryan. Such marks are not easily erased ; and for the rest, Loch Ryan is remarkable in being the only Scottish water in which oysters are still cultivated for the market.

Ryan is perhaps most remarkable in being the only " loch " on the eastern shore of the Firth of Clyde. It is indeed strange that few of us think of the long length of the Ayrshire coast on the eastern shore as belonging naturally to the Clyde system : so strongly are we attracted by the delightful arabesques of lochs and hills, islands and kyles, on the Highland fringe. It is easily seen from the map that a sort of bight cuts into the eastern mainland in the shape of a new moon, and that this is as indubitably a feature of the Firth of Clyde as the Kyles of Bute. It does not require a high degree of education in geography to know that the ports of Ayrshire —Ardrossan, Irvine, Troon and Ayr—are of some significance. Ships of size are built in two of them. Ardrossan and Ayr are both steamboat terminals, mainly for the connections with Arran. Ayr alone is a fish-market and coaling-port of importance.

Such towns seem to belong only remotely to the Firth of Clyde system for the good reason that the mainland railroad system from Glasgow and the industrial regions about that city renders them independent of the river steamer service. This shallow, sandy coastline is, with its golf links and beaches, one of the most popular of all holiday regions in Scotland. City-pent people find it simpler and cheaper to get to the edge of the sea and back by the omnipresent motor-coach. As we have noted, steamers of British Railways ply regularly from Ardrossan and Ayr, but in the first instance on the regular ferry service to Arran and, in the second, on daily excursions not wholly unrelated to the existence of a large and exigently-organised holiday camp in the neighbourhood.

This stretch of coast, however, is remarkable within the Clyde 'Sea Area in containing the longest stretches of fine bathing sands in all that wide-spread region. This may be a result of the persistent drift of prevailing winds from West and South-West into the mainland coast. It is a faintly melancholy fact that the shores of the Firth of Clyde are in the main notably hard, varying from rock to aggregations of boulders and then to shingle at the best. Along the Cowal shore and among the islands the pockets of golden sand are few and far between. There are some fine patches on the western coast of Bute and some others in the bays of the island of Arran and of Loch Fyne. Stretches of sand on the grand scale are, within the Firth, to be found on the Ayrshire coast alone.

Such, in outline, are the conditions prevailing within the 1240 square miles of salt water within the Clyde Sea Area. It is to be hoped that the general reader will by now have perceived it to be something like an inland sea of magnitude with, for a fairly populous region, a strangely diversified character, just as, later on, the uniqueness of the social and racial patterns along these goffered shores will be suggested. The almost purely oceanic character of this great sheet of water is suggested by the scientist himself.

He notes that the salinity of the Firth of Clyde waters— that is, the proportion of pure ocean water to infiltrations of fresh water from rivers and streams—is quite unusually high, even into the remotest recesses of the lochs. He observes, indeed, that when we read of sea-lochs being frozen over in a hard winter, it is very much a case of the lighter fresh water from tributaries, floating above the heavier sea water, being taken and congealed by low air temperatures above the surface.

The tides with this inland sea move gently on the whole. In the broad expanses and about the heads of lochs they rarely move at a speed of more than one knot in the hour. Through Narrows, such as at Otter, in the Kyles of Bute, and in the Rosneath entrance to the Gareloch, they may rip, especially on the ebb of spring tides at any rate from five to three and a half knots, and when a brisk wind blows against such a current the consequent "jabble" can be uncomfortable and even dangerous. It is most notable that full high tide over the Firth of Clyde is almost simultaneous, even to the most remote heads of the narrowest lochs. Within only 17 minutes of high tide in Lamlash Bay, Arran, all these arms of the sea are full to the brim. This does not apply to the Ship-Channel up to Glasgow. Through that narrow gut the flood tide moves slowly, and there is a difference of almost exactly an hour between high tide at Greenock on the estuary and high tide at Glasgow some 23 miles up-river.

On such seas and along such shores, then, was a special sort of life and culture to develop during the 19th Century.

CHAPTER II

The Coming of the Steamboat

THE specialised and complicated history of steamship building on the Clyde does not properly belong to this record, but that industrial development so profoundly affected social development along the shores of the Firth that we must understand the legend in outline at least.

Henry Bell, one has to say again and again, was not the inventor of the steamboat ; the *Comet* was far from being the first vessel propelled by steam-power, even in the Eastern Hemisphere. Much abler men than he had long before his time, and even in Scottish waters, contrived successfully to fit engines into hulls, and Fulton's steamboat was plying between Albany and New York on the Hudson for a considerable period before the *Comet*, on an August day of 1812, set off from Glasgow down-river to Greenock, a piper playing in the bows. Bell was not even an engineer in the sense of being but slightly skilled in metal-working or in the confinement and use of the power of steam. He was apprenticed a stonemason, had some brief experience as a millwright, duly studied the art of ship-modelling, worked for a space in London as a mason for Rennie, builder of the Waterloo Bridge, and in the early years of the 19th Century, after a spell in Glasgow, settled in Helensburgh as a builder.

The restlessness of this early career provides the clue to the sort of man he was. We can fairly see him as a rather attractive, fantastical, sanguine party of the speculative type. In Helensburgh he acquired the Baths (now the Queen's)

75

Hotel, its white front and castellated roofs still gleaming across nearly four miles of water in the direction of Greenock. His acquisition—one had almost said prefabrication—of the *Comet* was directly intended to improve the hotel business by the employment of a novelty. The rich of Glasgow and the hinterland were to be lured to the sea bathing at Helensburgh by this thrilling promise of travel by steamboat, just as an exploiter of the mid-20th Century, decreeing a pleasure dome on an island, might promise the customers exciting but reasonably safe transport by helicopter. Thus Bell persuaded the respectable boatbuilding firm of Wood in Port Glasgow to construct a wooden hull, 42 feet in length. He bought a steam engine from John Robertson, engineer in Glasgow. He found a boiler somewhere else, and these elements were somehow put together. Mr. Bell's business friends were all fated to wait a long time for their money.

Henry Bell was just in time, with only a few months to spare, in getting the *Comet* into the water and his name into the history books. We need not grudge him the laurels of enterprise, but we must see that he was truly the rather accidental and faintly comic herald of a natural surge of human progress. The real engineers, the shipbuilders of the future, were already at work, pondering with a caution poor Bell could never command the true problems of steam navigation. The first successor to the *Comet*, the *Elizabeth*, was in the water within months of the pioneer's appearance, and she was a much more stable, a faster and more efficient ship : an engineer's carefully-thought-out job. The pioneer was nominally this restless man, Henry Bell ; the true father of the steamship business was the Clydeside Engineer.

For a variety of historical reasons the springs of applied steam power released by the discoveries of James Watt were now starting to flow in force. It was a sudden and simultaneous upsurge of inventive enterprise. For fairly obvious reasons the

eager new engineers of Clydeside largely devoted themselves
to the science of applying the new source of energy to the
propulsion of boats. Nine of these fearsome vessels, " propelled
by fire and brimstone," as an older, Calvinistic generation
would have it, were launched in the year of grace 1814.
Britain was still fighting a desperate war against Napoleon ;
none of these ships was much more in length between perpendiculars than a cricket pitch, but they were all fiery particles.
Their success brought about one of the most sensational changes
in the balance of British industry : the shifting of the centre
of shipbuilding power from the ports of Southern England,
still devoted with proper English conservatism to wooden walls
and stout canvas, to the shores and embankments of a Scottish
estuary.

It was not long before steamboats out of the Clyde, mere
cockleshells in the familiar phrase, were venturing to Ireland
and the Mersey ports. Soon enough they were being exported
to the Thames. They plied on the North Sea route between
Leith and London, and one of them, the *James Watt*, in 1832
carried Walter Scott on his last journey home from London
to Leith : the journey that was so soon to end on " a beautiful
day—so warm that every window was wide open—and so
perfectly still, that the sound of all others most delicious to
his ear, the gentle ripple of the Tweed over its pebbles, was
distinctly audible as we knelt around the bed, and his eldest
son kissed and closed his eyes."

Scott's contemporary, John Galt, survived to write some
pieces about the coming of the steamboat, but these were the
facetious, journeyman productions of a novelist who had
already written himself out. There is almost no purely
literary record of Scotland's intense industrial development
during the 19th Century. This nation of craftsmen turned
its back on the arts and gave itself over almost entirely to the
job of working with machines.

The Firth of Clyde

The expanding metal industries called for more and more labour, and that was attracted, even imported in somewhat brutal ways, from the Highlands of Scotland and the bogs of Ireland. They concentrated in Glasgow and the coal- and iron-mining regions about that city to form what is nowadays called a connurbation of the most formidable dimensions : at the least, one-quarter of the population of all Scotland confined within that relatively small area about the bridgehead of the Clyde.

A truly fantastic paradox was thus created. Out of the slums in which they had to live this rough proletariat found the best way of escape in the steamboats of their own creation. They fled, if only on public holidays, towards the brilliance and beauty of the Firth of Clyde. They went " doon the watter," in the doric phrase, even if, given the regional defect of the glottal stop, it was more likely to sound like " doon the wa'er."

This complex of impulses was, in effect, to create a new social pattern. It was to foster what we would nowadays call a tourist industry. It was to create, especially along the northern shores of the Firth, sizeable pleasure resorts out of what had been before mere remote clusters of cottages with a couple of fishing smacks lying at a small stone jetty. It was to lead to the building of piers, hotels and villas ; to the working-out of navigational rules and to sharp interventions by the Board of Trade. Above all, it was eventually to display the perfect diagram of the social set-up in terms of Victorian industrialism : elegance and degradation, beauty and slovenliness, decency and debauch in fantastic but not wholly incomprehensible confusion.

The history of the Clyde passenger steamer is well-documented, and none of its numerous successors has superseded in value the book of that name by Captain James Williamson. This Captain Williamson, in his later years something of a dandy with a pointed white beard, was the complete product of the Clyde pleasure sailing business and one of its most distinguished figures. When the Clyde steamboat industry was in its infancy his father had left the freshwater shores of Loch Lomond to enter the new and rapidly-prospering trade on tidal waters. He succeeded, to the extent of becoming the owner of a small fleet of his own, and he brought up four sons to his trade.

James was remarkable among them in being both a qualified engineer by proper apprenticeship and then a skilled shipmaster, duly licensed as such by the Board of Trade. It is a remarkable and fortunate circumstance that from such an unlikely pen there came at length, if not a masterpiece of interpretative literature, an invaluable contribution to the social and economic history of modern Scotland. *Clyde Passenger Steamers* was published at 5s. or 6s. Thirty years later clean copies were selling as covetable rarities at 30s. With a good deal of attention to engineering detail that does not concern us here, Williamson's narrative, based both on family record and his own experience, covers completely and in intimate detail the mechanical and industrial developments in one sphere of nearly a century of what used to be called progress.

We are reminded how steamship building was originally an engineer's job, the mechanics, eager in competition, creating their beloved engines in the first place and then ordering from a boatbuilder the sort of hull most likely to suit the machinery. We learn how many of those individual engineers became shipowners, running their little vessels in sharp competition against the products of their rivals, with speed and comfort and cheapness always the counters in a nearly piratical game. We are told how so many of those primitive vessels were sold by devious means to run the Federal blockade in the American Civil War and how so many of them were to perish on the way—and still so many to make the perilous Atlantic passage and earn huge dividends for the spivs of the period. Williamson's account of the state of affairs on the Clyde, Ship-Channel and Firth, in the 1860's or 70's, is material for a dozen novels and two-score theses for the degree of B.Com.

This state was that of cut-throat private enterprise at its rawest—but also, let us not forget, at its most picturesque. Dozens of little vessels, individually owned by an engineer or an enterprising skipper, raced and touted for custom over many square miles of salt water. They raced with each other, barged each other at piers, exchanged insulting advertisements in the local newspapers, were fined for speeding down the Ship-Channel from Glasgow to Greenock and upsetting the navigational conventions of that tricky channel, and ruinously cut prices against each other. There was a time when the individual might have a whole day of sailing from Glasgow to Rothesay and back, a distance of some 80 miles, for a shilling. There were bankruptcies galore. This new ship and then that turned out to be " crank " or unaccountably slow or a glutton for coal—and was promptly sold to Italian or Turkish or Spanish owners. The skeletons of these old Clyde paddlers are still to be seen mouldering in creeks from the Great Lakes to Tasmania.

This regional trade was one of the crucibles in which the elements of an ultimately great shipbuilding industry were melted and fused. The little ships of the coastwise waters were the working models for the *Queen Mary* and the *Queen Elizabeth*. More to our present point, however, it had the effect of completely changing social dispositions and ways of life along the whole coastline of the Firth of Clyde and its lochs and islands.

The first of the effects was the development of pleasure resorts and of a catering industry. Small riparian communities, some of them mere villages, joyfully and untidily

SHORE ROAD: The typical West Highland track above the beach, southwards towards Otter Ferry on the eastern side of Loch Fyne.

LAWFUL OCCASIONS: The *Jeanie Deans* in L.N.E.R. colours at speed on the homeward journey towards Craigendoran.

expanded to make money out of the hordes from the Black Country up-river as the steamboat-owners chose the destinations of their excursions. Rothesay, on the island of Bute and at the head of a lovely and sheltered bay, was thus specially favoured ; so were Dunoon on the Cowal coast, Largs on the mainland seaboard of Ayrshire, and Millport on the larger of the Cumbraes. In places thus largely patronised by the mobs (and that harsh word is just in this context) the public houses proliferated and flourished ; the letting of rooms, with or without " attendance," became the economic stand-by of thousands of people, as simple in their own peasant way as the bovine trippers from the industrial concentrations.

At the same time, in that distant period of sharp economic and social differences, the well-to-do must have their own houses at " the Coast." The truly prosperous merchants of Glasgow had indeed enjoyed the delights of the estuary before the coming of the steamboat. There are extant several diverting records of elaborate journeys from the city to the sea, involving long hauls by carriage or coach from Glasgow to one of the Ayrshire ports, then the transfer of family, luggage, linen and servants into a fishing smack or gabbart, and then a long and stormy sail across the outer Firth, even to Arran. The large developments of the coast resorts followed that of the steamboat, and the rich went with the poor to the pleasant places. As we shall see in a later chapter, they sometimes chose the same places.

The coasts near Rothesay and Dunoon are littered with the heavy sandstone villas the new industrialists built for themselves. In other cases they created small, genteel settlements of their own ; Kilcreggan, Cove and Blairmore at the mouth of Loch Long are typical. Often enough these suburban extensions of the well-to-do were related to the new cult of yachting, another subject of still another chapter ; but the universal instinct of all classes of society on Clydeside during the 19th Century was to use the power of the steamboat to take them out of grey and crowded places to the agreeable shores of the splendid firth on their very doorstep.

No other estuary in the wide world was at that period so copiously, even redundantly, served by competitive shipping interests. It is fairly safe to say that there was never a coastal service so ample and so ridiculously cheap. Considering the size of the vessels employed in the trade, one is astonished by the bravura of the performance. Distances on this ramifying Firth of Clyde are formidable, but these cockleshells of the mid-19th Century were running daily from Greenock as far as, say, Inveraray at the head of Loch Fyne, or to Campbeltown just round the corner from the open Atlantic ; and that across leagues of nearly open sea. It was perhaps a unique case of a forceful new industry exploiting a territory uniquely suited to its first needs.

A contributing factor was that, in the native population of fisherfolk, familiar with all the navigational quirks of the Clyde estuary, its tides, narrows, landmarks and alarmingly sudden spasms of dirty weather, the engineers who built and exploited the steamboats had always a rich reserve of skilled labour, from mere deckhands to " skeely skippers." The greasy, grimy men in engineroom and stokehold came wholly of that other Scottish breed celebrated by Kipling in " Macandrew's Hymn " and " Brugglesmith "—the bastard but highly-individual tribe that evolved with the metal-working industries of Clydeside proper.

Thus and thus was the development of the Firth in its social aspects a distinctly haphazard affair, a pure product of what would nowadays be called *laissez faire* or an uncontrolled economy. In Captain James Williamson's classic work, however, and though he closed his record with that of the year 1901, we see through his shrewd eyes the shape of things to come.

The Coming of the Steamboat

By the late '70's of the 19th Century the individual owner-ship of small steamboats began, according to the inexorable laws of economics, to give place to small partnerships in small fleets or to the acquisition by family groups (like that of the Williamsons) of a few stout ships with their own distinctive colours on hull and funnel. At the same time, a new species of patron, evolving out of the same set of economic circumstances, was beginning to appear. He was the man of what is loosely called the lower-middle classes : the successful trades-man, the well-doing shopkeeper. He envied the rich, but could not afford their yachts and seaside villas. At the same time, and with some reason, he did not wish to take his womenfolk and children for a sail in a ship that, in its steerage department, would likely be packed with the very poor, the very rough, the very drunken—just as inevitable products of the system as himself.

Whisky . . . One is tempted into a lengthy digression, which might search quite profoundly into the diseases of a raw industrial civilisation and into the " furious " nature of the Scot. In any thoughtful reading of the history of the Clyde steamers a whole pattern of modern life is laid before us in daunting complexity. Whisky was the anodyne, the water of Lethe ; and it is to cut a long story short to say that the uprising of a class of " respectable " persons, even out of the mob, in the '70's and '80's started to insinuate another web into the social pattern.

Captain James Williamson himself worked industriously, even decisively, towards the improvement of general behaviour —and, whether he knew it or not, towards what we would call the " rationalisation " of the Clyde fleet of small paddle-steamers : that is, out of chaotic competition on the lines of individualism towards some sort of order and finally, for better or worse, towards nationalisation.

In the early '80's he was one of a syndicate, with the

83

charmingly antique title of the Firth of Clyde Steam Packet Company, formed to build and manage a graceful and famous vessel, the *Ivanhoe*. This was a ship of 225 feet in length, with two yellow funnels widely spaced and capable of a very fair turn of speed. The special interest of her, however, was that she was specially planned and equipped to cater for the newer, genteel sort of trade promised by the emergence of a substantial if nominally *petite bourgeoisie*. Her furnishings were " elegant " according to late Victorian lights. Much was made in advertisement of the " commodious " nature of the saloons. There was music, and the crew were so attired as to give the simple patron the illusion of travelling in a private yacht. Above all, this brave new ship voyaged unlicensed for the sale of intoxicating beverages.

She had her vogue. With the elegant, bearded figure of Captain Williamson on the bridge (his expert eye also on the engineering department) the *Ivanhoe* made her place in estuarine history. Alas ! however, for the vanity of human wishes and for the belief that popular catering can be contrived on teetotal lines. It was not very long before at least one astute spirit merchant in Glasgow had on sale the " Ivanhoe flask " for the benefit of male travellers in the vessel of that name. Within a few years the fashion had waned and the *Ivanhoe* was back with the ruck in the competitive business, and that with bars open to the convivial holidaymaker.

One is tempted to digress on the significance of this commercial adventure as an experiment in practical Calvinism, but it is enough that the vessel was probably the last and best expression of the purely private ownership of pleasure steamers on the Clyde. Much finer ships were still to be built, but with much more impersonal motives behind their building. As James Williamson recorded in the days of his maturity, new forces—and land forces at that !—were massing even in the heyday of the *Ivanhoe* to lay heavy financial hands on the breezy, untidy but delightfully coloured world of " the Boats."

Even the most casual student of British economic history knows that competition among the pioneer railway companies inclined to be at once fierce, expensive and often wasteful. Within the narrow realm of Scotland alone there operated before the First World War no fewer than five independent concerns. Of these three were of major stature ; and towards the end of the 19th Century all three began to interest themselves anxiously in the rich possibilities of the passenger traffic on the Firth of Clyde.

The companies concerned were the Caledonian and the Glasgow & South-Western, both with competing lines on the South bank of the Clyde from Glasgow down to Greenock, Gourock and parts adjacent ; the third the North British, with a monopoly on the North bank from Glasgow down to Helensburgh, opposite Greenock. For reasons too intricate to explain here this monopoly of the old N.B.R. was never even one-half so valuable as the traffic for which the Caley and the G. & S.-W. competed so bitterly on the other side of the Ship-Channel.

The Caledonian Railway, first in the field, completed its line from Glasgow to Greenock in 1841. The Greenock terminus lay in the centre of the town, and in so far as steamboat passengers were important, these must walk or be driven some 500 yards, through narrow, wind-swept and often rain-washed streets, to the Customhouse Quay, then the berthing place of both the Firth and Irish steamers. Nearly half a century was to pass before these urgent railway concerns began to perceive that there was a mint of money in the steamboat traffic, and that they could profitably exploit it only if their trains could be laid alongside the points of embarkation. The economic corollary was that railway companies should go into the steamboat business on their own account ; the principle of centralisation and somewhat remote control being thus justified to their own satisfaction in the earnest minds of the earlier capitalists.

Herein resided a delightful irony ; and within the period of competitive expansion the railway companies performed some remarkable acts of highly-expensive development. The nature of these was largely dictated by the obdurate character of the shape and substance of the land about the Port of Greenock. The necessity to drive long tunnels through the hard igneous rock upon which the town is built cost sums that would now be reckoned in millions. The series of tunnels on the old Caledonian line from Greenock Central to Fort Matilda extend over a distance of nearly three miles. The mazy and wildcat struggles of the promoters to establish themselves on the upper reaches of the Firth belong, however, to another history, and we merely note the fact that by the mid-80's they had succeeded in doing so.

The Caledonian concern had already built a line high along the slopes above Greenock to a railway pier at Wemyss Bay. The Glasgow & South-Western concern had come down the hills above Port Glasgow and driven its tunnels under Greenock to Princes Pier. The Caledonian company had extended its line from Greenock Central to Gourock and there built a railway pier. At Craigendoran on the opposite shore and hard by Henry Bell's hotel the North British undertaking had set up a rail-steamboat terminus with not a few physical disadvantages. Finally, and perhaps in retort to the Caledonian development at Wemyss Bay, the Glasgow & South-Western made use of piers at Fairlie and Ardrossan on the Ayrshire coast, somewhat exposed but convenient enough by rail from Glasgow and well-placed for steamer runs to Arran. . . . If these convolutions seem intricate and only to be followed by careful map-reading, they very prettily symbolise the outcome of the conflict between competitive expansion and the stubborn

The Coming of the Steamboat

topography of this south-western corner of Scotland. One wonders what a planner of the 1950 type would have made of the geographical problems alone.

Thus, at all events, the railway companies—most by then amalgamations and all now invested with the appropriate powers by Parliament—set up briskly in the steamboat business. The twilight of private ownership was about to fall, but competition at the sharpest pitch was to remain for many years to come.

The railways started by acquiring each a nucleus of sound vessels from private owners. Soon enough they were ordering new ships as their understanding of the requirements of the trade improved. Captain James Williamson took the *Ivanhoe* and himself as a Marine Superintendent of genius into the service of the Caledonian Steam Packet Company, with headquarters at Gourock. His brother, Alexander, accepted the same position at Princes Pier with the Glasgow & South-Western. A third brother went South also to engage in the management of pleasure craft. A fourth, Captain John Williamson, chose to remain independent and that with, as we shall see, interesting results.

That the Clyde steamer services were immensely improved by the intervention of the railway companies there can be no doubt at all. There was capital to spare, and now the little ships were well-found, amply manned by qualified seamen and engineers, brightly painted, kept clean, and run punctually to schedule, wind and weather permitting. When the railways started building on their own account, having discovered what types of vessels were best suited to the various branches of their trades, they built with distinction.

Each, indeed, evolved a type of its own. The Caledonian steamers gave the general impression of swift, slim grace, the illusion heightened by the apparent lightness of the yellow funnel and the slimming effect of black paint on the hull. The

South-Western boats, on the other hand, suggested bluff strength and forcefulness, as if they would cheerfully set out for New York to-morrow. This, again, was possibly an illusion created by the impact of a distinctive colour scheme —red, black-topped funnels above french grey hulls with a broad band of white intervening. The ships of the North British seemed somewhat nondescript and clumsy in comparison, though some of their later vessels, notably the *Waverley* of 1899, had both grace and speed.

Both the external and internal decoration of the ships was important in the competitive phase of Clyde steamer history, and the styles were distinctly Victorian in flavour. The first-class saloon of any paddler of the late 19th Century bore a close resemblance to the parlour, if not the drawing-room, of any mansionhouse ashore. Externally, the decorative instincts of the period went into elaborate and often handsome modelling and painting of the outer casings of the paddle-boxes. In the modern paddle-steamer the paddle-boxes are, as it were, built into the hull and their outward appearance is, as they say, purely functional. In the more spacious days any one of these little ships carried on its paddle-boxes the equivalent of an inn sign, in which a vast amount of crude heraldry and fine craftsmanship would be commingled.

Fortunately, at least two specimens of these decorative scrolls have been preserved. The Caledonian Steam Packet Company owned in the *Duchess of Hamilton* an unusually elegant vessel. She went to the wars in 1915 and was rather dreadfully transformed into a minesweeper ; and in November that year she was sunk—by a mine. Happily, the scrolls of her paddle-boxes in gilt and bright colours had been preserved, and during the years of L.M.S. control between the wars these were set up in cases for public viewing : one in the Central Station, Glasgow, its twin in Princes Street Station, Edinburgh.

Perhaps the finest expression of both the Victorian genius

for the production of fine engineering jobs and of the Victorian taste in what were called the " appointments " was in that famous, elegant and deeply-mourned vessel, R.M.S. *Columba*, the heroine of a legend.

The great Queen herself travelled her way. Throughout the summer months for decades on end the *Columba* maintained with quite remarkable precision the inner leg of what was widely advertised as " the Royal Route." Every morning she left her berth in the heart of Glasgow on the stroke of 7.11 a.m., made a call at Greenock's Princes Pier about one hour and a half later, proceeded to Gourock Pier, and then set out by way of Dunoon, Rothesay and the Kyles of Bute for Tarbert and Ardrishaig on arms of Loch Fyne, at the latter port linking with a service through the Crinan Canal and so, by another change of steamer, to Oban. She returned to Greenock about 5 p.m. and berthed again at Glasgow about 7 p.m.

It was a long day's work for ship and crew ; out of each day there were left only 12 hours for refuelling and revictualling at Glasgow. In the labour conditions of the period, however, all this was duly contrived, and men said fondly that you could set your watch by the movements of this beloved ship. They also said that she " ran like a sewing-machine," so smooth and relatively silent were her movements through water. David Macbrayne owned her : a man who, taking over an older company, built up a near-monopoly of the passenger and cargo trades on the seaboard of the Western Highlands.

The *Columba* was built in 1878 by J. & G. Thomson of Clydebank and thus came out of the yard that latterly produced the two great *Queens* for the Cunard White Star line. She was a big vessel in her period and class, fully 300 feet between perpendiculars. She had a cutter bow and sat low in the water with something of the grace of a racing yacht. Her oscillating engines of 544 h.p. drove her with speed and that always remarkable smoothness. In the *Columba* they made much of passenger comfort and solidity in the catering department ; and though, with her long-distance itinerary and her associations with journeys beyond the confines of the Firth, she hardly seemed to belong to the community of the inner Firth, she was certainly the finest expression of the pleasure steamboat driven by paddles ever conceived. When, after nearly 60 years of useful and decorative life, she went to the knacker's yard—in 1935, to be precise—men were moved actually to tears and to more columns of obituary notices than the passing of a great poet might have occasioned.

The existence of a cult of the Clyde steamer is a fact of much social interest. There exists a Clyde River Steamer Club, which sedulously collects and preserves and records the memories and emblems of the brave days of free enterprise on the Firth, when scores of little ships, each with its own interest as a job of shipbuilding and engineering, churned the estuarine waters and saucily competed for custom. The cult is a clear symptom of nostalgia ; it harks back to the days when life was cheaper, easier, simpler and brighter in colour. It recalls the youth of a generation only now middle-aged. It exists, as it were, to register a protest against change and to declare for values in danger.

The entrance of the railway companies into the passenger business on the Firth of Clyde did not by any means do away with wasteful competition. If the authorities in Glasgow or Edinburgh officially frowned on such cantrips as racing for piers, no Highland skipper of spirit, or his chief engineer from Greenock, could be prevented from seeking to show his rival on the same run what he could do in the way of speed when put to it. One has seen two railway steamers of rival companies racing along the Cowal coast for the pier at Innellan at a speed at least a knot above schedule, the washes on their funnels burned brown by the stokehold efforts to produce that little extra head of steam.

The Coming of the Steamboat

What such as Captain James Williamson would have thought of ultimate nationalisation and of a fleet so reduced that in 1950 it was barely sufficient for its tasks one cannot know. But even though, as Marine Superintendent of the Caledonian steamers, he was heavily involved in the competition among the three railway companies, he clearly perceived the shape of things to come and in his history was bold enough to write :

" Much of the service is superfluous and needless, the sole advantage derived from the running of three steamers where one would serve being to afford the public a choice of route. One has only to watch the converging of the steamers from the coast towns off Gourock on a summer morning between eight o'clock and a quarter past. At that hour there are in sight no fewer than nine steamers on five days of the week, and eleven on Mondays.

" This flotilla is employed to carry passengers who, in the aggregate, could be accommodated comfortably on board three steamers. The entire performance is in reality a continuation of the steamboat fight for supremacy, the only difference being that the combatants are now more formidable and the struggle more wasteful than it ever was before."

In the meantime, Captain Williamson's brother John, he who had remained an independent, dropped an explosive element into the accepted system of Clyde pleasure sailing.

Working on Tyneside, Sir Charles Parsons had perfected the turbine engine. The old but always progressive ship-building firm of Denny of Dumbarton on the Clyde, specialists in fast passenger vessels, were naturally interested in this development. In the issue there was formed " The Turbine Syndicate" which, in close collaboration with Parsons, built and engined for the Clyde pleasure service the *King Edward*, the first turbine-engined vessel to be put, in 1901, into successful commercial employment.

To those of us who were little boys at the time she seemed very wonderful and strangely beautiful. It was astonishing that a river steamer could do without paddles ; there was a dark fascination in the boards with the " Keep off Propellers " warning hung under her stern. She was lean and very silent in motion. Old hands in the engineering trades hinted sourly that there would be an explosion one of these days, with all that head of steam at high pressure.

The public meanwhile flocked to patronise the elegant novelty. She was put on the long run to Campbeltown and did so well that the Syndicate immediately ordered an improved consort in the *Queen Alexandra*. Shortly the two turbines were efficiently maintaining two long-distance daily services : to Campbeltown and to Inveraray at the head of Loch Fyne, the two longest excursions possible within the confines of the Firth.

The coming of the turbine steamer was, in fact, to sharpen competition and to have the effect of weeding out the more inefficient among the side-paddle-steamers. With its high speed and considerable length, the turbine was not suited for the short hauls of the pier-to-pier ferry service ; it was more naturally fitted for long cruises with few stops. Many men not yet old remember with pleasure how, on any Saturday afternoon in the season before the First World War, it was possible to enjoy a long and invigorating sail—from Greenock round Ailsa Craig and back, it might be—at a fare that, even with the cost of a meal thrown in, seemed ludicrously cheap 40 years later. The turbine was above all the ideal vessel to carry on the great Clyde tradition of the Evening Cruise.

In the labour conditions of the mid-20th Century it seems remarkable that it was ever contrived, but after the long day of voyaging to Campbeltown or Inveraray and back, the *King Edward* or the *Queen Alexandra* was turned about at Greenock, refuelled and revictualled, and sped once more down the Firth with another complement of people seeking but a breath of fresh air and the stimulus of the Firth's beauty, the German band ministering powerfully to the sentimental pleasures of the occasion.

These evening cruises were not, except on special occasions, of any great range. It might be down to Rothesay and back, with a look into the Kyles of Bute or Loch Striven ; it might be a turn up Loch Long or round the Cumbraes. It was a delightful form of refreshment, and it seems fantastic in our more complicated times that it could be enjoyed from Greenock for a shilling, with a penny or two dropped into the velvet collecting bag of the German band's second cornetist. On the strength of cheap railway fares from Glasgow, even the city-dweller could have a night out on the Firth for three shillings at the most, taken from the city about 6 p.m. and returned, rested and refreshed, little more than four hours later.

The Caledonian Steam Packet Company produced a notably fast turbine steamer in 1906, and the *Duchess of Argyll* is still in honourable service. On the whole, however, the railway companies were content for many years to leave the turbine monopoly to John Williamson's white-funnelled grey-hounds, failing to perceive, one may think, that the long-range cruising capacity of the turbine-engined ship, with its appeal to the average tourist, was to have the ultimate effect of by-passing the little communities made by the paddle-steamer. That the development of the turbine vessel started the slow decline of the Firth of Clyde as a pleasure ground, of its innumerable resorts and of the standing of its pleasure fleet, is a reasonably accurate generalisation.

As we shall see later on, many other social and economic factors were at work, but let us take it meanwhile in terms of estuarine shipping alone. One would suggest in the first place that the Clyde scene was at its brightest and best in, say, the year 1910. Edward the Seventh's unique creation of a general sense of comfortable grandeur, even if it was only a *folie de grandeur*, informed the behaviour of the masses of the British people. On Clydeside alone the workers were well placed, turning out the warships for the conflict that was to be the first step towards a decline. For their delight there plied on the Firth of Clyde the bright, bustling fleets of three railway companies. The white-funnelled turbines darted up and down the waterway. Macbrayne and a few other independent owners maintained among them at least a dozen vessels, Buchanan's black-and-white funnelled " Sunday-breakers " among them.

By 1910 the " Sunday-breakers " had lost most of their notoriety, as in 1950 even British Railways were Sunday-breaking with a will, but the survival of the phrase witnessed to the importance of the social change they symbolised.

Out of deference to Presbyterian feelings in these matters few of the independent steamboat owners of the old days worked their services on the Sabbath Day. As long ago as 1853, however, the owner of a vessel called the *Emperor* took to running his ship with Sunday excursions to Garelochhead. The local laird and owner of the piers at that once pleasant village, Sir James Colquhoun of Luss, objected to these weekly invasions of rough parties from industrial Clydeside, and on the 22nd day of August, 1853, he had a small army of policemen and his own gamekeepers down to deny the *Emperor's* rough passengers the right to land.

There was a fight in consequence, nearly a riot. Bottles and stones and lumps of coal hurtled from ship to shore and back again. There was a lively dispute over a long pole, which was used by the defenders on the pier to push the boat away. She returned, and the upholders of tradition were

forced by another fusillade of coal to take cover behind a
barricade Sir James had had prudently erected. This was
rushed by the mob from the steamer and overwhelmed. Sir
James shortly reverted to the ordinary processes of the law
and, after some years of litigation and the spending of much
money, secured the injunction necessary to protect the Sabbath
sanctity of his property and tenants.

It seems merely funny and considerably absurd now, but
the episode was significant in the terms of Scottish life at least.
It was in fact repeated in the last years of the 19th Century,
at Dunoon, when some of the local Presbyterian ministers
rallied forces and marched down to the pier to prevent, if they
could, the landing of passengers from one of the " Sunday-
breakers." Their effort was in vain. The invaders, mostly
from Glasgow and out of the claustrated labouring classes,
climbed the barricades and chased the defenders away.

It is all too easy to make fun of episodes of the kind. The
ways of the Presbyterian Kirks of yesterday form the easiest
of sitting-targets for the satirist. It is more important to
comprehend that " Sunday-breaking " was a phenomenon in
the social rather than the religious order of things. It represented the intense pressure outwards, towards fresh air, beauty
and light, of an overcrowded industrial population. And it was
these who mainly maintained the Clyde pleasure steamers in
their heyday.

It is all past now, for better or worse. Various pressures
and inclinations and imperatives developed to reduce both
the size of the Clyde fleet and its place in public favour. Two
wars took most of the paddlers away to serve as minesweepers
and such, and some were never to return. The railway
amalgamations of 1923 were a blow to individuality and
character at least. Those ancient rivals, the ships of the
Caledonian and South-Western fleets, were brought together
under the L.M.S. flag and rigged out in an unsatisfactory

colour scheme, including a yellow funnel with a black top and a red band intervening. On the other side of the Firth the old N.B. steamers carried on in their original colours but under the L.N.E.R. pennant. Perhaps it is hardly worth while asking now why all the Scottish railways were not gathered into one national group, but it is only worth recording that any man sensitive to the emanations of the *genius loci* began at that period to feel on his skin the cold touch of remote control.

To be sure, the L.M.S. policy during the decade following the First World War was progressive. It built and put into service several handy little paddlers for the ferry routes and at least two magnificent turbine vessels for long-distance cruising. But a second war and ultimate nationalisation reduced the fleet, in yellow and black-topped funnels, both in size and adequacy.

While, however, it is reasonable to suggest that the young British Railways had even by 1950 failed to get the measure of their task on the Firth of Clyde, it would be wrong to imply that the public demand for their services was what it had been in 1910. The people of the industrial hinterland had started to look beyond their native Firth for relaxation ; and this mass-movement, to be analysed later on, affected both the steamers and the destinies of many of those little riparian communities they had so greatly helped to create.

GOUROCK: Principal steamboat and rail terminal of the Firth, from the heights above Greenock, looking north-west towards the Holy Loch and the Cowal mountains.

MORNING AT HUNTER'S QUAY: The view eastwards from the famous yachting centre towards the entrance to the Clyde Ship-Channel.

ISLANDS OF THE OUTER FIRTH: Across the Greater and Lesser Cumbrae towards the peaks of Arran, from above Largs on the Ayrshire coast. Note left the monument for the Battle of Largs, 1263 A.D.

CHAPTER III

Towns of the Upper Reaches

I

EXCEPT those that are strung along the low and sandy foreshore of the Ayrshire bight—that is, from West Kilbride southwards to Ayr itself—the towns, townlets, villages and hamlets on the shores of the Firth of Clyde occupy sites of unusual distinction. Most are picturesquely built up steep, green slopes above the sea and, if not, on agreeable flats within the embracing arms of pretty lochs. The adventurousness of domestic building on abrupt hillsides is the prevailing *motif*, and it must all look very strange to an East Anglian, for instance, just as the Western Scot invariably feels that there is something wrong, if not positively dangerous, about the landscape of Holland.

The foreign traveller, coming up the Firth on a fine evening in a liner anchoring off Greenock, undoubtedly forms an agreeable impression of that town in its physical aspects. Especially with the lambent glow of a western sunset upon it, its situation appears to possess the nobility proper to a great harbour. Above its western suburbs there towers an outcrop of rock, jutting towards the West with the *panache* of a great galleon's prow : a huge Cross of Lorraine on the skyline intimating the importance of the port to the Free French during the Second World War. It is to be seen that the villas along the terraces above the sea are solidly, often elegantly, built in sandstone and pleasantly embowered amid tall trees. The middle parts of the town seem to clamber picturesquely to a height of nearly 500 feet along the escarpment of the sub-highlands of Renfrewshire. The eye is carried along miles of precipitous land most boldly built upon, and the imagination rightly envisages a range of unusually steep streets and rutted lanes.

Unfortunately, the noble appearance of Greenock and its satellites from the sea is sadly contradicted by the grim realities of the older and inner parts of these communities ; and hereabouts one may venture on an interesting if disputable generalisation.

Too often we are all prone to say that such-and-such is a pretty place, whereas the more exact statement would be that such-and-such is a rather slattern town in a lovely setting. This, unhappily, is only too true of too many of the Clyde coast settlements. On the east coast of Scotland—in such places so widely spaced as Dunbar, St Andrews, Montrose and Peterhead—the standards of civic decency in architecture and lay-out have the tidiness and often the loveliness produced by the keen burghal sense of the Teuton element in the population. In the west, on the other hand, where the Celtic lack of civic experience became a factor in a rapid and uncontrolled industrial expansion, the communal results were too often deplorable : slums proliferating in Arcady itself.

It is right to observe that during the period between the two wars the larger Clyde coast resorts strove admirably to clear up the meannesses that were their inheritance from the thoughtless expansionism of the Victorians, even if it was only in face of the economic pressure of competition from livelier and newer pleasure grounds in England and the Isle of Man. It is equally proper to state that Greenock was in two wars the melting-pot of the rough seamen of several nations, only too eager to blow off steam after stress and to spend accumulated wages. This town was moreover heavily bombed by the Germans in 1941, and it is of grimly ironical interest that, when a missile hit one of its tenement buildings built in the soaring Scots tradition on steep slopes, the ensuing concentration of casualties was apt to be lamentably high.

The accidents of war, however, cannot away with the civic sins of the past, and the contrast between the elegant solidity of Greenock's West End and the untidiness of its central and business parts is depressing. The town's site on a narrow riparian strip under high and steep hills has dictated that its main street must be tortuous, and it is quite hideously diversified by the competing fascias of multiple shops. (When tram-cars ran along it, the clangour and congestion were incredible in the modern understanding.) Despite a few occasional beauties, a few good buildings, some antiquarian oddities and many startling vistas, what one misses in the town of Greenock is any trace of a distinctive style or traditional pattern in its physical make-up. Of all the larger towns of Scotland it is at least the perfect example of what the Teuton-Celt conflict was bound to produce within the conditions of Victorian industrialism.

Above all, Greenock is not an old town deeply rooted in the life of Scotland. It was in the first place, in fact, an *ad hoc* creation. Until near the middle of the 17th Century it was little more than a hamlet of small fishermen. Then an enlightened laird, or landlord, of the native family of Schaw, conceived the idea of creating a harbour at this highest point of anchorage on the Firth of Clyde. From the restored Charles II this laird, Sir John Schaw, and his colleagues obtained the necessary warrant to establish Greenock as a Burgh of Barony, as the phrase then ran. Seaborne trade with the Americas was beginning to develop, however spasmodically. The herring fisheries were of increasing importance to the increasing population of the Scottish Lowlands. When the Union of the Parliaments of England and Scotland was consummated by the Act of 1707, the new Burgh of Greenock began to thrive as a seaport. Even then it set up in business as a shipbuilding centre. The considerable business of Scotts' Shipbuilding & Engineering Company, Ltd., the oldest ship-building concern in the world, still controlled in the hereditary line, derives from the small private boatyard set up by John Scott in 1711 for the fabrication of herring busses or, as we should say nowadays, fishing smacks.

Greenock enjoyed its brief golden age during the Napoleonic wars. The privateering system conferred on the merchant-shipowner remarkable opportunities of making a great deal of money, and for a score of years on end few ships out of the port sailed without a joint armoury of cannon and Letters of Marque. Prizes of fabulous value were brought in through the Western Approaches, and at the same time several of the merchant princes acquired valuable possessions in the West Indies—teak forests in the Honduras, sugar plantations in Jamaica. One of the largest concerns for a period stacked the island of Heligoland with coffee from its own plantations in San Domingo, selling it into Northern Europe through Napoleon's blockade. The sugar-refining industry, still one of Greenock's staples, developed largely out of these connections; the furniture manufactories of the nearby towns of Loch-winnoch and Beith were founded largely on the fine woods imported through Greenock.

These Greenock merchants of the late 18th and early 19th Centuries thought grandly of the future of their town. They were leaders in the movement that broke the East India Company's monopoly ; they promoted a Bill, luckless in the event, to establish a local university. The glory was short-lived. As soon as the merchants of Glasgow had contrived their Ship-Channel the fate of Greenock as a major port was sealed, and the larger cargoes sailed past her dockgates to be unloaded so much nearer the populous heart of Scotland.

Towns of the Upper Reaches

The local shipowning business was a long time a-dying nevertheless. Well towards the end of the 19th Century many fine ships, famous clippers among them, had Greenock as their port of registry ; Steele's of Greenock were among the most distinguished of clipper-builders. The inevitable drift towards centralisation, however, took the shipping trade to just a few main British ports—notably to Glasgow in Scottish conditions —and this town's shipping connections with the larger world dwindled to a coastal trade of moderate dimensions. Even before the Second World War it had ceased to be a pleasure-steamer terminus of any consequence.

Shipbuilding remained and remains, with engineering, the backbone of the town's economy, but highly productive as this is, it is but another phase of Greenock's destiny as a place most strangely cramped. In economic terms, it lacks the variety of industry that cushions other communities against the jolts of slump conditions in world trade. Just so, as even the stranger's eye may perceive at a glance, it is almost incapable of physical expansion : so steep are the slopes in the background, so wild and soggy the moors on the plateau over the skyline. By the middle of 1950 the planners were aiming to " decant " some 30,000 of Greenock's population into a new town to be created on the Renfrewshire uplands about Houston, while the local authorities were agitating to use their last possible line of expansion—the short stretch of the Kip Valley which, running south-westwards behind the butt on which the Cloch Lighthouse stands, could serve for little more than the easing of congestion. Expansion of a population of roughly 80,000 is virtually impossible, and Greenock thus presents the elements of a case of claustration, and frustration, almost unique.

From the sea, at least, the stranger's eye sees what he believes to be Greenock as an immensely long strip of " connurbation " under those glooming slopes of the Renfrewshire hills, but it is probably not explained to him that this settlement, strung along so many miles of coast, consists of three separate and independent burghs—Port Glasgow (with a population of about 22,000) to the eastward and Gourock (population about 9,000) to the West, with Greenock in between, its centre marked by the remarkably high Victoria Tower of its municipal buildings. Together the three communities, which are now completely fused in the physical sense, would make a city of much the same size as Dundee, but though the local authority of Greenock has more than once sought to bring about the merger, strong sentimental opposition from its neighbours, Port Glasgow in particular, has stood in the way of union.

Port Glasgow, as we have agreed, is not on the Firth of Clyde proper, but its ships and its shipbuilders had much to do with the making and shaping of the coastal community. Physically, it shares many of the qualities of Greenock : notably a rather grubby central area and solid, fine houses climbing up even steeper slopes towards the high farming country behind. Otherwise its interest is largely historical, and that in an odd context. The fine old Castle of Newark, now an Ancient Monument, broods in dark rose-red above the Ship-Channel towards the eastern end of the town, but the true interest of Port Glasgow is that it represents its parent city's last attempt to get a footing for its seaborne trade on deep water.

The efforts of the Glasgow merchants to secure a foreport for their merchandise both inwards and outwards would make the subject of a separate study at length. Their battle was a long and complicated one against the interests of several communities nearer the sea. During the 17th Century they encountered the trading prejudices of the Royal Burghs of Renfrew and Dumbarton, both just a few miles nearer the tidal sea. For a time they used the small harbour of Blackness on the Forth for their Continental trade. They took to employing the harbour at Irvine on the Ayrshire coast for their purposes of Atlantic commerce. They even hired vessels out of Whitehaven and other ports of Cumberland to carry their goods. And even although the first effort to deepen the Clyde was made in the 16th Century, it was not until near the end of the 17th that they agreed to take " ane peice land " from Sir Patrick Maxwell of Newark and there create, in deliberate challenge to the stubborn jealousy of the upstart Greenock, a new Port Glasgow of their own.

This was a successful venture. The first triumph of the Glasgow magistrates was to secure for their new creation the premier customs-house on the Clyde. That was an advantage in those days, and the building still stands in considerable dignity though its day is long past. Here they built the first graving-dock in Scotland. Their ships traded widely overseas, and shipbuilding flourished. Here was built by John Wood and his sons the wooden hull of the portentous *Comet*. Glasgow's new port never quite overtook the volume of Greenock's trade at the more convenient point of anchorage, but it served its day in considerable splendour. Its ironical fate was to be abandoned by its promoters once they had succeeded in opening their Ship-Channel, leaving it to share the commercial fate of its hated rival, Greenock.

Thus Port Glasgow has come to wear the air of orphanhood, as it were. Its harbours came to be of little account. A rather fine Town House in the Doric manner is much less handsomely matched by its environment of the obsolete harbour on the one side and tenement buildings on the other of the main road that must carry the heavy burden of Glasgow-Greenock traffic. Port Glasgow, once the pride of the City of Glasgow, was left at least with an extensive shipbuilding industry and a rope and sailmaking concern so venerable and important that it made the ropes for both the *Comet* and the *Queen Mary* and produced the big top for the Bertram Mills' Circus. It may be significant, however, that towards the middle of the 20th Century an industrial estate was set up on the high lands above the eastern end of the town to absorb the surplus labour of a community that was artificially created and then discarded by its creators.

Gourock, the smallest of the three conjoined burghs, has a longer history than its larger neighbours and differs from them in character in that it latterly developed almost entirely as a residential area and that its western portions look boldly across the Firth proper to the Highland hills. Manifestly, the bay in the shelter of the bold ridge that divides the town into two quite distinct parts must have been a better harbour of refuge from the prevailing sou'-westerlies than the less definite indentation before Greenock. Hence in 1494 sailed James IV of Scotland on an expedition to the Western Isles. Here was the base of a fishing fleet, and a perdurable legend maintains that on its shores the first red herring ever cured in Britain was experimentally " processed " : this interesting event taking place in 1688. In a hollow not far from the Greenock boundary, now an agreeable public park, the powerful family of Douglas had a small castle or outpost, though no trace of it remains.

The most interesting relic of the past in Gourock is a monolith of grey mica schist, some six feet high and known as " Granny Kempock." To the eye of indifference it looks a very ordinary lump of stone at a corner of a narrow lane amid undistinguished tenement buildings, but it seems to be a link between modern Gourock and pagan times.

It is on record that seamen, each carrying a basket of sea sand and chanting a rune, would walk round it seven times in an incantation for fair winds and safe voyaging. The circuit was also necessary to secure the bliss of newly-wedded spouses. In 1662 an unfortunate girl in her 'teens, Mary Lamont, is reported to have confessed at a witch-trial (which was no doubt part of a witch-hunt at that troublous period of Scotland's history) that she took part in " a meeting at Kempock, where they intended to cast the longstone into the sea, thereby to destroy boats and ships ; where they also danced and the devil kissed them when they went away." With other unhappy females she was duly burned at the stake.

Modern Gourock would hardly suggest to the stranger that it had any history at all. Such industries as it possessed departed during the 19th Century, being replaced by such activities as centre round a railway and steamboat terminus and, in the 20th Century, by its development as a seaside resort. The older parts of the town, on the leeward slope of the median ridge, look up the estuary and command some pleasant prospects, but only across the sidings and idle carriages and wagons of the maritime station. The modern town's fortunes are round the corner, so to speak, where beyond the railway pier the line of the coast swings south-westwards and opens up the view of the Firth proper. A promenade runs a mile and more along this front to the headquarters of the Royal Gourock Yacht Club, and the turnpike beyond offers a lovely walk by the shore to the Cloch Lighthouse.

Not every architectural prospect on this western side of Gourock Pierhead is guaranteed to please. The fatal slatternliness of the Celtic West is only too obvious at intervals along a bight commanding such brilliant vistas. Even so, Gourock's claims to a considerable share of the pleasure traffic is soundly based. It was, in historical fact, a favourite resort when it first became the fashion to go to " the Coast " for " the sea bathing." The rocky shore would not commend itself to the taste of the mid-20th Century, and an artificial pond can contain all who would venture into these cold and salty waters. The chief assets are plenty of fresh air, a sufficiency of organised amusement but, far and above all else, the view across and down the Firth.

The Firth of Clyde

There is to be discerned in this western part of the town one of the most urgent examples of that *motif* so characteristic of the Firth of Clyde communities—the piling, tier upon tier, higgledy-piggledy, of cottages and villas up steep hillsides, wherever the builders could find a terrace, or even a ledge, of ground on which a building could be placed with reasonable security. In the most westerly part of Gourock, called Ashton, this suggestion of a group of cliff-dwellings is even stronger than it is in Port Glasgow ; the lanes and steps that give access from the heights to sea-level are often of fantastic steepness. On the uppermost heights of all, the wealth of Clydeside has built from time to time many most desirable houses. The number of season-ticket holders from Gourock to Glasgow and back by a frequent service of fast trains is, in due proportion, equivalent to the weight of traffic from, say, Southport to Liverpool or even Richmond to Waterloo, especially since Gourock Pier receives the numerous, and hardy, daily travellers from Kilcreggan, Kirn and Dunoon on the other side of the Firth.

The prime asset is still the view northwards across the Firth. From the higher levels you look down on the sea as on a scene stereoscopically sharpened. The brisk ship life of the Firth is endlessly interesting. The eye may range on a fine evening round a semi-circle of hills at an average 3000-feet level, stretching more than half the breadth of Scotland, and all the colours of the rainbow upon their distant slopes and peaks in the hour or two before and after the long sun-setting of the North. Above the nearer peaks of Cowal the sunset can be fiery in the most melodramatic degree. For this revelation alone many men remember a not otherwise notably distinguished community.

It is indeed a very curious thing that, the case of Gourock apart, all the communities of the Estuary, as distinct from the Firth of Clyde, are artificial creations, their roots only shallowly embedded in the blood-stained soil of Scottish history, their fates always dependent on the growth of the industrial power of Glasgow, the big city at the bridgehead upstream. As we have seen, Greenock was independently established but had to bow to Glasgow's domination of the Ship-Channel, while Port Glasgow was created by the city merchants and duly discarded when the channel was opened to big shipping. From these slightly forlorn ports we now look across the estuary to a town most deliberately created in the late 18th Century to catch what it is fashionable nowadays to call " the overspill " of Glasgow in its gay period of expansion after the Act of Union with England. This community bears the clumsy name of Helensburgh.

The eponymous Helen was a daughter of Lord Strathnaver, of the family of the Earls of Sutherland ; she became the wife of Sir James Colquhoun of Luss, a family still most creditably connected with the western shores of Loch Lomond and quite notably intelligent in its dealings with the outward surge of popular holiday traffic from the industrial regions into its lands.

This Sir James and his advisers must have been shrewd people, acutely perceiving the inevitable drift of the well-to-do out of Glasgow and the industrial hinterland. They inserted in the *Glasgow Journal* of January 11, 1776, the following advertisement :

NOTICE.—To be feued immediately, for building upon, at a very reasonable rate, a considerable piece of ground, upon the shores of Malig, opposite Greenock. The land lies on both sides of the road leading from Dunbarton to Row. The ground will be regularly laid out for houses and gardens, according to plan. There is a freestone quarry on the ground.

For the accommodation of the feuars the proprietor is to enclose a large field for grazing their milk cows, etc.

N.B.—Bonnet-makers, stocking, linen and woollen weavers will meet with proper encouragement. There is a large boat building at the place for ferrying men and horses with chaises.

Perhaps it should be explained that to "feu" a piece of ground in Scotland is to take out a lease in perpetuity, a considerable variation from English practice in landholding : and that "Row" is now spelt "Rhu" in a slightly bogus Gaelic way : *rudha* signifying a promontory or spit such as runs out from the place of that name to form the Narrows against Rosneath on the other side of the Gareloch.

Sir James's enterprise was well rewarded. If there is no record that bonnet-makers and weavers flocked to the new settlement, the feus were taken up eagerly. Mr. Henry Bell's Baths Hotel became popular—as it still is under another name. To-day Helensburgh is an unusually tidy and attractive town of an almost purely residential character, its villas, climbing high up the agreeable slopes, substantial and often quite singularly handsome, their well-tended gardens delightfully blooming in a mild, moist climate that particularly favours the rose and the sweet pea. To fly over it is to see how its lay-out is regular without monotony—indeed a model of intelligent town-planning. Sound taste in local administration at one period lined all the broad upper streets with flowering trees, so that in spring these quiet roads are most happily lighted by the blossom of the wild cherry. The shopping centre is remarkably attractive for a place with a population of only about 9000.

Helensburgh officially advertises itself, with help from the railway authorities, as a pleasure resort. One has seen, and blushed to see, on the hoardings in a wayside station in southern England a poster that represented the place as a sort of Morecambe, with striped awnings, the ruddy domes of pleasure palaces in the 20th Century style, and a fringe of bright sand ; whereas the Helensburgh foreshore is an unfortunate combination of rock and weed, and the attractions offered to the beanfeaster are confined to a good swimming-pool, an unusually attractive public park, and a promenade along the front that commands attractive views and is separated from the busy shore road by green turf, much of it given over to putting-greens. The town is also advantaged by the facts that it lies only six miles over the hill from Loch Lomond, and that it is a convenient stopping place on a most popular road tour, that of the Three Lochs : Loch Lomond, Loch Long and the Gareloch.

On the whole, Helensburgh is the place for the day-tripper rather than for the long-term holidaymaker, so excellent are its connections by rail and bus with Glasgow. It is of much subtler interest that we see in this pleasant place an unusual variation of the social pattern made up by these estuarine communities. It is reasonable to suggest that the naturally conservative inclinations of villa-dwellers has tended to check, rightly or wrongly, development on " popular " lines. In the case of Helensburgh the compromise is certainly quite a satisfactory one.

It is repeated with slight and local variations up and down both shores of the Firth of Clyde. The villa settlements along the shores of the Gareloch are virtually extensions of Helensburgh, though both Rhu and Rosneath on the other side of the Narrows have interesting histories of their own as villages. Settlement hereabouts was favoured not only by the charm of the loch but also by its safety as a yacht anchorage. Most of the houses run to size, some of them to the dimensions of castles, and many of them have inevitably lost caste as boarding-houses or institutions. Even after the First World War the pressures of taxation and the shortage of cheap labour began to undermine the foundations of privilege and, as we have already noted, the creation of docks on the lochside during the Second World War vastly reduced both the social and property values in the region.

Another characteristic community within this general class, in many ways so like and in many ways so unlike Helensburgh, is that formed by Cove and Kilcreggan, over the hill from the Gareloch and looking boldly down the open Firth.

Helensburgh always seems a little withdrawn from the Estuary ; the shallowness of the waters before it appear to hold it slightly apart from the eager shipping life of the Tail of the Bank. Cove and Kilcreggan (which together form a police burgh for administrative purposes) belong to the open Firth, are mercilessly battered by sou'-westerly gales, and command such views down the Firth as, if comparisons in such matters were possible, are grander than most of the many grand prospects to be seen anywhere between Greenock and Arran. The townlets lie respectively on either side of Baron's Point, which marks the eastern entrance to Loch Long. Kilcreggan is on the southern, steeper side, looking across to Gourock ; Cove fills a gentler bay that looks across to the mouth of the Holy Loch. In almost any summer the grey seals of West Scotland may be seen basking on the rocks off Baron's Point.

This twin burgh was a later and less-carefully planned settlement than Helensburgh, but a vast amount of Glasgow's wealth went into its making. And if it has not the orderly lay-out of Helensburgh on its relatively gentle slopes, it has its own West Highland charm of steep irregularity. Here again in the early and middle decades of the 19th Century was a great building of vast houses and even castles, a great laying-out of private pleasure-grounds : such an expenditure of industrial wealth on the grand scale as must amaze even the professional economist. Here no development of popular facilities was permitted, if it was ever thought of, beyond a little modest boat-hiring. As in so many places of the kind the native population was mainly engaged in shopkeeping, jobbing gardening and domestic service. The livelier young men found employment in the yachtbuilding yards of the Gareloch or even in the Greenock shipyards.

There was a period when the economy of Cove and Kilcreggan looked in a fair way to collapse, when some of the larger mansions passed to their inevitable fates as hostels or convalescent homes. This was at that point in political time when both the pressure of taxation and the relative remoteness of the settlement threatened in combination to leave it in the air as a riparian colony flung just a little too far from its base. Big houses lay empty for years ; local values dropped. It is of much interest that Cove and Kilcreggan returned in the 20's and 30's of the 20th Century to popularity and prosperity.

The improvement of the motor-car had much to do with this, also the expansion of the average man's sense of distance through the reliability of the motor-car. The shortage of city housing was another factor in the theorem, not to mention the continuing urge of the well-to-do to move away from the crowded places. The last factor in this pleasant little community's recovery was the establishment of a frequent ferry service across the Firth to Gourock, so implementing the services of the railway steamers that a man of affairs could reckon to reach his place of business in Glasgow, some 30 miles away, within 90 minutes at the most.

We are all less fussy about daily travel than we used to be, but it is only necessary to make the generalisation here that men and women, whether in Greater London or on Clydeside, on Merseyside and Tyneside, are more and more inclined to sacrifice hours of the working day in order to escape into pleasant places from the places in which they make their livings. This, in brief, is the reason why the Clyde Coast developed as it did, though in so many enchanting variations on the main theme. It is of rather special interest that the dormitory towns tended to coagulate about the railway termini. Gourock and Helensburgh are cases in point. Another is the agreeable bit of the world known as Wemyss Bay, with Skelmorlie attached.

This settlement on the borders of Renfrewshire and Ayrshire takes a special character from three distinct elements —its setting, the prospect of the Firth and islands it commands, and the fact that it is built almost entirely of the Red Sandstone of the district. Apart from the affairs of the terminal station, the community is purely residential, and the tycoons of the day before yesterday built their seaside villas solidly, often handsomely. The site is a difficult one in that the main road by the shore passes for a space underneath what is virtually a cliff, and Skelmorlie thus curiously consists of houses on two tiers. Indeed, an hotel with an enviable position on the upper terrace operates a lift to take its clients from the shore level to its eyrie on the bluff.

Whether from the shore road or the upper terrace, the view northwards and westwards across the Firth is of startling splendour. Perhaps no other settlement on the Clyde coast commands so many of the region's scenic elements. It looks northwards towards the austere hills of Cowal and then, eastwards, to the dramatic tangle of mountains grouped about Loch Long. On a bearing slightly West of North it gazes towards the low profile of Bute and into the very entrance to the Kyles, the white pillar of the Toward Light just across the way. Southwards loom the green slopes of the two Cumbraes, and beyond these, the arrogant Alps of Arran. All the shipping that moves on Clyde waters must pass this way. The shipping scene is all the more intimate in that most of the many vessels built in the up-river yards run their speed trials on the Measured Mile which, as we shall see, is marked off by a series of tall white masts set against the Skelmorlie hills.

The community itself is a pleasant sight from the sea which stretches so widely before it to the shores of Argyll and Bute. The arrangement of Red Sandstone villas amid the copious greenery under the romantic fold of rock is extraordinarily pleasing. It is from the sea, however, that one perceives why Wemyss Bay and Skelmorlie, even if they wished, can offer little to the beanfeaster save a view. The position on a wide leg of the Firth is much exposed to the prevailing winds, and the shore is only for bathers and boaters of the hardier sorts. At the same time, though this is not a guide-book, the stranger could choose a less agreeable base for his explorations of the Firth at large. With the decline of middle-class wealth in the middle years of the 20th Century some of the great villas became, in the economic order of things, adequately good hotels. The steamer service from Wemyss Bay became under British Railways as good as any from any other pier on the Firth. There remains eternally the incomparable view.

Wemyss Bay-Skelmorlie—and is it necessary to say that Wemyss is pronounced *Weems*?—completes a grouping of communities that, however widely differing in individual character and physical colour, share much the same economic and social qualities. This derives mainly from their mainland positions about or near convenient railheads. Even if it may seem surprising that the large industrial town of Greenock should be included in the group, Greenock did, in the process of centralisation, become in the years after the Second World War a residential suburb of Glasgow to a considerable extent. These towns and townlets of the Estuary and the Inner Firth are distinctly apart from the communities that are pleasure resorts and very little else.

II

Not even the most popular resorts on the Clyde coast remotely approximate to Blackpool or Southend in riotous wealth of popular " attractions," and it used often to be said that the local authorities were backward in what was most obviously their chief business. It is fair enough to say that the Scottish caterer is a slow mover, but the relative peace of, say, Dunoon as compared with the clamour of Margate on occasions of high holiday is not to be explained quite so simply.

One important influence on the developments of the Clyde resorts was that of the landowners who, at one time fully armed with the restrictive powers embodied in the feu contracts they engaged in with their tenants, approached the noisier exploitation of their territories with not wholly unreasonable conservatism. Other restraining influences were simply those of geography—such as the steepness of the land, which prevented expansion over extensive levels ; and such as, also, the fact that boating and sea-fishing on Clyde waters are infinitely safer than from the shelving beaches of most of the popular English resorts : this interest cancelling out much of the popular demand for artificial amusement ashore. The last factor was that of the sheer power of scenery to divert even the idlest mind, along with the distracting interest of fine, rugged country behind.

One is tempted into a syllogism, which might run thus : Blackpool has a splendid beach but little else in the seaward direction or behind ; Dunoon has no beach but safe waters in front and lovely country behind. Therefore Blackpool expanded artificially while Dunoon remained, for practical purposes, in a natural state. That may not be the whole of it, but it is a fairly sound, rough statement of existing differences between two resorts that are closely comparable in their relationships to two large industrial aggregations.

The story of Dunoon's development is, in little, very much that of any of the Clyde coast towns. The place has a respectable history of its own. On a knoll to the westward of the modern pier are still faint traces of a castle that legend holds to have been first put up by Dalriadic chieftains in the 6th Century and then held for a space by the Scandinavian invaders. It is rather more certain that it became a seat of the Lord High Stewards of Scotland and even, in the 14th Century, a royal palace with the Campbells of Lochow as its hereditary keepers.

These Campbells, who duly became Marquesses and then Dukes of Argyll, were of an acquisitive breed, much involved in the larger politics of Scotland. In the middle of the 17th Century the Castle of Dunoon apparently ceased to be of much interest to them, however, and its glory departed. By 1822, it appears, much of its masonry had been carted away to build cottages, piers and what-not ; and as the castle had declined, so in that year of grace Dunoon had dwindled to the dimensions of a clachan, with a kirk, a manse, one or two decent slate-roofed cottages and rather more mean dwellings rudely thatched. It was merely, says an old record charmingly, " an occasional resort of invalids for the benefit of drinking goats' whey."

It is something of an irony that the eminence upon which the castle was once situated is now crowned by a fanciful effigy of another Campbell, that Mary Campbell who, reputedly born in these parts, is believed to have been the " Highland Mary " of some of Burns's more unctuous verses. Some exact historians are not quite happy about the validity of the legend, but there the statue stands, solemnly unveiled in the last years of the 19th Century, and to the simple Glasgow folk who throng the esplanade below it is of much more sentimental interest, of more tangible significance, than all the past splendours and spent powers of the House of Argyll.

The romantic history of Dunoon over a dozen centuries is, in short, nothing to the social history of its growth over 150 years of industrial expansion. The new steamboat saved it, made it, nourished it, and transformed it. In that fatal year, 1822, James Ewing, Esq., LL.D., took out a feu hard by the site of the old castle and built thereon " the handsome marine villa called . . . Castle House." His example, the influence of the new steamboats powerfully prevailing, was followed quickly by the prosperous merchants and manufacturers in and around Glasgow.

Solid villas proliferated along this pleasant stretch of the Cowal coast. At the same time, and in consequence, the old hamlet expanded into a small town, with a business or shop-keeping quarter that to this day displays all the stigmata of careless, clotted, higgledy-piggledy building by a people without the tradition of civilised architecture. Then the steamers kept pouring the masses on to a convenient pier in such a pleasant situation ; and in due course the well-to-do, armoured with the fantastic increase of Victorian wealth and ever more convenient means of communications, withdrew to more westerly positions.

The right man could make out of the development of Dunoon during the 19th Century a valuable thesis in political economy. He would note how the villas along the front now form a phalanx of boarding-houses or, as their owners prefer to define it, private hotels. He would at the same time report the appearances and flashy expansions of hotels proper : concrete and chromium laid on regardless of either tradition or taste. He should, delving a little deeper, know that a large number of visitors to Dunoon, possibly the majority over any holiday season, live in a scrambled sort of way in furnished rooms, with or without attendance in premises often humble, usually primitive, also that this is one of the larger local industries. He might, with a little more subtlety, touch on the irony in the fact that the exclusive " marine villa " of a West India merchant of 1822—James Ewing, Glasgow's Lord Provost, 1832-33, and latterly M.P. for the city—is now the very nexus of Dunoon's most popular asset as a holiday resort : the Castle Gardens. The building is a dun, castellated affair in the tradition popularised by Walter Scott.

The thesis would take heed of the building of fine esplanades round the horns of the two bays that divide the town into two parts, with the pier at the promontory between them, and of its ultimate extension so far as Hunter's Quay almost within the mouth of the Holy Loch : a splendid walk of fully three miles, if somewhat hard on the feet. It would note the clearing of an open space at the pierhead and the erection of a covered pavilion for dancing, concerts and the like—also, latterly, useful for political and trades union conferences. Dunoon is fronted by one of those knobbly and unsympathetic beaches so common on the northern shores of the Firth, but the creation of a Lido, so-called, at the farthest extremity of the West Bay would be duly noted. All the advances of popular catering, with the immigrant Italians making the running in the first place, would find a place in a scientific study of this town's development as a pleasure resort. It would, above all, be noted that Dunoon's greatest assets are plenty of fresh air and a lovely view.

The social structure of the place, however, remains complex. The very well-to-do may have left it for quieter hide-outs, but its stable population in the mid-20th Century still included a high proportion of substantial people, many of them retired persons but quite as many daily travellers to and from solid business in Glasgow. It developed as the administrative capital of the huge rambling County of Argyll even if, by a curious irony, the County Council took to sitting in Glasgow ! Let

The Firth of Clyde

hoi polloi pour in during two summer months, make a great deal of noise, behave like lunatics in rowing-boats and wear summer clothes of extreme absurdity, but a solid decency of native character has remained. The eastern extensions of Dunoon even rarify in social quality and solidity of domestic building as they swarm under and over the villa-garnished slopes of Kirn to Hunter's Quay where the headquarters of the Royal Clyde Yacht Club, in an imported half-timber style and yet curiously pleasing in the given environment, strike once more the note of a certain, not wholly unimportant patrician dignity.

It seems, again, to be impossible to create such as a Blackpool on the Firth of Clyde. Environment and racial inclination are against it ; for better or worse the geographical quiddity of the Firth imposes on the riparian resorts a quality of wildness that is not to be subdued. And this is not to overlook the purely social fact that a very large proportion of Scotland's industrial workers increasingly tended after two wars to prefer Blackpool.

The prospect from Dunoon is, directly, across three or four miles of sea towards where the stocky white pillar of the Cloch Lighthouse has the green and pleasantly wooded hills of Renfrewshire for background, and then down the expanse of the inner Firth to the islands. Out of sight, on the other shore but only ten miles away, there lies in a fold of the Ayrshire coast another pleasure resort with a character quite different from that of Dunoon and one of its most vigorous rivals for the patronage of the people.

Largs, with a resident population of more than 6,000 souls, occupies an odd situation in both the geographical and social senses. Just as Dunoon is a typical townlet of the Highland mainland, Largs is a typical small town of the Lowland mainland. Even so, it is rendered curiously remote by the nature of its communications.

Its most important axis, to use the military term, is the shore road from Greenock. It is also directly connected with Glasgow by rail, but the hills behind the town are so high and steep, the line has to run as far southwards as Ardrossan and round this buttress of high ground northwards again through West Kilbride to Largs : the journey from the city occupying 80-90 minutes on the average. The town station is thus a terminal point but not a terminus, nor is the pier an important one on the Clyde coast steamer routes. If ever a place was specially favoured by the development of popular road transport it is this pleasant town of Largs, since the distances by road from the industrial aggregations about Paisley and Greenock in particular are short in modern terms. The motor-coach, cutting over the hill into the Garnock valley, can beat the detouring train on the way to Glasgow.

Although it was one of the many places on the Clyde coast to which the fashionable once flocked " for the sea bathing," in which the wealthy built their large and often pretentious " marine villas," Largs retained into the early years of the 20th Century much of the character of a small market town. Its traditional St Colm's Fair was of great antiquity and interest until it fell into desuetude under the impacts of commercial centralisation and improving communications. Largs, though rather a late-comer in the field, chose between the two Wars to develop its economy in the fields of catering.

Its natural assets in this department are considerable. From the sea the town, built largely of the native Red Sandstone, particularly effective in church steeples and such, wears a very pleasant air of charming solidity in agreeable colours. From the promenade the place commands another of those glorious Clyde views—as it were, the view from Dunoon in reverse. This is limited in the first place by the soft and pleasant outlines of farming lands on the greater of the two Cumbraes, and then the prospect expands across the width of the inner Firth to the Cowal hills, the green, recumbent silhouette of Bute and then the frieze of Highland hills in the background : the tower of the Toward Lighthouse raising a monitory white finger in the middle distance. From the top of the steep Haylie Brae behind Largs this prospect (as so very many not very good artists have endeavoured to show) takes on a sensational character especially in sunset conditions, the islands and even the coastline seeming to be laid out like pretty models on a gleaming mirror.

It is one of the fortunes of Largs that the overlapping of the northern promontory of the Greater Cumbrae encloses a most pleasant sheet of sheltered water, as safe for boating as any reach of the Clyde may be. It is one of its misfortunes that the foreshore is of hard shingle all compact. This township, however, is peculiarly favoured in the inevitable comparison with Dunoon in its position on a relatively broad stretch of flat ground, or raised beach, under the foothills.

This has allowed for the creation of spacious esplanades, putting greens, gardens, pavilions and the like, so that towards the middle of the 20th Century Largs came to wear a brighter, more sophisticated air than any of its rivals. Its governors were not afraid to lay on plenty of coats of good white paint, cheerfully lifting the face of the old market town, so to speak. If the tourist must have a bit of Scottish history thrown in, Largs could outdo Dunoon in being the scene of that great Battle of Largs, in 1263, in which the Scots under Alexander III of Scotland routed the Norsemen under Haco III, thus demolishing the suzerainty of the Vikings over the northern and western fringes of the country. The scene of the battle was a stretch of flat ground at the southern end of the modern town, and monuments here and there duly celebrate the event.

III

Largs and Dunoon make up with Rothesay the triumvirate of large popular resorts within the inner Firth of Clyde, but the rather special case of Rothesay can rest until we come to consider the Island of Bute as a separate entity. It is more to the point just now to understand in a general way the provenance of a dozen small settlements up and down these coasts that had become in mid-20th Century little more than vestigial : created in the mighty flood of Victorian prosperity, left stranded and slightly pathetic in the ebb.

These are the hamlets in which the industrial magnates, and even their modestly successful foremen, built their seaside villas and cottages—the little places that never, like Dunoon or Largs, could attract people in masses and, with the general recession of means, have tended to become slightly pathetic backwaters, however picturesque.

It was usually a case of the strong Victorian arm reaching a trifle too far. Northwards from Cove-Kilcreggan on the eastern arm of Loch Long is a widely-spaced extension of large villas, almost running into the redoubtable bases of Highland hills. This is Coulport. It was grandly planned as one of the new " watering places " in the eighties of the 19th Century. A pier was built, and only the landward stump of it now remains. The situation is delectable, the outlook charming, but this long range of large houses by the sea still wore the look, in 1949, of something that had not quite come off and had been written off. Even in a period of desperate housing shortage it was obviously just a little too far from the economic bases of such a society as might have kept it in healthy being.

The Victorian, and even the Edwardian, fashion kept on establishing and even seeking to maintain those nearly impossible outposts. Within the dark arms of Loch Goil there still stand villas, if only a handful, of preposterous solidity in such a remote and rocky place. Opposite Coulport on Loch Long proper a late spasm of Victorian expansionism created out of a mere clachan the place now called Blairmore, with a pier and a kirk and all the rest of it. Marine villas of great size were built hereabouts ; the place shaped to become exclusive in the extreme. It was most strangely overlooked that Blairmore, in the shadow of steep hills rising to the 1500-feet level, loses the sun at quite an early hour of even the longest day of a Scottish summer. At the least, expansion on popular lines was impossible and the decline of the original splendours inevitable.

This error of siting was not made in the case of its neighbour, the village of Strone, which straddles the bold promontory that separates Loch Long from the Holy Loch. In this splendid situation, commanding heroic views both up and down the Firth, some extremely agreeable and solid houses were built in the palmy days, and it is much to the point of the argument that these notably retained their site-values when those of corresponding dwellings in Blairmore tended to flag. A retired person might look far for a more agreeable resting place than Strone, the shipping and yachting life of the Firth always before it ; the local golf course almost in the Alpine class of hazard.

Strone and its opposite number on the other shore, Hunter's Quay, mark the limits of expensive development within the short arms of the Holy Loch. Above the main headquarters of Clyde yachting the joint settlement of Sandbank-Ardnadam wears a faintly industrial air. Hereabouts, in fact, is a busy centre of the charming crafts that minister to yachtsmen, and the trend of Victorian expansion was rather towards cottages than villas. Nearest the head of the little loch, on the northern shore, Kilmun is also largely an aggregation of cottages but this hamlet has an atmosphere of its own. Given its position within six miles of the smoke and bustle of Greenock, it seems curiously remote and withdrawn, as if it belonged not so much to the Firth as to the thinly-populated countryside of Cowal. This impression is no doubt rooted in the fact that Kilmun has a history of some ancientry and interest.

As the name indicates, it was the cell or church of Mun— more correctly St Fintan Munnu, a Columban missionary of the 6th Century. In this holy place, in mid-15th Century, Sir Duncan Campbell of Lochow founded a collegiate church for a provost and six prebendaries, and its square tower remains. Thus Sir Duncan's descendants, the Dukes of Argyll and their duchesses, are brought hither for burial, far from their capital at Inveraray. The original church received in 1661 the head-less body of the Marquis of Argyll, executed by the restored Royalists, and it is of grim interest that the head was returned for burial with the rest three years later. The dead chieftains of Argyll and their ladies now lie in a not notably distinguished mausoleum built in 1794.

Another interesting example of what we may fairly call the vestigial settlement is Innellan on the Cowal coast just four miles west of Dunoon, with which, in fact, it is spasmodically linked by a chain of unusually large villas : most of them private hotels and institutions by the middle of the 20th Century.

This was, in the first place, a settlement created by the well-to-do of Greenock. Again it is very much an affair of villas built tier upon tier on a steep slope that has, once more, the slight disadvantage of cutting off the sunlight at a relatively early hour of a summer evening. The views, however, are again superb, and Innellan is one of the places on the Clyde coast that has positively benefited by the coming of the motor-bus, especially since, possessing a strip of real sand, it takes a considerable overspill of visitors to Dunoon. The place has no history of the romantic kind, but some may care to know that here were written the words of the hymn, *O Love that wilt not let me go!* a hymn still well-beloved in the Scottish churches at least and above the average in quality. The author was the blind parish minister, the Rev. George Matheson.

Blinded at the early age of 18, Matheson was then still a young man, and it is believed that his verses were inspired by an emotional experience of the personal kind. The hymn was written, he said, in just a few minutes ; " I was suffering from extreme mental distress, and the hymn was the fruit of pain." The extremely popular, if somewhat fulsome, tune to which it is commonly sung was composed by Dr. Peace, organist of Glasgow Cathedral, when on holiday at the manse of Brodick, Arran, in 1884. Matheson went on from his simple charge at Innellan to become minister of St Bernard's, Edinburgh, with a congregation of 2000, and so to be a notable preacher and a scholar of real distinction : a big man in the religious world of his day. Another of his hymns, " Make me a captive, Lord," sung to the tune *Leominster*, is also still in popular circulation.

Beyond Innellan, going westwards along the shore road, there lies at Toward Point and behind its lighthouse a small community which is as a mark of the limit of expansion along one stretch of Clyde coast. Here is quite a small clot of villas and cottages, pleasant in themselves and most pleasantly surrounded, that nevertheless have the air of an outpost, as it were. There was here a pier, regularly used by the Caledonian steamers and as regularly ignored by those of the Glasgow & South-Western, but it was demolished many years ago. Despite the buses, despite an extremely pleasant stretch of sand on the shore looking across to Rothesay Bay, this little settlement could not in any way develop. It was at a dead end in terms of Victorian transport. Here a communal impulse, a fashion if you please, petered out.

By the middle of the 20th Century the fabled Kyles of

Bute had taken on something of the same quality of abandonment, the most dramatic case being that of Colintraive.

This pleasant hamlet on the mainland shore of the eastern kyle was for many years a resort highly favoured by middle-class families. Rich persons, enchanted by the Swiss-like prettiness of the country about the Narrows, built large houses in a style deriving from the Elizabethan, and a row of solid sandstone villas in the purely Scottish tradition developed along the shore below the pier. The latter was touched at by more than a dozen steamers every day ; the bay was much favoured as a yacht anchorage. It was possible to think in 1910 or thereabouts that Colintraive was marked for development, and about that period, indeed, there was a speculative building of a row of small villas in a variation of the Tudor manner that might have graced a garden city in the South.

The fate of this row, not offensive in any way if a trifle out of keeping with the environment, suggests that the period in which they were built actually marked the turning of the social and economic tides along the Clyde coast. These pretty little houses were never taken up in a substantial way. From period to period their prices fluctuated wildly, sometimes down to bargain figures.

Colintraive was not, in fact, marked for development by the mysterious gods of progress. Soon after the Second World War its pier was closed for lack of revenue to keep it in repair, and while the hamlet is still popular with a handful of people —and is likely always to be so for the peace and charm of it— it was fated to become another lost village : its communications limited to bus, car or lorry up the Bute coast from Rothesay and so across the ferry at Rudhabodach, or the long haul through the hills and over narrow roads from Dunoon. The steamers pass it by.

On the western kyle there used to be three piers in urgent daily use—Tighnabruaich, Auchenlochan and Kames, the last the terminal of the popular Kyles of Bute run. Of these only Tighnabruaich pier is now in use, the imperative of economics laying it down that it is cheaper to run buses from one pier to two other places near at hand than to stop and start a vessel of 300 tons three times within a distance of so many miles. These settlements overlap and merge. At one time a gunpowder factory in the country behind Kames provided a certain if small amount of industrial employment, but the three communities conform to the pattern so common on the outer shores of the Firth of Clyde.

These are sub-Highland places in which the urge outwards from the dark, satanic mills prompted the building of seaside villas and cottages. They have remained primitive so far as shopping facilities and all the other accepted services are concerned. They rest in lovely surroundings. In relation to the forces that created them they are, however, exhausted and remain rather as memorials to a communal urge now, not so much spent, as diverted.

CHAPTER IV

Coasts of the Outer Firth

THE encircling arms of the Firth of Clyde are widely spread when they have come to embrace the Isle of Arran. From Ayr on the mainland to Campbeltown on the Kintyre peninsula the distance is fully 36 land miles, and these coasts are as often as not out of sight of each other in the prevailing weather conditions. This is deep, nearly open water, its Atlantic character unmistakable. It separates regions that are in different worlds : the industrial Lowlands on one side, the sub-Highlands on the other ; though, as we shall see, Campbeltown and parts of Kintyre have been "contaminated" by influences from across the outer Firth.

The great bight of Ayr, made up on the map by Irvine and Ayr bays, hardly seems to belong to the Firth as we have noted. Its shelving beaches and flat riparian lands have little in common with those pretty convolutions of the northern and inner parts of the Firth the traveller sees from the steamers. Even though it stares that splendid island in the face, it seems to have little relationship to Arran, even less to the more suave graces of Bute. The hinterland is largely industrial in character, and some of the coastal towns, justly popular as holiday resorts, are also busy harbours and shipbuilding centres.

The complex and relatively sophisticated structure of the human society along this bit of coast—that is, in contrast to the pattern of life along the coasts of Argyll on the other side of the Firth—is easily understood in terms of simple geography. This area did not need to be opened up by the steamboat. By

rail and, latterly, by bus the communications with the industrial concentration in the Clyde Valley are easy across the
base of that triangle of high country, of which Greenock forms
the apex. Its shores are lined with such long stretches of fine
sand as are comparatively rare in Scotland and blessed by
(what is perhaps still rarer in Scotland) a relatively dry, sunny
and bracing climate. If coal and iron could be profitably
worked in the background, that stretch of coast from West
Kilbride down to Ayr itself was bound to be a natural playground for rich and poor alike.

So it has naturally developed, with many surprising and
delightful contrasts everywhere. The very agreeable town of
Troon, for instance, seems at one end to consist of a snug
harbour and a prosperous shipyard and, just down the road,
to be a most elegant place of residence for the well-to-do ;
while no fewer than five golf-courses, one of them in the
Championship class, are neighboured by two popular beaches.
The traveller by car may occasionally curse to be halted at a
level-crossing and to await the passing of a slow mineral train,
only to be enchanted in the next minute by the emergence
from a side-road of the Eglinton Hunt in all the excitement of
red coats, mettlesome horses and eager hounds.

Much of the fortune of this coast lies in the dunes that
surge behind the sandy beaches. If these, at the northern end
near Stevenston, must shelter an enormous explosives factory,
elsewhere they have been used mainly as golf-links : all of
merit, whether municipally-owned or maintained by private
clubs. Between West Kilbride and Ayr, and within as many
miles of coastline, there are 20 golf-courses ; and hereabouts
any man with a bag of clubs can have the time of his life. The
phrase may seem a cant one, but golf in Scotland is still a much
more democratic and inexpensive business than it is elsewhere,
and any man with reasonable references may easily follow in
the footsteps of Vardon and Walter Hagen across the lovely

Highland Harbour: Yachts in East Loch Tarbert, Loch Fyne. The ruin on the headland is of a castle used by Robert the Bruce.

Highland Capital: Inveraray, Loch Fyne: seat of the Dukes of Argyll and ancient capital of Lorn, from the south.

SALT AND SUN: Summer forenoon at the bathing-pool, Gourock.

greens of the Old Course at Troon or essay the " Cardinal " hazard at Prestwick that once cost James Braid the Open Championship. Any one of the municipally-owned courses is a good course, and on these pleasant fairways the visitor may at any time encounter that friendly representative of golf in Scotland, that mighty swiper before the Lord, the artisan player. He is also likely to receive much useful, if sardonic, advice if he chooses to employ a caddie.

The four sizeable towns of this seaboard are Ardrossan, including Saltcoats ; Irvine, Troon and Ayr, including Prestwick. Of the quartet Ardrossan and Troon are relatively recent and nearly artificial creations, while Irvine and Ayr are Royal and extremely ancient burghs, their histories entangled in the very roots of that of Scotland itself. In spite of several common elements and interests all differ distinctly in character, one from the other.

The social student with a bent towards economic history might be most interested in the Ardrossan-Saltcoats grouping. Saltcoats, as its name suggests, was originally a place of salt-pans, and it was by all accounts a mean enough settlement in its original state. On the other hand, Ardrossan owes much of its development to more than one Earl of Eglinton in the late 18th and early 19th Centuries, and then to the reckless competition of the early railway companies.

The first Eglinton involved was an enthusiast of canals during the brief vogue of that mode of transport, so soon and disastrously to be overtaken by the railway development. A canal was to be cut from Glasgow by way of Paisley to the Ayrshire coast, and Ardrossan was to be its terminal. The canal was indeed cut from Glasgow as far as Paisley, where a local poet of merit, Robert Tannahill, drowned himself in one of its last extensions. (It was out of such operations, by the way, that the word " navvy " originated. Because of the nature of their work the Irish labourers employed on these schemes were facetiously nicknamed " navigators," and the contraction has duly found its way into the O.E.D.) Like so many of its kind, the enterprise petered out. The canal was filled in and shaped to carry railway lines.

The work at Ardrossan, however, went on. The fortune of another young Earl of Eglinton was pledged to the building of harbours, quays and breakwaters. One railway duly reached the port and another followed its rival in the 1880's. A ship-building firm solidly established itself in the place. A town with somewhat monotonously wide streets intersecting at correct right-angles developed behind the harbour. A port was thus created about the site of an ancient castle.

Ardrossan provides the material for an interesting study in industrial development. The enterprise of the Earls of Eglinton has not gone unrewarded by any means. The piers of Ardrossan are busy terminals for steamboat connections with Arran, Ireland and the Isle of Man ; the inner harbour makes at least a good enough fitting-out basin for locally-built ships. But one has to see here how wastefully two competitive railway companies built separate piers, each with an abominably awkward approach from the town proper : each planned in idiotic rivalry to get the city-dweller into the ships so many minutes earlier than its competitor. The clutter of sidings and sheds towards both pierheads hands the Socialist planner an object-lesson and an argument ready-made.

This town of Ardrossan, though with many pleasant extensions in three directions from the docks, seems a rather bleak, wind-swept sort of place ; and its geographical position fates it to take the full force of sou'-westerly gales. Even so, a great many people from the industrial hinterland came to regard it as an agreeable holiday resort. Its hotels and its boarding-houses proliferated along the bay it shares with its neighbour, Saltcoats. The two communities make a strange pair of twins, for while industry made Ardrossan, Saltcoats is a place in which industry, in spite of several attempts, notably failed to establish itself. On the contrary, its holiday trade has become brisk and profitable.

The holiday habits of the Clydeside working folk are often incalculable. It is the experience of the catering industry that they tend to move in cycles of fashion, as if a bush telegraph were at work. This year the main current will flow towards the Fife coast, the next towards Aberdeen, and the next towards Blackpool. Wherever they go, these urban folk mostly prefer places in which, along with the attractions of a beach, the gregarious conditions of life at home are reproduced. They do not share the poet's taste for rapture on the lonely shore ; they opt for the hearty, hugger-mugger sort of resort in which cafés, picture houses and pubs are to be found hard by the lodgings.

Thus, in spite of competition, Saltcoats has long commanded the steady loyalty of many plain people. The swimming pool, the putting green, the paddling pool—they are all there. If there is little or no boating on this exposed coast, there is always the beach, and if it rains (though this is a dry region in the West Scottish scale of things) there are the pictures and the pub. The inner town is one of those clotted, unplanned congeries in the mode of the West, but its narrow streets have bustle and colour at the time of the Glasgow Fair, and here the social observer with the senses of humour and tolerance can vastly enjoy himself for an hour or two.

Only a few miles down the road the town of Irvine, which is most curiously situated on a loop at the intersection of the Rivers Irvine and Garnock and is only reached from the North by a wide inland sweep of the coast road. . . . Irvine is quite another sort of place.

Here is a Royal Burgh with a charter dating from the 13th Century and renewed by Robert the Bruce in 1308 for services rendered to his cause, of which Ayrshire was the springboard. Here, with a population of some 12,000 souls, is one of the oldest of Scotland's western harbours, still busy. Here is a considerable aggregation of industrial power, mainly of the iron-working kinds, with chemicals and some shipbuilding thrown in. Robert Burns set up in Irvine as a flaxdresser in his early manhood, his shop being burned down in the aftermath of a carouse. A lesser but not negligible poet, James Montgomery, was born here. So was John Galt, one of Scotland's few considerable novelists. And in this grey town, no doubt a much bewildered child, Edgar Allan Poe dwelt awhile with Scottish relatives. Not far away, in 1839, the legendary Eglinton Tournament was elaborately mounted.

In spite of surrounding patches of industrial working, the town of Irvine still wears an air appropriate to its old distinctions, and the approach along the shore road going inland, lined with douce and solid villas, has a curiously dignified or processional quality. It is rather on the outskirts of the town that we discern, however, that Irvine is the very centre of a whirlpool of highly variegated activity. Here a golf-course marches with an ironworks, there a racecourse is just across the river from an explosives factory. More golf-courses adjoin military training grounds, the confused scene diversified by settlements of huts, shacks and caravans in daunting masses. We should, however, try to see these shaggy settlements as another of the odd social-industrial phenomena of the Clyde Basin, representing both the decent impulse towards the sea of townsfolk on the lower income levels and their instinct towards the ownership of property, however humble. The factors conflict again to produce quite another sort of result in Troon, far and away the most compact example of the fusion of the social (as distinct from the industrial) influences that operate along this Ayrshire coast. Here is a fine beach and that golf-course in the Championship class. Here many of the well-to-do commercial people of Glasgow and thereabouts have their permanent homes in villas for the most part elegantly architected and agreeably spaced, while with the usual popular amenities the municipality attracts in increasing numbers the working-man and his family out for a day at the Coast.

We have therefore hereabouts a quite unusual medley of human activities within a relatively small space, the special interest of it being that there is singularly little overlapping or conflict among them. It remains remarkable that in this singularly fortunate place the harsh industrial workings about the harbour hardly affect the amusements of either group. This industrial area is detached and not by any means without its own distinctive, individual character as that of any proper seaport. In many ways it is reasonable to think of Troon as a good example of town-planning, however accidental.

Two influences were at work to produce this result. The first was that of Nature, which threw out at this point of the Ayrshire coast a crescent or horn of rocky land to form a creek with its mouth opening northwards and its back to the prevailing sou'-westerlies. Here was a natural harbour in an unexpected place. Before the Ship-Channel of the Clyde was even dreamt of the Magistrates of Glasgow coveted Troon as the site of a fore-port ; their repulse by local forces impelled them to create Port Glasgow, which we have already visited, in a much less favourable situation.

Then, towards the end of the 18th Century, a Duke of Portland started the development of the natural harbour on his own account. He built sea-walls, piers and breakwaters, and the tongue of land lipping the shallow seas of the Ayrshire bight duly became a port of consequence. The building of the villas along the gracious length of the South Bay about golf-links in the first class, and then the popular use of the beaches—these things followed in the inevitable order of 19th Century expansion.

The Firth of Clyde

What the Dukes of Portland, the Cavendish-Bentincks of Welbeck Abbey, have to do with this coign of Scottish soil is the matter of a dynastic story that hardly concerns us here. A young economist in search of a thesis might, however, consider the part that the landed gentry played in development during the 18th Century before the pure industrialists arose in their glory.

By the shores of the Firth of Clyde alone we have already seen that Sir James Colquhoun of Luss, Sir John Schaw of Greenock, the Earls of Eglinton at Ardrossan, and now the 3rd Duke of Portland at Troon fathered notably beneficial enterprises in the fair way of business. It is in the meantime pleasant to record that the Lady Isle, lying about a couple of miles offshore from Troon, was in 1948 or thereabouts leased by the Portland Estates as a bird sanctuary to a body of enthusiasts at an annual rental of thirty pence.

This range of interesting and complex communities culminates at the southward end in the county town of Ayr itself, Prestwick intervening. Prestwick and Ayr have tended between and after two Great Wars to expand mightily in several directions so as to form a settlement stretching along fully six miles of coast. By the middle of the 20th Century it had become rather hard to discern the quiddity of these ancient places through the numerous layers of change that " development " had so rapidly imposed upon them.

It became during that period an almost uncanny experience to stand by Prestwick's ancient and well-preserved Mercat Cross and realise it to be but a shard of ancientry, piously preserved by the force of a slightly bogus sentimentality, a bit of mere jetsam amid the tides of buses and cars that flow endlessly past it, nearly in the volume of London traffic along the Strand.

Shops and inns are crowded about it, just as a market cross

should be surrounded, but the business of these is alien, mainly given over to the service or exploitation of the holiday-maker. The ancient village is wholly engulfed in bungaloid extensions and obliterated by them ; at every other turning a harsh and metallic municipal sign points " To the Beach." Entertainment has become Prestwick's business, and this it does very well according to our modern lights, with one of the most spectacular bathing pools on the coast and all manner of aquatic diversions thrown in, most of these favouring the more exhibitionist sort of nubile humanity.

The apparent social disparities between Prestwick Golf Club and the Prestwick Swimming Pool were suddenly and surprisingly obliterated when, during the period between the two wars, the airport at Prestwick acquired international status. The expanses of flat land inland from the golf-courses could take the largest types of transatlantic aircraft.

During the last two or three years of the Second World War the airfield at Prestwick, almost completely free of fog from one end of any year to the other, was the favoured terminal of the gigantic air traffic to and from Canada and the United States. One has stood by the runways in the darkling and heard as many as a dozen huge aircraft cruising overhead after their long passage above the ocean and waiting for permission to land : the tired eyes of the pilot always on the dial that measures his dwindling supplies of petrol. One has seen American ambulance planes loaded at midnight with those G.I.'s who, grievously wounded on the Western Front, might at least decently be ferried home to die and be buried among their kinsfolk.

> *Keep us, O Thetis, in our western flight!*
> *Watch from thy pearly throne*
> *Our vessel, plunging deeper into night*
> *To reach a land unknown.*

135

The Firth of Clyde

And how strange that the poet was a child of industrial Renfrewshire, for a time a teacher in Greenock, and at length a suicide from the rocks of Cornwall !

The brisk community of Prestwick, so much taken up with the business of catering, is nowadays merged for all practical purposes into its large neighbour, the county town of Ayr. The connurbation, as they say, is complete. There are almost more buses than private cars along the length of road that unites these two centres of population. And in Ayr itself, all the elements that form the character of this section of the Firth of Clyde coast are completely, finally merged.

This is a town most remarkably well-favoured in all its circumstances. It lies open to the sun and enjoys a mild, dry climate. Its harbour at the mouth of the River Ayr is a natural one and busy, whether with the export of coal or the intake of herring. It is the inevitable market town of a wide and rich farming district. Robert Burns endowed it with a literary identity ; it has its own antiquities, latterly preserved on a slightly belated wave of local pride. Some of its architecture is rather highly distinguished, notably the fine mass of the County Buildings at the seaward end of Wellington Square, a gracious fragment of planning, marred nowadays by the gilt signs of insurance companies and such that have supplanted the gentry of Ayrshire in their grave town houses. Ayr has its industries, its quota of near-slums and perhaps rather more than its quota of multiple shops, and still it remains a very pleasant place to visit and to live in.

A large number of persons with business in the Glasgow and Paisley areas so use it. The railway connections are fast and frequent, the ramifications of the bus system incredibly complex, cheap and efficient. Ayr's development as a purely residential area for what the Scots call " incomers " was rapid between the two Wars, occasionally not a little garish, and property values in the pleasant southern extensions of the town ran relatively high. At the same time, there are a beach, ample lodgings for the working folk of the Clyde Basin, wide links for their family picnics, putting greens, municipal golf-courses and what-you-will in the way of entertainment. The town's balance of trade, so to speak, is for all these reasons distinctly favourable. Arran and Ailsa Craig are always there to seaward.

It is one of the minor curiosities of literature that Robert Burns, though born virtually within sight and sound of the sea, seems to have been completely uninfluenced by it ; you will search the large body of his poetry in vain for any impression the rolling leagues of the outer Firth may have made upon him. The man's eye was at once microscopic and bucolic, concerned closely with the details of the country scene. The analogy might be used to suggest that, when we are considering the character of the Clyde Sea Area in particular, our concern is not at all with the rural scenes of a poet's young manhood. It is quite impossible, however, to move through Ayr southwards by the coast without having some concern for the scene that inspired so many lovely lyrics, so very many spirited chronicles and satires in verse.

Two of his monuments are in the very heart of the town of " honest men and bonnie lasses "—Ayr itself. By the coast road the traveller must pass over the " New Brig " which, in the poem, exchanged so much of philosophical and social comment with the " Auld Brig " that, though nowadays limited to the use of foot-passengers only, still stands in its agreeable ancientry. The Tam o' Shanter Inn, from which Burns had Thomas Graham of Shanter Farm starting on his fearful ride home in one of the most brilliant short stories in verse ever written, is still at the receipt of convivial custom, its low-browed façade and thatched roof enduring amid the bustle of the High Street.

The shrine of shrines, the cottage in which the poet was born, is easily reached in a short bus run to Alloway, a hamlet

The Firth of Clyde

latterly threatened by the suburban extensions of the county town. This humble dwelling had to be rescued from its fate as a public-house in the 1880's, and the atmosphere of restoration is inescapable. Here, however, the pious may recapture much of the richness of association ; and the museum, containing for instance the original MS. of *Tam o' Shanter*, cannot be seen without emotion by those who understand something of the nature of the poetic genius and the peculiar pathos of this single poet's life. The ruins of the Auld Kirk of Alloway are near at hand, with the graveyard in which Tam o' Shanter beheld such an alarming convention of spectral figures. The group of shrines about Alloway is completed by the Burns Monument on the banks of Doon, overlooking the old Brig o' Doon : a remarkably successful exercise in the Grecian manner with, again, a museum of some interest.

Pilgrims to the other places of association with Burns in the hinterland will not lack for copious and exact guidance on the spot. The area is easily covered from Ayr by frequent and inexpensive bus services. Indeed, it is curious in the mid-20th Century to measure the limited geographical range of a highly gifted man of the late 18th Century.

The Burns Country, to use the convenient phrase, is a triangle of mainly agricultural country with its apex on the coast at Ayr. This region is watered by the twin rivers, Ayr and Doon, the latter in particular a charming stream of the fabulous " banks and braes." The countryside immediately behind Ayr is passing rich nowadays in the agricultural sense, but while it remains green and pleasant and varied all the way inland, it duly rises towards the high ridge on the Ayrshire-Lanarkshire border. The farms thereupon decline in size and richness, and the small towns of this marginal countryside have become mainly mining communities. If it were permissible to take account of the effects of economics on the life and work of a poet, one could find the matter of an entertaining thesis

138

in the fact that, for sheer lack of capital to rent farms in good heart and keep them in good heart, Burns and his father and brother were condemned to such grudging holdings as Mount Oliphant, Lochlea and Mossgiel, as wore them all out prematurely.

All these farms, now healthy under a vastly improved system of cultivation, are within the convenient triangle, and nearby are the townlets that were the small capitals of the poet's turbulent reign. From Lochlea he held court in Tarbolton and there formed his Bachelors' Club : the original building now in the care of the National Trust for Scotland. From Mossgiel his metropolis was Mauchline, with Poosie Nansie's inn and all its associations with *The Jolly Beggars* still in use and, across the road, the churchyard that holds the bones of so many of his " originals " : not least that Mary Morison who inspired perhaps the loveliest of his love-songs. Southwards, near the coast again, is the village of Kirkoswald. Here is another old churchyard containing the bones of Tam o' Shanter and Souter Johnny, here another cherished possession of the National Trust for Scotland : Souter Johnny's thatched cottage. It is but a step over the hill to the shores of the Firth and Shanter Farm on the green braes above the fishing village called Maidens.

Immediately to the south of Ayr, in fact, not far beyond the Burns cottage at Alloway, the character of the coast suddenly changes from the mild-and-sandy to the bold-and-rocky. The point of change is marked where the Heads of Ayr rise like a banner unfurled above a castle, the besieging seas always foaming at their base. Even if the spine of the Heads was occupied after the Second War by one of Mr Butlin's massive and mass-motivated camps, it so happens that in one brief moment of scenic glory this eastern shore of the Firth of Clyde takes on the quality of grandeur again after the gentle interlude of the bight. The bluffs rise high above the turbulent sea, the white farmhouses seem to cling to remarkably green hillsides. For miles on end southwards from Ayr there are no human settlements of size worth mentioning.

This coast road all the way to Stranraer, a distance of more than 50 miles, is one of the finest of its kind in all Scotland, so grandly does it soar over a series of headlands, cut down wooded glens and, at one point, run so close to the sea through a rocky pass that the wind-screen of a car may be misted by the spray from even a moderate sea. It includes that oddity of a hill known as " the Electric Brae," the topic of innumerable Silly Season newspaper stories and Letters to the Editor. The joke is that a car *seems* to be going downhill when it is in fact climbing, and the other way about. The prosaic explanation is that the illusion is purely optical, created by the fact that the hedges and ditches by the turnpike run at eccentric angles to that of the modern road surface.

This section of the highway is a good deal more interesting when, at a height of 430 feet above the sea, it soars to command an expanse of shining salt water and, on a bluff below, the fine Adams building of Culzean Castle (pronounced Cull*ane*) the seat of the Marquesses of Ailsa and nowadays, with its flat set aside for the personal use of General Eisenhower, in the care of the National Trust for Scotland and so open to public visitation at appropriate times.

There are few settlements of size along this green coast, indeed, but there are some of much interest and charm.

A few miles south of Ayr is Dunure, with its castle ruins and the appropriate legends, but rather more interesting for its snug little fishing harbour, the base of one group of those ring-net fishing boats that, run strictly on family lines, so expertly and industriously supply the British market with herring. Just beyond Culzean Castle the little harbour and settlement of Maidens (usually referred to as " the Maidens ") shelters and mans another little fleet of the elegant ring-net boats—a pleasant, mild place notwithstanding the busyness of the main road that runs behind it.

This village, for all its modern bungalows, is unusually interesting in that one Marquess of Ailsa here first established the shipbuilding firm that is now such an important part of the economy of Troon. The original slipways are still to be seen, and an improbable tenement building at the head of the pleasant harbour, rather like a barracks, was in fact built in the first place to house the artisans of this far-flung outpost of the Clyde's major industry.

And only a mile or two down the road, at Turnberry, the note of industrial sophistication is heard again.

Here in the brave days of cut-throat competition the Glasgow & South-Western Railway Company, challenging the Caledonian Company—and perhaps inspiring it to the *ersatz* creation of Gleneagles—decreed another pleasure dome of the expensive sort. A luxury hotel was built on the green slopes ; an excellent golf-course was laid out on the links behind the lighthouse. In the incredible irony of circumstance both were fated to be casualties twice over in two World Wars : the hotel as a hospital, the golf-course as an airfield.

In spite of the prosperous villas that were built in relation to the links, Turnberry has the faintly jaded air of a resort that has somehow lost the place and can never quite make up the leeway. Perhaps it is just a little too far beyond the reach of even the fastest car out of Glasgow. The philosophic traveller may discover an agreeable irony in the fact that it was from Turnberry Castle, its ruins on the fringe of the golf-course and hard by the lighthouse, there flamed the signal-fire that, for better or worse, called Robert the Bruce from exile in Arran to the conquest and Throne of Scotland.

The more practical eye will note that the soil hereabouts is red, obviously rich, most intensively cultivated. This is in fact the region, remarkably free from frost, in which Britain's most adventurous exercises in the growing of early potatoes are conducted. They will think nothing hereabouts of planting in February, with the reasonable hope of lifting in early June and taking the market by storm. This district of Carrick, with so mild a climate and amenable a soil, is one of the few Gardens of Scotland, and it is hard elsewhere in the country to find such a variety of fine vegetables as, in the season, are displayed in the shop windows of Girvan.

This is a douce little town, somewhat straggling in length, somewhat misshapen about the top end of the harbour, and then a thought bleak in the regularity of its western streets, regularly lined with houses mostly of only one storey in height. The harbour itself is interesting : a real fishing port manned by stout seamen before the Lord and, as we shall note, the port for Ailsa Craig. There is again a beach ; and Girvan, though some 63 miles by rail from Glasgow, is a coast resort with a loyal army of patrons. The country immediately inland, though no concern of ours here, is enchanting, and it is surprising how little known to the general run of travellers are those Carrick Highlands, rising in The Merrick just over the Kirkcudbrightshire border to a height of nearly 3000 feet.

Following the coast as we must, however, the glorious shore road cruises by the water's edge through Lendalfoot and then goes soaring over Bennane Head, the lop-sided shape of Ailsa Craig playing hide-and-seek with the wayfarer's eye all the time. This road drops steeply again to the agreeable settlement of Ballantrae out of which Robert Louis Stevenson alleged that he was stoned as a vagabond, and from which he got the title of an excellent romance. As a holiday resort of the quieter kind, eternally ventilated by the fresh airs off the outer Firth, this village has its great merits : the more so in that the road eastwards by the River Stinchar is of delicious charm and that the main shore road, climbing inland in a loop to come down on the quiet shores of Loch Ryan at length, is equally entrancing, if in a bolder fashion.

We have already peeped into Loch Ryan, a mild and shallow arm of the sea, its mouth facing northwards against the run of most of the Clyde lochs, its amenity not at all improved by the construction of that military harbour on its eastern shores during the Second World War. And here, in the town of Stranraer at the head of Loch Ryan, our journey along the eastern coast of the outer Firth of Clyde comes to an end. Stranraer has a faintly Irish look and not unnaturally so, since the rich pasture lands of Galloway behind it are largely peopled by farming folk of Northern Irish stock or with affiliations in that direction.

Portpatrick on the other side of the hammer-headed peninsula was designed to be the terminal of the swift steamer-crossing to Larne, but the beat of the sou'-westers across the North Channel was too much for Portpatrick as a harbour, and the railway vessels have for many years past run from Stranraer out of the quiet waters of Loch Ryan. The town of Stranraer has therefore much of the air of any railway terminal and, at the same time, the authentic atmosphere of a market town serving one of the richest agricultural regions in Scotland : a region of notable dairying and cheese-making, in which the average farm may carry 100 and more head of milch cows of the handsome Ayrshire breed.

At this latitude, however, we are outside the Firth of Clyde proper. The Rhinns of Galloway look westwards to the coasts of Antrim, and the Scottish farmer about Lochnaw sees at night the blink of The Maidens light a few miles to the north-wards of Island Magee, with Cushendall and Ballymena not far behind on that alien coast. The course out of Loch Ryan to Campbeltown lies N.N.W.

It is convenient meanwhile to include Loch Fyne in this Outer Firth area, and it would be wrong to pass over the almost unique interest of the small town of Inveraray near its upper end. Here towards the end of the 18th Century a Duke of Argyll lavished a fortune on the building of decorative bridges, arches and what-not about the approaches to his castle with its pepper-pot turrets, and these architectural whimsies have in the course of time so charmingly blended with the wooded scene as to give this little place the air of having been translated from the Italian lakes. The ramparts of an old county prison on the very edge of the blunted promontory support the illusion, and the average quietness of Inveraray and its soft, moist climate complete a sort of Ruritanian illusion, proper to a ducal capital in a gentle decline.

Inveraray was once a place of great consequence in the West Highlands. From hence the powerful Campbells wielded almost monarchical influences in the politics and little wars of Scotland. It was at one time the effective county capital, and there still stands by the white arches the old courthouse in which James Stewart of Appin was condemned, by a Campbell jury, for the alleged assassination of a Campbell of Ardbreck : the episode that gave us the tale of " Kidnapped." Another novelist, Neil Munro, fashioned many of his stories about the character and " characters " of this old town, so like a pretty old lady counting her last days hard by the banks of the lovely River Aray. During the Second War it was most noisily invaded by Poles, Wrens and the hard experts of Combined Operations, but that fierce tide duly receded as the tides of ducal influence, county power and of a tidy fishing industry had more quietly ebbed long before.

Its history apart, Inveraray is worth looking at as a good specimen of the old Scots county town, the Lowland note of " lands " or tenement buildings prevailing in this Highland setting. White-washed, these communal dwellings with their nicely-placed windows are agreeably arranged along two extensions of a central square, in the middle of which stands

AYRSHIRE COAST: The 6th hole of the reconstructed golf-course at Turnberry, used as an airfield in two wars. The Shanter Farm of Burns's *Tam o' Shanter* is on the foothills nearby, north of the railway hotel behind.

MILLPORT, ISLE OF CUMBRAE: The trefoil bay of a popular island resort, looking south towards the Arran peaks.

THE HOLY ISLE: From the slopes above Whiting Bay, Arran. Lamlash Bay on left.

ROTHESAY BAY AND PIER: Capital of the Isle and Shire of Bute on a summer morning, from the east.

the considerable bulk of the Parish Kirk. An old story tells that a convivial party, colliding with the western pillars of this solid building, complained that this was "a hell of a place to put a kirk." The temperate traveller should be more interested to know that the single edifice is divided into two parts. The English-speakers worship at the northern end, the Gaelic-speakers at the other : a solid wall between their petitions to the universal God.

Down the handsome length of Loch Fyne from Inveraray there are various settlements of interest, few of them of size and all a little moribund since the fishing industry concentrated in the ports of the outer Firth proper. Ardrishaig, at the eastern end of the Crinan Canal, grew up a thought untidily as a terminal of that old-fashioned waterway and is of rather less interest even than its neighbour, Lochgilphead, which has at least a faded charm as it looks across the sands that dry out so far over a tiny arm of the sea. The country about these small ports, however, is delightful, and they both keep their places, even if in a considerably run-down economy, as small markets and resorts still popular with people of quiet taste. They are true West Highland villages, and no pierrot ever strutted on their foreshores.

Within Loch Fyne, as we have seen, Tarbert is the most considerable settlement, cosily arranged about its little land-locked harbour, still a herring port of some, if diminishing, consequence, still a market for the surrounding district of Knapdale.

It is hereabouts, however, that the peculiar geography of the Kintyre peninsula dictates a swing of human interest away from these western shores of the outer Firth of Clyde. At Tarbert the main road crosses the isthmus and runs down the outer, Atlantic side of this strange tongue of land. There is indeed a secondary road down the inner, eastern side of the peninsula, but from Tarbert southwards on this route and within the sphere of our concern here there is very little along nearly 40 miles of coast but a few pleasant fishing villages, such as Skipness and Carradale. The life of Kintyre comes properly to the boil in the strange and interesting port of Campbeltown.

This may fairly be described as a slightly untidy but agreeable town of Lowland character at the head of a pleasant little Highland loch, but it wears a larger air of consequence than many more populous places. Its population in 1950 might be estimated at 6500. It is indeed a regional capital, the seat of a Sheriff Court, an important fishing harbour, a not unimportant naval base, the natural market town of a prosperous farming region, an airport of British European Airways and an industrial centre in its own right. The villas on the shores and slopes about the head of the loch bespeak a solid prosperity. In its geographical position near the tip of a thinly inhabited peninsula the reality of Campbeltown comes as a surprising oddity.

Its industrial history has been a peculiar one. Until the slump year of 1922 there was a shipbuilding yard here, employing a considerable number of men and capable of building sizeable vessels up to 4000 tons. It was once a whaling station. In the nineties of the 19th Century twenty distilleries were in copious production, their output in 1897 rising to the intoxicating peak of 1,810,226 gallons. A colliery was worked for a number of years and then closed down. A networks grew out of the fishing industry. Several passenger and cargo vessels plied regularly to Greenock and the Ayrshire ports. A light railway ran from Campbeltown across the green waist of lower Kintyre, carrying passengers to the fine beaches and golf-links of Machrihanish on the Atlantic coast.

The economic and political variations of half a century changed all this and created quite a new balance of trade. The light railway disappeared, to be replaced by buses. Rightly or wrongly, the British Transport Commissioners decided that the steamer services were uneconomical and decreed that goods must be carried mainly by road 160 miles to and from Glasgow over highways less than first-class and several mountain passes ! Of the brave score of distilleries of 1897 only two remained working in 1950. The whaling ships went with the wind long ago. And then the local resources, duly reorganised, balanced these apparent losses that had seemed so formidable in times of inter-war depressions.

The networks survived to build up a valuable export trade. Immediately after the Second World War a private company reopened the colliery workings, and the National Coal Board, impressed by the richness of the deposits still to be worked, so developed the field in due course that, by July, 1950, the Argyll Colliery was producing 1500 tons of fuel a week : enough to supply all regional needs and to leave a fair balance for export to Ireland by direct shipment. It was reckoned that this weekly output might rise within a measurable space of time to 8000 tons. The oddity of Campbeltown within the Firth of Clyde system would thus be considerably enhanced.

The harbour remains the centre of the town's life and interest. It is a sight to see when, in the season, the tidy vessels from all the fishing fleets of Scotland cram it cheek by jowl.

The figures relating to the Campbeltown fleet alone illustrate again the curious overturning of economic circumstances during the first half of the 20th Century. In 1888 there were registered at the Port of Campbeltown 646 boats employing 2185 men and boys ; by 1950 the numbers had dropped to 35 and 200 respectively. The contrast seems alarming, but it is again a simple case of cause and effect. The boats of 1888 were sailing skiffs, pretty models with brown sails, using the slow drift-net. (A great fleet of them in sunset waters made a lovely sight, and after the type was superseded, many were converted into cruising yachts.) In 1870 a smack of this kind could be built for £30, its nets and other gear costing £20. The ring-net boat of 1950 cost about £7000 to build, the net about £300 to buy.

The revolution has been one of technique, and the various methods of fishing are explained in another chapter. It is sufficient here to know that ring-net fishing, very much a speciality of the Clyde Sea Area, is the deadliest of all netting methods, and that the numerically small fleet of 1950 had at least the same killing-power as the 2000-strong fleet of 60 years before.

As we shall read in a later chapter, Campbeltown was sending to the fishing grounds boats of some 55 feet in length, driven by diesel engines of 120 h.p., armed with wireless sets for transmission as well as reception. Whereas his grandfather followed the gannet or the whale in search of the herring shoals, and his father used a fine and heavily weighted wire slung overside to feel their presence, the modern ring-net man has his depth- or echo-sounding screens to *show* him where the shoals may be crowding.

Thus and thus Campbeltown became an up-to-date place in an unexpected geographical position, a much more solid community than one would expect to find in Highland territory. It is as if one of the Ayrshire ports had been ferried overnight across 30 miles of stormy Firth. (The analogy is strengthened by the fact that the farms of the country behind were at one time invaded and largely occupied by scions of the canny farming families of the mainland.)

This is always a brisk town, not lacking in the roughness of any seaport when the seafaring and mining folk have money to spend on a Saturday evening. The inevitable Main Street is bustling, and at its Quayhead end stands a Celtic Cross with unusually elaborate ornamentation and obscure lettering : the multiple shop and the ancient monument symbolising the complex character of the community.

Campbeltown Loch is short but sufficiently deep for the

most serious maritime purposes, and its entrance is picturesquely blocked by the lumpy mass of Davaar Island, its central peak rising to nearly 400 feet.

This small island carries a lighthouse, but much of its interest has latterly been created by the odd act of a native of the town at the head of the loch.

Some time during the late eighties of the 19th Century a young local artist, Archibald MacKinnon, painted on the naked rock of one of the caves of Davaar Island a picture of the Crucifixion. Over a long period of years this painting, in such an unusual place, acquired a *mystique* of its own. If that were not enough, MacKinnon returned to his native town in 1934, an old man after a long sojourn in England, and considerably repainted much of his early work, which is in fact a creditable job in the Italian manner. It attracts yearly hundreds of those people who, despite its largely industrial character, regard Campbeltown and its environs as a pleasant region in which to spend a holiday.

And with that we pass out of the defined boundaries of the Firth of Clyde. To the southwards, just off the southernmost tip of the Kintyre peninsula, lie the island of Sanda and its satellites. Here is a lighthouse of much importance on the North-Western Approaches. The island, with a central hill rising 400 feet above sea-level, makes with one of its calves an excellent sheep-farm. Its outlying skerries are monstrously dangerous to small and casual shipping.

Hereabouts, however, the intimate Firth of Clyde is merged into the Atlantic, and beyond the Mull of Kintyre, the rocky hills rising 1400 feet behind the lighthouse, there is nothing to the westward but 2000 miles of cruel and indifferent ocean.

CHAPTER V

The Islands: Bute and the Cumbraes

IN ANY writing about the islands within the Firth of Clyde the comparison must be between the two largest, Bute and Arran. This is a sharp one.

As against the leonine majesty of Arran, Bute lies relatively low in the water and wears for the most part a far gentler air of the pastoral sort. It is much more populous than Arran, the resident population of the county capital of Rothesay alone being some 9350 as against Arran's total population of about 4500. As a holiday resort Rothesay attracts in any summer thousands to the hundreds that may visit Brodick or Lamlash.

This comes largely, but not entirely, of Bute's nearness to the mainland and the industrial region about Glasgow. The rail-and-steamer journey from city to island town can be contrived well within one hour and a half. At one acute period of railway competition in the early 20th Century the Caledonian Railway authorities undertook to transport the traveller from Glasgow to Rothesay within the hour by way of the pier at Wemyss Bay by an afternoon train. The undertaking was duly honoured, but the antics of the trains rushing downhill from above Inverkip to the coastal pier so alarmed elderly and important gentlemen of the merchant classes that the experiment was dropped after a few weeks of high excitement and corresponding blood pressure.

Long before then, Bute and Rothesay in particular were the obvious targets of the early steamboat owners and skippers. The placards of the early 19th Century show that the run direct from Glasgow to Rothesay (at a fare of only one shilling !) was the standard excursion of the period. A lively paddle-steamer could make the passage in little more than two hours and display to the passengers the beauties of the inner Firth. Allowing for the return journey in the evening, the excursionist could enjoy a long day in happier and lovelier surroundings than he could ever know in his tenement building. Given the natural beauty of Rothesay Bay and the sober charm of Bute as an island, it is not surprising that Rothesay developed mainly as a pleasure resort, Dunoon its only significant rival.

Considered purely as a geographical entity, Bute is an island with an extreme length of $15\frac{1}{2}$ miles and a breadth that varies from rather more than six miles to rather less than one. Including that of its calf, Inchmarnock, the total area is nearly 50 square miles. As the map shows, the northern snout of the island thrusts deep into the mainland of Argyll, two narrow arms of the sea, forming the Kyles of Bute, separating the masses of land. Only at this northern tip, and again briefly at the extreme southern tip, has Bute any sort of wildness. Even so, the highest hill on the island rises to only 911 feet— a mere protuberance in the Scottish scale of things.

This northern end of the island, however, has its own rugged charm. It excellently matches the loftier, steeper mainland hills that unite with it to form the unique feature of the Kyles. It contrasts dramatically with the orderly, industrious and successful husbandry of the farms that adorn the median belt of Bute. Up there, on the shores of the Kyles of Bute, you are in the Highlands ; only a few miles away you might be in the fertile lowlands of Ayrshire ; while in Rothesay on a Glasgow Fair Saturday you might be in Govan. The Highland-Lowland dichotomy of Scotland, spiritual as well as geographical, was never more neatly produced for the general consideration than in this Isle of Bute.

No road runs completely round the circumference of the island, the steep and rocky nature of the knobbly North End neither allowing nor demanding the convenience. On the western side a rough road running northwards from Ettrick Bay peters out at the farm of Kilmichael, and near the sites of the Grave and Chapel of St Michael, where a local burial ground hangs most picturesquely on a bluff above the western kyle. On the eastern side, that is, north-westwards out of Rothesay, the narrow shore road ends at Rudhabodach opposite Colintraive on the mainland coast. Here is an ancient ferry. In the days of cattle-droving the bestial were swum across the narrows on their way to the mainland markets. In July, 1950, a vehicle capable of carrying six cars was put into service, giving Bute a direct link with the mainland, of which the consequences, potentially important for the island, are not yet measurable.

The importance of the vehicular ferry apart, this northern third of Bute is remote, much given over to sheep-farming and the rearing of hardy cattle. The road system of the island from Rothesay tends mainly in two separate directions—westwards across the narrow waist of Bute towards the sandy bays of the western coast, and due southwards towards Kingarth and Kilchattan Bay and the bleak extremities of the island, the Garroch Heads. This latter road down the eastern side of Bute is the only one rated first class or nearly so by the Ordnance Survey.

Following these axes in this order : the island's waist may be described as lying roughly between Rothesay and Kames Bays on the eastern side and Ettrick and Scalpsie Bays on the other.

Now, this is very charming country of the milder sort and quite remarkably fertile. Farming in Bute is an important industry conducted on the highest level of competence. These are sizeable farms of both the arable and dairying sorts. Notable strains of Ayrshire cattle and Clydesdale horses are bred to prizewinning standard in this region of excellent pasture. As compared with Arran, Bute is in this respect incomparably the richer. The traveller will note the oddity of the mainly Celtic names of these farms, such as Ballanlay, Ballycurry, Kilwhinlick, Creslagvourity and Quochag. He may be even more impressed to hear how the natives pronounce these eccentric place-names.

This is long-settled country, industriously tilled through many centuries. Its archæological interest is remarkable. Few stretches of British soil are so closely littered with circles of stones or trees, with the ruins of the chapels or cells of saints, with crannogs, tumuli, vitrified forts and other shards of remote and mysterious civilisations. The holy men of the early Christian era, and perhaps before it, seem to have found Bute a pleasant place. More likely, coming in from the West, the missionaries found in Bute a better tactical position in relation to the mainland than that provided by the safer but more isolated bulk of Arran. It is just worth noting in passing how many names of Saints are associated with the island— SS Ninian, Michael, Blane and Colmac, their various shrines closely concentrated on the western side.

This coast, southwards from the lower end of the western Kyle of Bute, is remarkable within the Firth of Clyde in being indented by three sandy bays. Two of these, St Ninian's and Scalpsie Bays, are a little remote from the main holiday traffic of the island and have not been notably exploited. Of these two indentations the former is rather the more remarkable in drying out for a great distance behind the low peninsula that bears the ruins of St Ninian's Chapel and in being a prolific bed of cockles. Every visitor to Bute, however, is apt to hear much more of Ettrick Bay to the northward and roughly on the same parallel of latitude as Rothesay.

Here is a wide expanse of safe and shallow sands, open to the salt waters that extend between Bute, the Kintyre mainland and the peaks of Arran. About the turn of the century, when the pioneers of the electric tramway were almost as enthusiastic as the men behind the early railways, it was widely intimated that Ettrick Bay and its glorious sands were to be opened up and developed to form a sort of Blackpool in Scotland : as, no doubt, free and ruthless enterprise could have made it. Certain local prejudices, however, both religious and signeurial, intervened ; and though the tramway was duly laid and the cars from Rothesay plied successfully across the island for a long period of years, there was never to be a Blackpool on Bute except in so far as Rothesay itself can modestly compete with that astonishing and disconcerting town.

The old tram cars across the waist of Bute from Rothesay to Ettrick Bay were delightful in their period. They were single-deck vehicles, open at the sides in fine weather, with a toast-rack arrangement of hard wooden seats. It was an odd experience to go hurtling across green fields and through fine pastureland ; the marvels of electrical power always in the innocent Edwardian mind, the as-it-were Mediterranean illusion created by the open sides of the cars always enchanting.

It was a fleeting glimpse of splendour, however. The trams had hardly 40 years of life before they must give way to the motor-coach. As for Ettrick Bay, it never got far as a *plage* ; a municipal shelter, a few booths, a miniature railway, a few ponies and donkeys for hire—little else except the vast stretches of excellent sand which, to be just, the holiday crowds from Glasgow have for two generations found sufficient for their needs. There is always an enchanting view.

One is tempted to linger over this persistent Scottish backwardness in the exploitation of holiday resources : not that one might, personally, have it otherwise. Undoubtedly, the influences of the Landlord and the Kirk rightly or wrongly checked such blatantly commercial development as one may see at Southend, Margate, Brighton, Southport, Morecambe and Skegness : even, in Scotland, at Portobello, in some of the Fife and Ayrshire coast resorts. One would best like to think that the scenic splendour of the Firth of Clyde was in itself enough for most people. The facts remain. The national character and the physical conditions have somehow combined to preserve a certain order of natural balance. It is still remarkable that the terrific power of the thrust outwards from industrial Clydeside has produced, relatively, so little of wholly vulgar artificiality.

Within this Isle of Bute the powers of an aristocracy in a changing world may, as it happens, be studied with some particularity and, one hopes, with patience and justice.

As we have seen, the best road in Bute runs down the eastern side of the island from Rothesay to come to an end at Kilchattan Bay. Of this settlement there is little enough to be said. It is just another of those pleasant hamlets that once shaped to be popular watering-places and now, the social urge in that direction dwindling, wear a faint air of remoteness and neglect. It is remarkable how the obsolescence of its pier can take the life out of such a place. This eastern side of Bute is best served with communications largely because they lead towards the palace of the native aristocracy, Mount Stuart, the fabulous seat of the fabulous Crichton-Stuarts, the Marquesses of Bute.

The road-map shows how the main road and its secondaries must go in wide loops about the private grounds ; and that is not at all to sneer at privilege. It is rather to admire a magnificence unique in the middle of the 20th Century. Here is aristocracy to the *n*th power. This Bute family disposes of nearly a dozen titles of great antiquity. It owns about 117,000 acres of land in Great Britain. At one time, at least, its wealth through the ownership of the Cardiff dock area was fabulous. The family seat is fabulous in proportion, and its story is interesting in that it is one of the last expressions in its kind of aristocratic wealth and power.

The Firth of Clyde

The original house of Mount Stuart was destroyed by fire in December, 1877, though the plate, most of the furniture and the pictures of fabulous value, a Rubens among them, were providentially saved. Also spared from the flames was a resplendent Catholic church or chapel : the third Marquess having gone over to that faith in 1868. The rebuilding of Mount Stuart was entrusted to Mr. Rowand Anderson, and it can fairly be said that he seized the opportunity with both hands, producing what the popular works of reference still describe as " a magnificent Gothic pile." It is remarkable in every sense of that word.

Of the three stories of the mansion, the first two are built as to the outer walls in red sandstone, while brick is used in the third. External features are " the high-pitched roofs and dormers, the angle turrets, the corbelled oriel windows, and a stone balustrade in front of an open gallery." A central entrance hall some 60 feet square is surrounded by a Gothic arcade in various marbles. The chief public rooms are each about 20 yards long. The total cost of rebuilding Mount Stuart in the late 70's of the 19th Century is said to have been rather more than £200,000—or, shall we say, a million to-day ? The highly decorated Chapel is reported to have cost another £100,000.

The politicians can no doubt enjoy themselves vastly in a gloating over this splendiferous expression of privilege and wealth. The more detached historian may be more interested in the creation of such an effulgent pleasure dome towards the end of the Victorian era, though he should be careful to note that the industrial magnates were still, with much less sanction, to build on a scale proportionately magnificent. It is to the point here that in Bute, as in Arran and elsewhere on the Clyde coast, the influence of landowning aristocracy remained powerful as against the demands of popular taste and those who catered for it.

The Islands : Bute and the Cumbraes

The experience of that Sir James Colquhoun of Luss, who sought in vain to push a " Sunday-breaker " off his pier at Garelochhead, has been repeated in much subtler forms at many points up and down the Firth of Clyde. This arises out of the very character of land-holding in Scotland, and that should be understood.

The old order of things had begun to change even before the Second World War, but as distinct from the leasehold or copyhold systems common in England, a man building a house in Scotland took from the landlord what is called a feu. This, as we have noted, is a lease in perpetuity of a piece of ground with none of the ruinous " falling-in " that so disturbs property values South of the Border. At the same time, the Scottish landlord customarily imposed on the feuar in the contract quite a number of onerous conditions, most of these designed to conserve amenity. If you took out a feu in a residential area, it must be solely for the purpose of building a dwelling-house ; you could not run up a slaughterhouse or a tanworks as fancy might dictate. Thus, though the feuar had complete security of tenure so long as he paid the feu-duty, the landlord or his agents could intimately control the details of what we have learned to call "development."

This set of circumstances considerably modified the exploitation of all the shores of the Firth of Clyde for the benefit of the mere beanfeaster. In both Arran and Bute, as elsewhere, there were many collisions between the interests of the landowners, on the one hand, and those of ambitious local authorities and of relentless private enterprise on the other. No doubt something like a Blackpool or a Southend could have been laid out on the Clyde coast, but it is at least arguable that, given the great natural beauty of the scene, the conservative instincts of a Duchess in Arran and of a Marquess in Bute have resulted in quite a happy compromise.

The Bute family has, in fact, an admirable record in the

157

preservation of the native decencies. Whatever we may think of the Victorian excesses of Mount Stuart, the Crichton-Stuarts have most admirably preserved and lived in two of the most delightful old houses in Scotland. Both are near the county town of Rothesay, nearer its northern satellite, Port Bannatyne. One of these, Kames Castle, consists mainly of a square 14th Century tower with a low range of dwelling-houses attached to it. Within the same grounds is Wester Kames, reputed to be the oldest inhabited house in Scotland. Once the home of the family of Spens, for a time a ruin, it is a sort of peel, much decorated with crow-stepped gables and pepper-pot turrets, and altogether a gem of native architecture intelligently restored and preserved.

To return to Mount Stuart : its grounds, or " policies " as they say in Scotland, are on the whole rather lovelier than the Victorian palace. Here are avenues, gardens and woodlands of singular luxuriance. These could not have been grown in anything but a very mild climate, and Bute enjoys in fact so much mildness that palms grow easily in the public gardens of Rothesay and that ambitious town likes to advertise itself as " the Madeira of the North." The metaphor is hardly scientific ; it might be more illuminating to compare Rothesay with Falmouth, but even then strictly *pari passu.*

No place in the West of Scotland can ever escape the fact that it is drenched each year by relatively large precipitations of rain. If palms and fuchsias and rhododendrons, ferns and creepers and roses, grow in lovely profusion, it is because one of the northern eddies of the Gulf Stream favours the region with precisely the conditions of moist mildness that makes vegetation of these kinds grow in abandonment. Outside the Firth of Clyde, in the southern Hebridean island of Gigha, for instance, the palms and gigantic banks of fuchsia and great drifts of montbretia flourish wherever they are protected from the killing winds off the Atlantic. On the island of Tiree again, with one of the highest sunshine records in Scotland, it is hard to grow even a row of lettuce, except in exceptional shelter.

Bute is almost wholly sheltered, and therein lies much of its fortune. South of the knobbly northern corner of the island only one ridge of fairly high ground intersects it on the axis NE-SW, this nicely dividing the rich farming waist of the island from the wooded and privileged regions about Mount Stuart. These little hills do not run high in the Scottish scale of things ; at their very highest about 500 feet above sea level ; but they are interesting in that they contain a chain of lochs that at once provide the community with an excellent water supply and contribute a pleasant touch of the sub-Highland to the island's scenery.

The largest is Loch Fad with an auxiliary dam on a slightly lower level towards Rothesay ; Loch Ascog is about half a mile away eastwards towards the Firth. The chain ends in little Loch Quien, which is slightly wilder and darker than its neighbours and contains a crannog. Many people have written with vast enthusiasm of the loveliness of these quiet lakes. The more detached and experienced traveller might prefer to say that they are charming without being notably exciting. This is scenery on a distinctly equable level. It includes, however, one showpiece with a distinctly odd provenance.

This is a house among trees on the western shore of Loch Fad, popularly called Kean's Cottage, though its prosaic name for practical purposes is Woodend. Nor is it a cottage by any means ; most of us would describe it as a small country house in the Georgian manner. Hither, however, the tempestuous tragedian Edmund Kean did choose to retire during one of the many stormy passages of his life, building his villa in this improbable place so that he could declare : " How glorious from the loopholes of retreat to peep on such a world ! " It was latterly lived in for a time by a lesser dramatic figure,

Sheridan Knowles, a more ambitious than successful dramatist : probably during the period in which he conducted a school of acting in Glasgow. Woodend is now in private occupation, but the pilgrim may stare with melancholy surmise at the pillars of the main entrance gates, each topped by a bust of a great English dramatist.

At the northern end of this diagonal ridge across the island, Rothesay's excellent municipal golf-course occupies a noble position commanding noble prospects. From various points on this bold shoulder of land it is easily seen why the bulk of Bute's population and commerce should be concentrated hereabouts. Rothesay Bay and its lesser neighbour, Kames Bay, are fine harbours of refuge, sheltered, safe and attractive. The former, which has inspired so much sentimental minstrelsy, is fully a mile deep within two points about one mile and a half apart. As one gazeteer helpfully puts it : " Its shape resembles what mathematicians call a semi-ellipsoid." There are fine woods at points about this deep crescent ; the view over to the Toward shores of the Cowal peninsula and the lands about the mouth of Loch Striven is delightful.

Here the Royal Stewarts of Scotland, their origins and bases in the West, had a seat from an early period of recorded Scottish history. The title of Duke of Rothesay has much the same significance in the Scottish context as that of Duke of Cornwall; it falls to the male heir-apparent and reverts to the Crown in the absence of a prince in the direct line of succession. It was often used by the Duke of Windsor, formerly King Edward VIII, on his Scottish tours, his interest inspiring the design of a Rothesay tartan. Thus the original village grew about a castle, its earliest parts dating from the late 11th Century, and then the modern town about its ruins.

The stranger may not find these remarkably impressive. Within a moat the central feature is a massive circular building in a dark pink stone once flanked by four round towers of which only one survives. The walls of an ancient chapel are to be found within. A later addition, in another sort of stone, much battered and called " the Palace," is believed to have been built by Robert III of Scotland (*c.* 1340-1406) and within these walls that feckless monarch died. The stronghold suffered in Scotland's various defensive wars against both the Norsemen and the English. Cromwell's troops despoiled it, and finally one of the Argyll family reduced it to ruin in 1685. . . . It is of much interest that so many of the fine old buildings of Scotland were battered out of existence by Nonconformist armies : just as, in an ecstasy of masochism, the Reformed Scots themselves raped the Cathedral of St Andrews.

Rothesay Castle is now in the care of the Ancient Monuments Department of H.M. Ministry of Works. It might not be even in such a fair state of preservation had not the Bute family spent considerable sums out of their private fortune during the 19th Century to clear up the mess of neglect and overgrowth. It is a bitter fact that, after the Union of the Crowns, the religious wars of the 17th Century and then the Union of the Parliaments in 1707, the Scots lost pride in their national possessions or lacked the power to preserve them. It was probably a case of devitalisation by the strifes involved in maintaining the independence of a small nation ; and when the Industrial Revolution rolled over Western Scotland, terrible as a black army with black banners, the old and gracious went under right and left. Here is an old ruin, the people seem to have said in the urgency of the new enthusiasms ; let us bottom our new roads with the stones, or build a pier or, at the very least, a byre.

The Castle of Rothesay, interesting and impressive enough, is a fair symbol of this conflict. It lacks somewhat in both impressiveness and charm precisely because the dignity of site was taken from it by the industrial growth of Rothesay as a town ; because it was ringed round in Victorian days by the grey and workaday cliffs of tenements in the old tradition of Scottish domestic architecture.

Rothesay's industrial history is much more interesting than that of any other resort on the inner Firth of Clyde. As an island capital, it shaped in the second half of the 18th Century to be a considerable centre of the textile industry. The manufacture of linen was started about the middle of that century, and then there was a turn towards cotton : the great David Dale in command and some 800 hands employed in several mills. (What is claimed to have been the first cotton mill in Scotland still stands in Ladeside Street, Rothesay.) The industry died under the influences of centralisation ; so also tanning and boatbuilding. A State bounty encouraged the herring fishing industry for a while, but that again had to pass largely to the ports of the outer Firth. By the middle of the 19th Century this town of Rothesay, the pleasure steamers from Glasgow and Greenock pouring more and more trippers into the place, had accepted its destiny as a holiday resort, its pier far and away the busiest outside the mainland terminals, and the largest.

Rothesay Pier is one of the sights and promenades of the place. It can take at least three sizeable paddlers or turbine steamers along its northern front and still accommodate two or three more at its ends and inner sides in moments of crisis. These have been rare since the period between the two Wars, for reasons already suggested and to be discussed more fully later on. It is a typical product of Victorian expansion, down to the rustic-Gothic tower that caps the administrative buildings. It is the harmless fashion of the holidaymaker to pay a modest pier-due and parade the length of the quay, backwards and forwards, whether to greet new arrivals to the Madeira of the North, wave to departing friends or simply to enjoy the brisk sociability of an obvious point of congregation.

The Islands : Bute and the Cumbraes

Is it necessary to explain that a Clyde pier is not as those elongated erections over shallow waters that are among the advertised attractions of such as Brighton and Southend, with bands playing at intervals and curious peep-shows along the route ? The Clyde pier is strictly functional, as they say. It is a point at which steamers put down and pick up passengers. Except here and there, the average Firth pier is not required to run hundreds of yards over sands or mud. Where it has to do so, it still sticks to its proper business within the regional transport system : the river steamer being in these variegated regions of more importance than it is anywhere else in the British Isles : so many islands complicating the problem.

For many people not yet old in the mid-20th Century the pier at Rothesay was the very symbol of the bustle and colour and fun of the daft days of competitive shipping on the Firth. There was not a moment from early morning until late evening when some gay-funnelled steamer would not be coming or going : two or three at a time in the busy hours of the day. Those were the times of the lyrical Heather Jock and the Pointing Porters in their white jackets. Every departing steamer rang the brazen bell under the break of the bridge ; and there once lived in Rothesay a blind girl who, with the sense of absolute pitch that often compensates persons thus afflicted, could tell which out of a score of steamers using the pier daily was eager to depart.

Those colours have faded, those echoes died away, and it may be that the establishment of the vehicular ferry at Rudhabodach may still further reduce the importance of Rothesay Pier. However that may be, the pier and the early steamboats made Rothesay what it is. As the steamer sweeps past the point at Craigmore, the local iron pier long dismantled, the experienced eye may see at a glance the panorama of social change within a century of industrial history.

163

The Firth of Clyde

This island capital is laid out in the inevitable pattern of the West Highland community. The nexus of tenements and streets beyond the pierhead betray in their clotted confusion and in the narrowness of the shopping streets the inability of the Celt to deal handsomely with an urban problem. This patch of near-slum, however, is handsomely offset by the bright openness of the front ; a line of hotels and gay shops that, as the traveller disembarks and passes the inner harbour, has a faint but agreeable suggestion of the Baltic about it. There are then the inevitable extensions of villas along both arms of the bay, with others climbing up the steep ground behind and seeming to perch on ledges.

These were the villas of the well-to-do in mid-Victorian times ; almost all, hundreds of them, are boarding-houses or, as it latterly became proper to say, private hotels. Catering is the staple industry, and the local authority has not failed to keep down the rates by providing gardens, bathing stations, putting greens, bowling greens, an ample hall for the inevitable concert party, and all the other devices of the trade.

The curious traveller from outside the area may be most interested to observe that the hiring of rowing boats and motor boats within this notably safe bay is a major local industry. The stances line the western arm of the bay beyond the pier, the wooden slips awash, the pretty craft prettily riding the little waves as they wait to be hired, even if the standard of popular oarsmanship on Rothesay Bay hardly matches the trigness of the long-suffering craft. It is significant that, with the decline of the railway steamer services, some of these Rothesay boathirers have found it profitable to build and run diesel-engined vessels capable of taking fully a hundred passengers on long trips up the Kyles of Bute and elsewhere about the island.

From Rothesay Pier the extensions in both directions differ subtly in social significance. The very architecture of the

164

villas along the fine front eastwards towards Craigmore—the façade of a gigantic hotel, once a polite hydropathic, looming over all—suggests the genteel, the refined, the prosperous. This settlement of Craigmore was at one time, in fact, what was called select, and it is still favoured by substantial persons in retirement. Its remarkable display of Victorian architectural styles as applied in solid sandstone to domestic building is wonderful enough, but it is excelled in grandeur and comic variety by the glories of Ascog, round Bogany Point and facing eastwards across the Firth towards Largs. Here the very well-to-do built their mansions on the lavish scale and set them in large plots of private ground ; and we must see them now as monuments.

By the middle of the 20th Century few private incomes could support these coastal palaces as well as dwelling places in city or town ; the labour of gardeners and domestic servants was simply not available. The terms of the theorem are recurrent, the conclusion is always inevitable. The stately pleasure domes reverted to the pool of things as hotels or convalescent homes. In the special case of Rothesay, the building of marine villas on the lavish scale was encouraged by the fact that the island town was for many years the head-quarters of Scotland's oldest yacht club, the Royal Northern. It is equally interesting that, before the Second War, the Royal Northern had withdrawn from the all-too-popular resort and hoisted its flag at Rhu on the Gareloch, within easy car-run of Glasgow.

The extensions of Rothesay westwards from the pier are less distinguished. The original Rothesay fades out quickly short of a stretch of ragged and rather notorious woodland on the western side of the bay, and where the line of dwellings is resumed again about Ardbeg Point we are in quite another community. This is Port Bannatyne, so named after the original and extinct lairds of the region, in a pleasant bay of its own,

Kames Bay, opening rather more directly eastwards than Rothesay Bay.

There is not a great deal to be said about Port Bannatyne except as in comparison with Rothesay. It has its own vague individuality : that of a West Highland village as compared with that of a county town. Its older and inner parts about the pierhead are faintly shabby and tortuous in the Celtic manner, but it is much more curious that the villas along the front were obviously built during one of the more depressed periods of Victorian taste : the high-arched Alpine gable all too common ; and it is clear that the development of Port Bannatyne was quite independent of that of its greater neighbour. Briefly, the Craigmore extension of Rothesay represents a reasonably intelligent deployment of wealth in the matter of domestic building by the large employer, while Port Bannatyne stands for the subtly humbler effort of the under-manager or foreman to stake his claim with the assistance of the speculative builder, working industriously without the guidance of an architect.

The fantastically intricate social pattern made up by the Clyde coast resorts takes on another twist when, leaving Bute, we arrive at Millport, the only town of the twin islands called the Cumbraes : the accent resting on the first syllable.

Between Rothesay and Millport there are some obvious similarities. Both surround safe and even cosy bays, Millport Bay lying more openly to the sun than that of its larger neighbour. It is made up, moreover, of three separate little bays, each with its own character. These bays have sandy shores, and the sum of them is diversified by a group of low, rocky islets. But the West Highland *motif* recurs again in Millport—the clot of indifferent streets and housing about the pierhead, the villas strung along a wide crescent. The most interesting difference is that Millport, with a population of just over 2000, does not naturally command the resources of the larger town on the larger island, so that the " improvements " or " attractions " are inevitably on a more modest scale. It is probably fair to suggest that Millport is a rather specially interesting case of the compromise between the relative sophistications of Dunoon, Largs or Rothesay and the more careless freedoms of the Arran villages. It certainly commands the most affectionate loyalty of its regular summer visitors.

This little town of Millport has one or two odd distinctions. The physical and social conditions have made it so that the houses do not hang by their foundations on perilous ledges but are rather more graciously spaced in length along the curves of the clover-leaf bay. Then, the Episcopal Church in Scotland, backed by the influence of the Earls of Glasgow, chose this small island town to be the see of the Bishop of Argyll and the Isles, and a collegiate church designed by Butterfield in 1849, but after the 13th Century manner, is one of the show-pieces of the place. At Keppel, a trifle to the North of the town, is an important Marine Biological Station with a fascinating museum attached. The golf-course on the slopes above the town commands views of the Firth that make putting seem an irrelevance. Finally . . . one hopes it is true, and the authorities are firm on the point . . . it was from the pulpit of the parish kirk of Millport that, in the early 19th Century, the Reverend James Adam habitually offered up a prayer " for the Great and Little Cumbrae and the adjacent islands of Great Britain and Ireland."

This greater Cumbrae is a rather mild sort of island, its highest point just above the 400-feet mark. It has its quota of standing stones, cairns and whatnot, and some dim traces of the Norse occupation, but one sees it mainly as a pleasant and reasonably fertile place of rose-red rocks and bright green fields, its affinities rather with the Ayrshire mainland than with the Highland and Hebridean characteristics of Arran and the distant Kintyre shore.

The Firth of Clyde

The sea passage between the Cumbraes and the mainland about Largs is feasible even for ships of size, but the fairway of large shipping in and out of the Clyde lies between the little islands and Bute. This fact confers on the Little Cumbrae a special importance.

The Wee Cumbrae, as they say, is a rougher entity than its parent and seems to stand higher out of the water : an illusion arising out of its lesser size. It is roughly farmed, but its most numerous inhabitants are rabbits and lighthouse-keepers. On an islet close into the eastern shore a small castle or watch-tower may have been set up as an outpost against Scandinavian raiders ; it was certainly raped in due course by those ubiquitous gangsters, Cromwell's troops, and wears the pathetic charm of all such relics. On the hillside above is the site of the chapel of an obscure missionary, St Vey or Beya, and above that again is the stump of the original lighthouse. This was set up in 1750, the second of its kind in Scotland. It burned coal to provide the warning light.

The modern lighthouse stands on a bluff at the western-most point of the little island. It is of the first importance within the Clyde lighthouse system and is elaborately equipped. When an inward-bound ship has the Cumbrae light abeam to starboard it is home again. The vessel outward-bound here makes its last signals and puts out the log. Beyond are the deeps and galloping seas of the outer Firth and then the great, cruel swells of the North-Western Approaches.

CHAPTER VI

The Islands: Arran and Ailsa Craig

THE Isle of Arran is far and away the most arrogantly brilliant feature of the Firth of Clyde seascape. A romantic view might hold that the lone monolith of Ailsa Craig, which rises out of the same under-water ridge, is unique, but it is only so in its kind as a sort of freak. Arran is infinitely more distinguished in its large size as an island, the great height and ruggedness of its mountains ; in its variety, the interest of its natural history and the charm of its coastal settlements. This is not to mention the fascination it has exercised on generation after generation of holidaymakers, so that a devotion to Arran has become a *mystique* or cult with its own esoteric understandings and odd social consequences.

Arran and its calf, the Holy Isle, are pervasive in almost any view of the Firth. In reasonably clear weather, no traveller by road up or down some 60 miles of the Ayrshire coast can expect to lose sight of it : the angle and aspect changing almost from moment to moment ; the slant of sunlight or the play of cloud varying as in a motion picture in colour. Many hundreds of artists, good and bad, have painted thousands of pictures with but the one title, " Arran from the Ayrshire Coast." Even from the upper Firth, behind the natural screens formed by the Cloch Point or the Rosneath peninsula, a man has to climb only 400 feet or so until, pointing to gilded peaks in the distance, he can exclaim to his companion—and he usually does so with a strange excitement—" There's Arran ! "

In the strict geographer's sense, Arran is an island that lies plumb in the fairway of the outer Firth of Clyde almost due north and south, is about 20 miles in length, and between eleven and eight miles in extremes of breadth, its total area being about 165 square miles. The road round the circumference of the island covers a distance of 60 miles. The mountains at the northern end of the island run nearly up to the 3000-feet mark. As we have seen, the resident population is in the neighbourhood of 4500.

These facts are of some general interest, no doubt, but they are as nothing in face of the sheer physical splendour of this island. For if hills rising to near the 3000-feet level are not out of the way in the Scottish scale of things, their formation and their arrangement in Arran are peculiarly theatrical—one had almost said operatic in the Wagnerian tradition.

These mountains at the north end have teeth in them : jagged ridges to test the most experienced climber, also to fret the skyline with a remote and Alpine sort of beauty. The ascent of Goatfell, the highest hill of all (2866 feet) is within the compass of children by a well-worn path, but the peak remains a monstrously dominant landmark, and the ridges running northwards and westwards are formidable. Even the tourists, comfortably cruising round the island in car or bus, may see on almost any ridge the alert and curious heads of red deer, staring down from their heights on the ant-like antics of *homo sapiens*.

It is undoubtedly this clot of mountains at the northern end which gives Arran its leonine majesty as a distant spectacle, but it really misrepresents the wholly charming, often pastoral. character of much of a delightfully varied island.

On the western coast, for instance, the broad, green plain watered by the Machrie and Black Waters is studded with sizeable farms of a patently prosperous sort. The short glens at the southern end suggest Devon or the Isle of Man in their richness of verdure in high summer, and the existence of a

The Islands : Arran and Ailsa Craig

large creamery of the Milk Marketing Board hereabouts witnesses to the existence of a solid dairying industry. The short glens and streams of the eastern seaboard can be cosily charming ; the botanical richness of Arran, encouraged by the soft, mild air, is indeed remarkable. All the colourful trees and shrubs—the fuchsia, the rhododendron, the forsythia, the honeysuckle, the azalea and the rest—blaze seasonably on all the lower levels, and in August the high ground glows everywhere with the warm purple of heather : the marshlands green and fragrant with bog myrtle and orchis.

It is most useful, however, to take Arran for what it really is—a Hebridean island that, within easy reach of the Lowland industrial regions and enormously popular, has miraculously retained its Highland qualities ; an island that, unlike Man, has no Douglas or Ramsey or even a Port Erin ; an island of which it can be said that even if its chief industry, apart from agriculture, is that of catering for the tourist, somehow retains a powerful native identity—as if its beauty and quality were too much for the gregariousness of the masses or, it might be, had enchanted them into decency. And if it be that the policy of the landowners in succession discouraged " development " on popular lines, then one may fairly say that the policy was wise and to the general advantage. All over Arran, in fact, the ordinary citizen enjoys a remarkable freedom of movement.

This blessed island was inevitably one of the targets of the early steamboat owners, and piers were built. In the golden years before the First World War it enjoyed a frequent steamer service, for not only did the rival railway companies run regular services from Greenock and Gourock, a swift cross-channel service from Ardrossan on the Ayrshire coast was maintained, and steamers making for Campbeltown landed passengers at several points along the north-eastern shoulder of the island. The circumstances of the pre- and post-Second

War periods sadly reduced these amenities, and it was left to internal bus communications to take up the slack as best they could. Here we are only concerned with the fact that inconvenience did nothing to abate the annual flow of long-term holidaymakers into Arran. It is perhaps an irony of the period that the establishment of one of Mr Butlin's camps in a former naval station at Ayr notably increased the number of day-trippers.

As the map shows, the natural ports of Arran are mostly on the eastern seaboard—Brodick Bay, Lamlash Bay and Whiting Bay. The indentation of Lochranza at the north-western corner of the island forms the only feasible harbour on the rather exposed western coast. About the heads of these harbours the largest settlements naturally took shape.

Brodick is the island " capital," and a very pleasant place it is indeed. The bay is an almost perfect crescent, with a stretch of good sand at the top : this diversified by something unusual in Scotland—a row of striped bathing-boxes. Over the northern arm of the bay looms the mass of Goatfell, the red castle of the Duke and Duchess of Montrose among fine woodlands at its base. Even so, Brodick Bay has an agreeably open aspect, for though the hills run high behind it, three glens, Rosa, Shurig and Cloy, cut large notches in the back-cloth, so to speak, and let in plenty of western light to play on the green flats above high water mark. The village and pier are on the southern arm of the bay, the former trig and clean and amusingly varied as to architectural styles. Between the First and Second Wars, and even after the Second, Brodick developed its resources for the entertainment of visitors, and all the newer hotel buildings are very decent in their styles and, no doubt at the instance of the landowners, admirably spaced in wide, bright gardens.

Hereabouts the sensitive traveller may catch a subtle " atmosphere " that is recurrent throughout the island.

Brodick is obviously a West Highland hamlet that has grown up under the patronage of townsfolk, mainly of the middle-classes, but on a bright day, when the young people are milling along the shore road in their coloured garments and colour is blazing on the hillsides round about, one gets the feeling of an element almost Mediterranean in the scene. Here there are golf and tennis to be played ; here you may swim and go boating or sea-fishing ; here may be your angling or mountaineering base. But there are no fun fairs, no helter-skelters. At the height of the season a mobile cinema may operate twice a week, alternating with free-for-all dances in the public hall. The rest is as natural, even primitive, as it may be in the 20th Century. The compromise is singularly happy.

Every visitor to Arran automatically goes round the island at least once. The bus and taxi services are ample. Assuming the vehicle to be heading south-about the next port of call is Lamlash, a village rather larger than Brodick but hardly its match in situation, style and tone. Before this point is reached, however, a traverse of one of Arran's exciting passes must be made. No road on this island can be anything but narrow and tortuous ; no native driver is anything but pragmatical in his approach to the use of clutch and gears. Thus even this brief journey of four miles or so can be an exciting affair as the road winds under trees, over mosses flecked with lint, and the vehicle must slow down continually to let another pass or allow a Blackface ewe and her lamb or even a Highland cow to rise at leisure from their resting places on the warm tarmac.

The descent into Lamlash is spectacular not for any special dizziness of the descent, steep though that may be, but because one suddenly sees how splendidly the high hump of the Holy Isle at once encloses and embellishes the very fine natural harbour of Lamlash Bay.

Some people feel that Lamlash is too warmly enclosed by the tall island on the seaward side and the high hills inland. These hills crowd closely on the village, but again there are twin glens, Benlister and Monamore, to lighten the little patch of flat green land by the sea. The bay has the largest sweep of any on Arran, and it is completely protected from all winds save those from two fine points of the compass. Especially before the First War it was much used by the Royal Navy, and at one period of post-war shortage the longshoremen of the district turned an honest penny by trawling for the tons of coal that had been lost overside in the processes of bunkering.

Lamlash village is much less compact than Brodick, less distinguished in its architecture and lay-out. It seems to straggle, and for some not easily discernible reason it has always tended to attract holidaymakers on subtly lower income levels than that of those faithful to its more fashionable neighbours. It may be surmised that it is a much older establishment than either Brodick or Whiting Bay—a surmise well-rooted in its distinction as a harbour of refuge—and that it was, as it were, slightly industrialised before its neighbours waxed on the tourist trade. It remains a very pleasant place on a bay of singular beauty and nobility. The enclosure of salt water between the green foothills of the Arran mainland and the grey screes of the Holy Isle has at once the boldness of the sea proper and the charm of a fjord.

From Lamlash the narrow road runs inland for a space and then turns sharply left and by grinding slopes to cut across high country to Whiting Bay, the third largest of the Arran resorts. In doing so, it runs behind the point of King's Cross, one of those numerous places on the outer Firth of Clyde traditionally associated with Robert the Bruce's campaign to secure the Scottish throne for himself. He is said to have sailed hence towards his destiny in 1307 to descend upon the Carrick Coast of Ayrshire, its green slopes and even its ploughed fields clearly seen in fair weather from Arran across 14 miles of salt water.

The character of Whiting Bay differs distinctly from that of its neighbours. It is less cosy, so to speak, than Brodick and Lamlash, much less a natural harbour. The curve of the bay is rather flat ; the exposure is to the east. In a sense it consists of two bays separated by the mild promontory from which the pier extends. Both have patches of fine yellow sand, and as the name suggests there is good fishing in the offshore waters, and there are flounders to be speared over the sand inshore.

This wide bay is partly overlapped by the southern tip of the Holy Isle, the white lighthouse buildings always startling against the greys and greens of scree and bracken, but the general aspect is open to the wide, occasionally wild stretches of the outer Firth, and all the considerable sea traffic of a great harbour is to be seen passing up and down the fairway for ocean-going vessels. In a word : as distinct from those of Brodick and Lamlash, the atmosphere of Whiting Bay has an oceanic quality.

The human settlements along these pleasant shores are extensive in terms of mere length and considerably varied as to architecture. Here is clearly another case of a tiny hamlet having been developed by forces from outside itself ; for Whiting Bay was never a small capital like Brodick nor a harbour like Lamlash. The dynamics were provided by the industrial folk of the mainland, always seeking their ways of escape, and it is of mild interest that in the closely-marked scale of social values rigidly applied on an island mainly patronised by the middle-middle and lower-middle-classes— and very little by the working folk, for fairly obvious reasons— Whiting Bay was for a long time, but a time now passing, regarded as having more " tone " than its neighbours.

The settlement is unique in Arran in that it repeats the *motif* more obvious on the inner Firth—the higgledy-piggledy piling of dwelling-houses in irregular terraces on steep slopes. A middle-aged man might be incapable of handling even a putter by the time he has contrived to the level of the golf-course above the roofs of the highest cottages. But if these slopes behind the village are abrupt and knobbly, Whiting Bay has always that open front to the open sea, while it is illuminated from behind by the gap of Glenashadale, an attractive glen with a double-flatted waterfall fully 150 feet high and paths that make an agreeable walk from shore-level through the lush vegetation of the West Highlands. Just below the mouth of this stream, from the agglomeration of rocks that marks the southern end of the bay, the view northwards to the Holy Isle and the clot of peaks about Goatfell is in the order of the theatrical.

Southwards from Whiting Bay the road soars and relapses, twists and tumbles towards the last considerable settlement on the eastern side of the island, the village of Kildonan.

This is a little place of cottages and villas, favoured by family parties of quiet tastes. The outlook is purely oceanic ; Kildonan stares down the outer Firth past Ailsa Craig to the open sea. It is of some importance as a coastguard and signalling station, and the place and its surroundings are much favoured by retired mariners, in the long sunset of the north watching the ships coming in and the ships going out. The tiny island of Pladda with its lighthouse lies offshore, so closely attached to the mainland by a reef that it seems hardly an island at all, while it perfectly symbolises the traveller's feeling of being here, at the southern tip of Arran, at a sort of land's end.

As it is, the main road snakes westwards from Kildonan and then northwards into and out of little glens, with small farms on the hillside but not a settlement of size for miles : here a parish kirk by the wayside, here a school, there most surprisingly the busy depot of the Milk Marketing Board ; but no more. The sea recedes, and it is surprising to come to

PADDY'S MILESTONE: The lone, unique cone of Ailsa Craig, rising 1114 feet above the sea in the Outer Firth and the home of countless seabirds.

CULZEAN CASTLE: Seat of the Kennedy's, the Marquesses of Ailsa. A fine Adams building of the 18th century, it is now in the care of the National Trust for Scotland and includes a flat for the exclusive use of General Eisenhower during his lifetime.

LAMLASH, ARRAN: The old stone pier. Sheltered by the Holy Isle, the bay is a recognised anchorage for naval vessels.

ISLAND GLEN: Glen Sannox, **Arran**; the typical glen of the islands, rising steeply from wooded, pastoral country to barren peaks.

the place called Lagg, which is little more than a hotel, deeply embowered among tall trees by a pleasant stream. It is surprising because it does not seem to belong to a Hebridean island, because you get in this enclosed and often stuffy place the feel of being in Devon or Wales. Out of this dip, however, the road up the western coast of the island traverses, with just one or two delightful breaks, a coast considerably harsher than that so sweetly indented by the three bays which face the Ayrshire mainland.

For a space the turnpike runs high above the sea in the Norwegian manner, the hillsides above it thick with bracken and round stones that seem likely at any moment to roll down upon the invader. At another point to the northwards it may be seen how the potatoes of the small farmers or crofters have to be grown in drills of almost pure shingle, so poor the land between the beach and the red cliffs that once contained the sea. This western coast has its own holiday popularity, its own following of devotees, and Glasgow families are as faithful to Catacol or Pirnmill as others are to Brodick or Whiting Bay. The relative austerity remains ; the boating, for instance, is hardly so safe on that exposed coast as within the eastern bays. There are on this western coast, however, two surprising breaks of greenery and sophistication.

It has already been noted that between two groups of high hills a triangular stretch of arable land, traversed by the Machrie and Black Waters, slopes gently to the sea—the channel between Arran and the Kintyre mainland called the Kilbrennan Sound. This wide and fertile vale has its proper " capital " in the hamlet of Shiskine, but at the coastal village of Blackwaterfoot it blossoms into a holiday resort of unexpected radiance.

Blackwaterfoot is a simple enough little place, stone built and clean. For its own sake the traveller would hardly linger here. But there is a view, and there is a beach ; and, above all, the most skilful use has been made of the natural features of the riparian lands running northwards. These are links of fine, hard turf and make an excellent golf-course. Against a range of low cliffs hard by the clubhouse runs a series of tennis courts. On a fine summer's day this aggregation of elements has the air of a planned Lido or country club, and that for the most interesting reason of all.

Blackwaterfoot is, as a holiday resort, virtually governed by the regular summer visitors from Glasgow, Paisley, Greenock and parts adjoining, who form what is in fact a local improvement association. Here, in this remote corner of the remarkable Isle of Arran, there has been established a convention rather more powerful than those of the natives. Here is a club in effect ; and as we shall see later on, the social structure of Arran is based to a remarkable extent upon the needs and demands of its summer patrons, mostly of the industrial and professional middle classes.

Lochranza at the north-eastern corner of the island has none of the glitter of Blackwaterfoot. It is a more real sort of place, so to speak. The loch itself is barely a mile in length and just about half as much in breadth, and it is steeply enclosed by high hills : a cosy little harbour. A feature of this harbour is a gravelly spit which nearly cuts off the head of the bay. This is a pleasant feature when the tide is in ; hardly so pleasant at the ebb when it dries out in mud, in spite of the interesting ruins of an old castle upon it. When the herring fleets of the outer Firth were much larger than they are now, Lochranza was a fishing port of some little consequence, and the graceful, brown-sailed smacks would be moored by the dozen behind the castle in the off-hours. But the herring fishing has gone from Arran, concentrated in just a few mainland ports, and Lochranza in consequence wears something of the air of a small seaport turned part holiday resort and part a place of refuge for retired sea captains and chief engineers.

The Islands : Arran and Ailsa Craig

As a holiday resort it cannot compete in popularity with Brodick or Whiting Bay, for so its position, its difficult communications and its relatively austere character dictate. Lochranza has, of course, its devotees, as what humblest hamlet of Arran has not ? What was once its inn or hotel became a Scottish Youth Hostel, and hikers and mountaineers are much in evidence in the season. The detached traveller may probably be most interested to see the place as a sort of sport from the general pattern of the island : as it were, something Scandinavian and antique, slightly rough and cold within an agglomeration that has so many gentle and even elegant passages.

The square-towered Castle of Lochranza on the spit is probably of no great historical, as distinct from romantic and architectural, interest. It appears to have been built as a sort of hunting-lodge by the Stewart kings of Scotland in the 14th Century.

The Western Islands of Scotland are littered with such shards of the past, the historicity of most of them dubious, to say the least of it ; their stories by no means clarified by the romantic inventions of Walter Scott and his followers in the monarchical tradition. Even within the wide and secure arms of the Firth of Clyde, the islands of Arran and Bute and the Cumbraes, the mainlands of Ayr and Argyll and even Ailsa Craig itself, are studded with ruins, incomplete circles of standing stones, the caves of saints, vitrified forts and relics vaguely ascribed to the " Druids." We need only note here that the South-Western coasts of Scotland, in a recurring pattern that might be worth the study of an expert, seem to have been the point of attack favoured by the strategies of various intrusive bodies, from the Columban missionaries by way of the Norse invaders to the ambitious Robert de Brus.

Out of the bowl of Lochranza, going by the clock, the road climbs high through a pass between the main mass of Arran's hills and those which tower above, to the height of some 1450 feet, the island's most northerly point, the Cock of Arran. It is a soaring pass, rising to 654 feet at its highest point, and on the northern skyline at any moment the traveller may again see the apprehensive but inquisitive heads of red deer. On the right there are always the operatic peaks of the high hills in their intricate arrangement, and as the road begins to tumble down into the recesses of the northern arm of Glen Sannox, almost unpopulated, one has the feeling of having for a brief space of time sojourned in Greenland or Iceland. Then the road falls sharply to the eastern shore of the island, and all is bland and comfortable again so far as Corrie.

By the middle of the 20th Century this hamlet had come to wear a faint air of the vestigial. In the great days of free steamboat competition on the Firth the Arran steamers from Greenock and Gourock halted here, where there was no proper pier, to disembark or embark passengers and their luggage into and out of a monstrous wherry rowed by stout islanders. The coming of the motor-coach put an end to that picturesque sort of thing, and Corrie's communications had to run through Brodick, five miles away by road. The relics of a small harbour in red sandstone remain, but the native fishing vessels it once sheltered have long departed. Corrie is left to the holiday-makers, many of them mountaineers.

The hamlet has, however, a sort of double on a terrace of high ground above shore level, and this dispersed settlement of High Corrie commands, with Corrie proper, the fidelity of those who, year by year, return to their chosen corner of this favoured island—as if it were a profound heresy to desert Corrie for Brodick, Whiting Bay for Blackwaterfoot.

Hard by this hamlet in rose-red and white, a few miles up the coast northwards, are the Fallen Rocks : one of these geological freaks that contribute so much to the mysterious quality of the island. This is a fantastic aggregation of chunks of old red sandstone, so abundantly released by a landslide, that they lie in infernal confusion over many acres of ground right down to the water's edge. It is all the more interesting that this shambles was not the outcome of a prehistoric geological convulsion but of the collapse of an overhanging cliff within, it is believed, the period since 1700 or thereabouts. These Fallen Rocks are easily enough approached, by a rough track along the shore from the mouth of North Glen Sannox, but various persons have met death on the way, and the explorer should move circumspectly.

The shore road from Corrie southwards to Brodick is level and pretty, running most of the way among woodlands, whether natural or artificial. The Firth is always there on the left, inescapable and majestic. Even so, the whole character of Arran, which has to be so largely expressed in topographical terms, is not wholly understood. This hilly island is remarkable in that across the belt of it, over high passes, two lateral roads remarkably connect the eastern and western stretches of the main road by the shore.

The first of these is conveniently called " The String." It runs eastwards out of the strath of the Black and Machrie Waters and then, under the hills and to a height of 768 feet, tumbles down Glen Slurig to the levels about Brodick Bay. The other, the Ross Road, leaves the main road just beyond Lagg at the south-western corner of the island and goes climbing up Glen Scorrodale to a height of 989 feet before it plunges down the Monamore Glen to the fork between Lamlash and Whiting Bay.

No understanding of the topographical variety of Arran is possible without a traverse of these fantastic passes, even if it is easily compassed by motor-coach. The mere convenience could never abate the loveliness and wonder of these Highland roads, their character at once offsetting the purely marine impressions gained from the shore road and completing the balanced picture of a surprising island.

The highest authorities on the subject, from Geikie and Bryce in the 19th Century to Dr. G. W. Tyrrell in the 20th, have found in the complex geology of Arran the matter of some of the most important, even classic, studies in that general subject. So with botany, mineralogy, zoology and archæology on the island. As Bryce the geologist remarked, every specialist who visits Arran "is tempted to write about it and finds something to add to what has already been put on record." The specialist will find in the bibliography appended a selective list of these authorities. The general reader will find the physical features of the island adequately described in Mr. R. Angus Downie's popular but excellent little book, *All About Arran* (Blackie, 1933).

Here our interest is in Arran in its special relationship to the economic and social history of the Clyde Sea Area as a whole.

Its dynastic tale is much clouded in legend and other mists of history, but it is perhaps best seen simply as a strategical point in what we have learned to know as amphibious warfare. The Norsemen held it uneasily enough from time to time in their struggle with Somerled of the Isles and his successors in the line of Scottish patriots until, in 1266 or thereabouts, Arran somehow came under the authority of the Scottish Crown. Thereafter it was for a time the refuge and rallying point of Robert the Bruce, eager to pounce on the mainland and the Crown he coveted ; and hence he sailed on his ultimately successful expedition, beckoned towards victory at Bannockburn by a signal of fire from Turnberry on the Carrick coast. On any fair day the white pillar of Turnberry lighthouse is clearly visible from King's Cross. A Douglas had held the island for the Bruce ; it fell at length into the hands of the powerful Hamilton family. Its reigning and benevolent monarch in mid-20th Century was Lady Mary Douglas-Hamilton, the Duchess of Montrose. The line of possession has thus been remarkably steady over some 600 years.

This island had once upon a time its considerable fishing industry. It still has a useful farming industry. Its chief industry, however, has become that of catering for the holidaymaker.

Once the small wars had died down with the Jacobite failure in 1745, Arran must have been a poor sort of place in the economic sense. Below the ennobled gentry there can have been but one or two bonnet lairds, or considerable farmers, and below these again nothing but crofters and fishermen on the barest level of subsistence. We may imagine that the native economy might have improved with general progress in the early 19th Century, but there can be no doubt at all that it got its chief stimulus from the development of the steamboat on the shores of the inner Firth and on the banks of the Clyde Ship-Channel up to Glasgow.

This stimulus was, as it were, naturally selective. The smallest and earliest steamboats could not safely compass the voyage into nearly open waters ; few industrial wage-earners of the early 19th Century could afford the fares. Arran was thus fated to be a paradise of the more prosperous industrial classes. The well-to-do merchants came first and built their " marine villas." The slightly less affluent followed to build or buy their seaside cottages. Conditions subtly changing, decent middle-class folk from Clydeside took to the regular renting of furnished houses for a month " at the Coast."

A local industry was born thus. All over Arran there were to be seen, even five years after the end of the Second World War, villas, farmhouses and cottages with tarred shacks behind or beside them, into which their owners retired for the season while the visitors from Glasgow or parts adjacent occupied the main premises, paid their substantial furnished rents and provided a considerable proportion of the island's internal revenue.

Even if there was an inevitable levelling-out of economic and social forces under Britain's first effective Labour Government, Arran strangely remained the shrine of a cult, largely middle-class in structure. Year after year the same families went to the same hotel or boarding-house or rented the same villa. You were faithful to Brodick and despised Lamlash, or you were one of the Blackwaterfoot crowd, looking down your nose on any patron of the eastern bays. Cliques and snobberies abounded ; within the Arran cult there was among the young people, so happily circumstanced, much lovemaking and engaging in the serious business of marriage. One has known of three generations of a Glasgow family finding its mates on its own social levels in the long and lovely evenings of the North on an island singularly blessed.

A novelist with the right sardonic touch could have a lot of fun with the doings of a suburban Glasgow family on its annual holiday on Arran. He or she would still have to account for the superb quality of the scene, the setting and the circumstances ; also, a much more difficult matter, the loving fidelity of a great number of sensible people to an island in the fairway of the outer Firth of Clyde.

It is pleasant to reflect that the name of Arran is familiar in an unexpected context of tens of thousands of people in Britain who have no interest in the island as a geographical entity. These are the farmers and gardeners who annually plant one or other of the long series of seed potatoes of the " Arran " strain—Arran Comrade, Arran Pilot, Arran Banner and the rest. These were the productions of a remarkable man who, beyond the award of the O.B.E. in his old age, never had his meed of public praise : not that his modest temperament would have welcomed it.

Donald Mackelvie came of an old island family. As a

young man he was trained as a chartered accountant in Edinburgh, but he returned to his native village of Lamlash to take over the family business in grocery and bakery. It was in the early years of this century that he became interested in potato culture, conducting his experiments on a series of plots within the narrow limits of a croft behind the village. His approach to his subject was detached. (He was also a highly successful breeder of Highland ponies.) He was almost merely the enlightened amateur, and commercial people made much more money out of his potato strains than he. Even so, Donald Mackelvie won the Lord Derby award for the best new variety of potato eight times : this supreme prize being awarded only after extensive field trials at Ormskirk in Lancashire. No other grower has ever won it so often. The achievement was, in the right sense of the word, unique.

Mackelvie played his modest but effective part in local affairs, and it is a pleasing circumstance that the secondary school he did so much to secure for his native island stands on the site of one of his experimental plots. He died in 1947, blind and a bachelor, aged 80. Less useful men have earned longer and more fulsome obituaries in our newspapers than this quiet scientist of an island in the Firth of Clyde.

The Holy Isle contributes its own powerful notes of boldness and variety to the Arran scene. Barely two miles in length and on the average half a mile in breadth, it rises to a height of 1030 feet. Both the eastern and the western shores are precipitous, but access is easy by motor-boat from Lamlash to the northern end, where there is a small farm and a patch of workable ground, or from Whiting Bay to where the lighthouse buildings stand at the southern end. The ascent of Mullach Mor is a fairly easy scramble from either point. The island carries a small population of wild goats, but not so wild that some of them, at least, have not learned to wait at the head of the landing stage by the lighthouse and nudge the members of picnic parties for a share of their provisions.

Its natural distinction apart, the chief interest of the islet and the explanation of its name is a cave on the western shore. Carefully excavated in 1908, this is an excellent specimen of the typical cell of the Culdee recluse—in this case St Molio, or perhaps more correctly St Maol Jos. Slightly below ground level, it is 13 yards in length and four in breadth, and it is fairly clear from the reports of the excavators that the outer part was the saint's living place, the inner his place of worship and meditation. Crosses cut by pilgrims are there to be seen, interspersed with the runic inscriptions of later Norse invaders : the latter historically valuable as confirming the fact that the Viking fleet lay in Lamlash Bay before proceeding to defeat at Largs. These redolent symbols must, of course, compete with the initials of trippers, rather less interesting figures within the canon of human history.

Near the cave is the inevitable well, endowed by legend with curative qualities of remarkable extent. More interesting is a chunk of sandstone hard by, popularly called " St Molio's Table " or the "Judgment Stone." This presents a most interesting puzzle of the speculative sort. The stone, almost correctly circular, is seven feet high and of the same diameter across its flat top. It is vaguely marked to the expert eye with crosses, but it is more interesting in that four seats are cut into the sides at the top level. Steps lead to this level from the ground on the south side, while at the other end of the diameter is a palpable stay for the human grip and again a step. The modern fancy may dwell endlessly on the purpose of this arrangement, but "Judgment Seat " seems the likelier of the two popular names. One may reasonably surmise the stone to have been a place of penitence, confession, and perhaps punishment.

The family likeness between the Holy Isle and Ailsa Craig

is plain, and they belong to the same system in the oceanographer's sense in rising out of the same relatively shallow ridge, of which Arran is the most notable feature. The Craig, however, stands in such isolation among the waters of the outer Firth that it is a more dramatic object than the Holy Isle in the lee of Arran. One always thinks that its nickname " Paddy's Milestone "—a somewhat satirical reference to Irish immigration—is singularly apt. This pyramidal chunk of rock has the look of an outpost or an elaborately-contrived seamark. As seen from the long Ayrshire coast it has, like Arran, that odd quality of appearing to turn up in the most unexpected aspects and surprising angles : as if the island were moving about the sea and not the traveller along the convolutions of the coast.

Ailsa Craig is slightly less in both length and breadth than the Holy Isle ; its summit is slightly higher than that of Mullach Mor. It boasts almost no cultivable soil, and its western cliffs are sheer in an interesting columnar formation. Access from Girvan during the summer months is quite easy by motor-launch for those with reasonably good stomachs, and there is even a small tea-room on the islet. The only feasible landing-place is at the northward end, hard by the lighthouse buildings.

From this point a rough track leads southwards and then in a zig-zag up and across the eastern slope to the summit, 1114 feet above sea-level. In doing so it passes the ruins of a sort of square tower of doubtful historicity, possibly one of those minor watch-towers or peels so lavishly distributed by medieval chieftains throughout West Scotland, possibly a hermitage ; and it is always surprising to discover a small loch half-way up that rough track across one of the shoulders of what is not much more than a solid chunk of syenitic trap.

Ailsa Craig, briefly, is an almost wholly maritime phenomenon. There are wild goats ; there are rabbits, too many of them ; there are rats, the prudent evacuees of wrecked vessels.

A legend that consistently recurs in the Glasgow evening newspapers during the Silly Season suggests that the rats and rabbits of Ailsa Craig interbreed, but this is obviously only such a legend as accretes about a place so strange, lonely and mysterious. It is more interesting that a small industry in the production of curling-stones is carried on here, and on family lines. A seam of reddish granite at the north-western corner of the island is regularly quarried. This raw material, in circular chunks roughly about the size and shape of cottage loaves, is ferried over to the mainland to be dressed and buffed under trickles of water in Ayrshire towns. Curlers, even in Canada and the States, set much store by the qualities of Ailsa Craig stones.

The island otherwise belongs to the sea-birds. In days gone by, when pleasure steamers occasionally sailed round the rock, it was the custom of the mariners to fire rockets and let the passengers wonder at the white clouds that would rise like thick whorls of wood smoke from the immediate nests on the ledges and within the crevices of the columnar rocks. This specialised matter of bird-life within the Firth is dealt with in another chapter.

Ailsa Craig, with its small population of human beings, remains aloof, monumental, a little cruel. It is quite outwith the social system that has so far been our main subject of study.

CHAPTER VII

Loch Lomond: A Sport

TO COUNT Loch Lomond as part and parcel of the Firth of Clyde system has ample scientific warrant. The oceanographers invariably account for this great sheet of fresh water in their surveys of the Clyde Sea Area, and Mill observes wistfully that, given an alternation of its level in relation to that of the sea by only 30 feet or so, it would be the deepest of all the salt-water lochs in the region. A sounding of 105 fathoms has been taken in the middle reaches of the lake, only two fathoms less than the deepest hole in the bed of the Outer Firth. That Loch Lomond did at one time belong to the salt water system is accepted.

It is thus a peculiarly interesting phenomenon of Nature ; and it is also quite remarkable for its natural beauty and for its consequent importance in the social life of the crowded industrial area that extends almost to its lower, southern end. It seems an almost fantastic circumstance that such a very beautiful and extensive pleasure ground should lie before Glasgow's doorstep, as it were—as if the English Lake District were moved southwards to end near Wigan in relation to Liverpool and Manchester.

Loch Lomond is the largest sheet of fresh water in Britain, its size within what used to be called the British Isles exceeded only by the expanses of Lough Neagh in Northern Ireland. Unlike that Irish lake, it is a long trough between ranges of hills running up to and beyond the 3000-feet line. As the crow flies it is just over 20 miles from Ardlui at the head of the loch to Balloch at the bottom. Following the bends, the distance is generally reckoned at 22 miles. The track of the steamers that ply on these waters from pier to pier on both sides of it covers 24 miles. The area of water is reckoned to be 17,420 acres—some 27·22 square miles. Out of these waters rise 30 islands, some of them large enough to be habitable and capable of cultivation in a modest way. The loch discharges itself into the Ship-Channel of the Clyde at Dumbarton through the River Leven, a short passage of some five miles in length. It is of much interest that the migratory salmon and sea-trout to be taken in the loch must cruise past the industrial ports of Greenock and Port Glasgow and through the industrial effluents that pour into the Leven before regaining the ancestral home, where they provide very good sport of a sort. The loch finally gave its name to a song that has almost as much validity as *Auld Lang Syne* on convivial occasions.

As the map shows, this fabled loch has roughly the shape of a very much elongated isosceles triangle. It broadens so much towards its base that the pretty intimacy of its middle and upper parts is almost lost in such an expanse of waters as prompted William Wordsworth to animadvert, a thought peevishly, on the large " proportion of diffused water " and to wish for " a speedier termination of the long vista of blank water." But Wordsworth was always comparing Loch Lomond with his beloved Lakes, and if he had travelled in modern conditions, by steamboat on the loch itself or by motor-coach along the shore roads, one may fancy that his complaints might not have been so mournful. For only a mile or two above Balloch, at the lower end of the loch and the terminal for railway, steamer and bus services, a clot of islands suddenly and most picturesquely complicates the passage northwards : fully a dozen islands of size, like floating tufts of woodland in the fairway. On a nice point of taste, it might be allowed that the lower extremity of Loch Lomond suffers from " diffusion "

in the Wordsworthian sense. It can be quite a dangerous sheet
of water for canoeists and such, and annually it claims its meed
of victims from among the foolhardy and the adventurous.
That any man with eyes in his head, however, should on this
small account seek to dismiss the glory of Loch Lomond seems
incredible.

Of the many islands in the waist of the loch it would be
tedious to discourse in detail. Mainly, as we have noted, they
are either pretty tufts of wooded land or places of residence on
a small insular scale ; they are either " preserved " by the
riparian landowners or they are islets occasionally visited by
picnic parties. Few are more than a mile in length ; the
dimensions of most are to be measured in furlongs. Some have
small histories of their own ; some bear in the ruins of castles,
monasteries, neglected graveyards and the like the marks of
civilisations much older and calmer than that which now
surrounds the loch during the industrial week-end.

We see them nowadays as elements in a scene of astonishing
beauty. Here is a prettiness—and the word is used deliberately
—of a special quality. Queen Victoria was reminded of the
Swiss lakes ; Tobias Smollett told in *Humphry Clinker* how
he had " seen the Lago di Gardi, Albano, de Vico, Bolsena
and Geneva, and on my honour I prefer Loch Lomond to them
all . . ." Smollett was a near-native of Loch Lomondside and
no doubt a prejudiced party, but it is significant that he refers
particularly to " the verdant islands that seem to float on its
surface, affording the most enchanting objects of repose to the
excursive view."

This miniature archipelago, as we have noted, fills most of
the lower half of the loch. The last of the larger islands,
Inchlonaig—said to have been planted with yew trees by
Robert the Bruce for the armament of his archers—lies opposite
the village of Luss, which, from the point of view of the
traveller along the shore road, is not much more than the

beginning of his journey northwards. It is just beyond Luss and the romantically wooded Ross peninsula that the loch begins to take on more of the Highland and less of the Italian character. Most notably the scene is dominated henceforward by the mass of Ben Lomond on the eastern shore : 3192 feet of mountain so placed by the accident of geography that it is a landmark for scores of miles around.

Its domination over the Loch Lomondside scene is so remarkable as to suggest an optical illusion. The mountains on the western side of the loch are not to be despised for height, most of them running well above the 2000-foot mark, but Lomond and its knobbly outliers are so placed relatively near to the water's edge that they command in the most picturesque way a long stretch of the loch below. It is faintly discouraging to know that the well-worn path to the top of the Ben from the hamlet of Rowardennan, though a long walk, is not difficult for even ageing persons.

Much of the grandeur of Ben Lomond's appearance is undoubtedly due to its setting. (It is still a notable and isolated peak as seen from a distance of 30 miles eastwards.) It is perhaps peculiarly attractive in that, as it plunges into the loch, its skirts are attractively trimmed with woodlands : conifers, scrub oak and hazel proliferating in the damp mildness of the prevailing climate. It has the special advantage, as that of a film star, in being seen mainly across a pretty foreground of lake water. The main road follows the western shore ; that up the eastern side of the loch under the haunches of the Ben is a *cul de sac* of secondary quality, which carries nothing like the weight of traffic surging up the other side.

The dominance of Ben Lomond meanwhile confers upon the middle stretches of the loch a subtly more austere quality than that which prevails in the belt so prettily diversified by the many islets. Beyond Luss the perceptive traveller should begin to feel that he is making rapid progress in terms of

ISLAND CASTLE: The old peel at Loch Ranza, Arran, and old-time fishing boats within the spit.

DISTANT VIEW: Arran, seen eastwards across the Kilbrennan Sound from the Kintyre peninsula, in time of harvest.

LOCH LOMOND: The tricky, winding road up the western shore of the freshwater loch. On the other side rises the northern shoulder of Ben Lomond, 3192 feet.

latitude, out of the Lowlands into the sub-Highlands. The prettiness endures for miles northwards of Luss, the winding road discovering here an enchanting bay, here the white-washed walls of a wayside cottage splashed with the bright red of *tropæloum speciosum*, there the mouth of a glen, or a rushing stream that hints at moorlands and corries high above. At Tarbet, the last settlement of size on the western shore of the loch (and little more than a mile from Arrochar at the head of salt-water Loch Long) there is again a surprising note of prettiness : the big hotel in sandstone against the white cottages of the hamlet, a few solid houses among large trees, the greenness of lawns and fields between the main road and the pier combining in a sweet and elegantly-harmonised cadence.

Here the main road dramatically divides, its left arm to stretch round the head of Loch Long and so across a high pass towards Inveraray, Campbeltown and the lands of Lorne ; the right to follow the western shore of Loch Lomond to its head and then, by Crianlarich and Tyndrum and the Moor of Rannoch, to Glencoe, Fort William and Skye itself. At this point of divergence the loch appropriately takes on a new character ; it ceases to be Italian or even Swiss and becomes frankly Norwegian. It narrows, and it is hereabouts that it reaches its maximum depth of 105 fathoms. The hillsides fall steep-to, the air seems darker. For now the peaks on the western side begin to match Ben Lomond in height and outdo it in ruggedness. The peak of Ben Vorlich stands only 100 feet lower than that of Ben Lomond and far exceeds it in the quality of the rugged if not in that of mass.

The last considerable settlement on the eastern side is Inversnaid. From the main road it looks across a mile of deep water a thought craggy and bluff : another large hotel dominating the scene. In fact, Inversnaid hardly belongs to the structure of Loch Lomond in its social aspects, at least. It has no communication by road with its neighbours along that steep eastern side of the loch. It is actually the *cul de sac* of a coach-road that comes out of the Scottish midlands by way of the Trossachs and the complex of Glasgow's water supplies. Hereabouts, however, the pious may decently bow, for it was at Inversnaid that William Wordsworth (critical as he was of Loch Lomond in comparison with his beloved Lakes) perceived the sweet highland girl.

In the passage of three miles or so from Inversnaid to Ardlui at the head of the loch the scene becomes more and more austere ; or one would rather say, more decisively northern in character, until the loch at length ends in a series of wet flats and the road thrusts uphill into the wilds of Glen Falloch with its waterfalls. The whole nature of this upper end of the loch, however, was radically changed towards the middle of the 20th Century, when the hydro-electric developments of a post-war age ordained large operations at this upper end of the loch on its western side.

The eager eyes of the engineers fell on the catchment area about Loch Sloy, a fresh-water loch at an altitude of more than 800 feet under the western slopes of Ben Vorlich. There they made their dams, bored tunnels through the mountains, and generally bulldozed a region that, in the quiet days of 1914 or even 1919, seemed as safe for the golden eagle and the mountaineer as any place in Scotland could be. A power-house now stands on the shores of Loch Lomond not far from its head, pumping electric energy over miles of cable to places far away. This project greatly alarmed sentimentalists when it was first outlined, but it has since been recognised, however unwillingly, that the forces of nature in the West Highlands are apt to be more overwhelming than the mechanical works of man, and that even a power-station with a dazzling capacity on paper can look a little harmless, clean thing under the masses of the mountains. Scenery, be it not positively out-raged, is not always enough.

Loch Lomond : A Sport

With one exception, the settlements on the shores of Loch Lomond are small. Balloch at the southern end of the lake is in itself partly industrial and within the industrial area of the Vale of Leven. It is definitely more important, however, as the terminus of communications from Glasgow : a busy place of hotels, boat-hiring establishments and so on. It is the anchorage for most of the motor-boats and yachts that sail among the islands and beyond, and it is specially remarkable in Scotland in sheltering within the mouth of the River Leven a large colony of houseboat-dwellers. (A smaller colony in a quiet bay below Luss made the subject of a brilliant picture in the French manner by that gifted artist, the late Leslie Hunter.) At Balloch again is a fine public park in the care of the Corporation of Glasgow, so popular that during summer week-ends the buses from Glasgow run backwards and forwards at intervals of only a few minutes. One may fairly think that Balloch is to Glasgow what Richmond or Hampton Court is to London.

Northwards from Balloch the settlements are all small and pretty. On the eastern shores of the loch, where the road peters out in the foothills of Ben Lomond and the road from the Trossachs is only an intrusion, Rowardennan is the base for the ascent of the Ben, and Inversnaid, as we have seen, is little more than the terminal point of an old coaching route : both little more than hamlets clustering round a sizeable tourist hotel. Luss, Tarbet and Ardlui are their counterparts on the opposite shore, and it is a very remarkable fact indeed, and well worth some discussion later on, that at no point have the shores of this loch been outraged and vulgarised by brass-necked exploitation. In that respect alone Loch Lomond remains a modern miracle.

For good reasons, Luss is one of the most popular and busy places on Loch Lomondside, but it remains small and unspoilt. . . . It is an irony that Luss most notably failed to please the

Wordsworths, critical in their inability to perceive that the primitive economy of the Highlands could in their time hardly match the order of the contemporaneous economy of even North England. Perhaps they were having a bad time with Coleridge. They complained of the crude smallness of the inn ; they remarked sharply on the absence of gardens about the rude cottages. . . . It would be an interesting exercise in the correction of prejudices if the fair-minded spirit of Dorothy could be evoked to look on Luss in the mid-20th Century. For Luss is generally regarded and much written about as one of Scotland's " model " villages.

No doubt it took time for the Scottish economy, especially on the Highland fringe, to allow a catching-up with the English order, but one of the Colquhouns of Luss in the mid-19th Century rebuilt the tiny capital of his realm wisely and well. Rows of neat cottages in a version of the Tudor style that admirably suits the surroundings stand back from a side-road, which, under a huge tree that performs the useful function of a traffic " roundabout " runs down to the water and the pier from the main road. The gardens thereof are almost fiercely competitive in the splendour of spring and summer. Whatever the reason may be, the cottagers up and down Loch Lomond-side tend their gardens with a care perhaps unusual in rural Scotland, and in May and June it would be hard to find elsewhere such a proliferation of azalea and rhododendron ; shrubs highly favoured by a relatively damp climate and peaty soil.

The transformation of Loch Lomondside into a vast pleasure area, virtually a national park, was vastly hastened by the inventions and social pressures that declared themselves between the two World Wars. When motoring became popular and approximately inexpensive, the run up the western shore of the loch was the most obvious of all the agreeable expeditions out of the crowded areas. Northwards from Luss the highroad is inevitably narrow and tortuous ; it requires cautious driving at any time. When, in the palmy days before 1939, it carried on any fine Sunday afternoon a flow of cars at the rate of 500-*plus* in the hour, this stream complicated by the sinuous processions of cycling clubs and clots of hikers and then by many cars unimaginatively parked, the best of drivers had much less pleasure in the outing than their passengers. Thus, however, the automobiles first opened up the whole territory to people within the higher income ranges, and then the motor-coach conferred the same benefits on people of modest means. The main invasion was powered by something more subtle and interesting than the internal combustion engine.

Whatever the reasons, the '20's of the 20th Century saw at work a powerful instinct among the young workers of both sexes to escape from the cities and enjoy the open air in lovely country. This may have been positively stimulated by political teaching and by the formation of such bodies as the Youth Hostels Associations. On Clydeside it was certainly encouraged mainly by the incidence of long and bitter periods of unemployment. One may think it was greatly to the credit of the young workless of these times that so many of them refused to hang about street corners and spend the dole in billiard rooms but took to the hills instead. They began to form the first main body of hikers in Scotland, at least. Some of them so finely polished the art of hitch-hiking that they would cruise for months on end round the whole of Britain, living on the land and their wits : accepting casual employment now and again and then, with an itch in their feet, move on. Some took to mountaineering on the expert scale, learning their craft on the peaks about the head of Loch Long, and one of the toughest climbing clubs in Scotland was formed by unemployed artisans and such, its leading spirit a crane-driver from the Glasgow docks out of work.

This invasion of privately-owned lands was on a large scale, and the possibility of serious clashes was always present during the period of adjustment. Fortunately, two factors united to bring about a singularly happy solution of the problem.

In the first place, the Law of Scotland differs from that of England in its attitude towards Trespass. Trespassers cannot, in Scotland, be prosecuted out of hand ; the private landowner must first go to the courts and secure an injunction against the chronic trespasser ; and this provision, wise or unwise, tends to ease frictions. In the second place, the private landowners along the shores of Loch Lomond were remarkably temperate in their dealings with the new invaders. The exemplar was the late Sir Iain Colquhoun, 7th baronet of Luss. No doubt he was shrewd enough to perceive that the outward pressures from the industrial areas could not be stopped, but he was in his own right a fine sportsman, a believer in vigorous recreation and a counsellor of broad vision. His example was to propose to the roving townsfolk a sort of gentleman's agreement.

This was roughly to the effect : Go where you please, but in return please have the most careful regard for the rights of the landowner and his tenants. Do not disturb livestock, tramp on growing crops or leave gates open. In return for the freedom of the hillsides and moors, seek to respect the landowner's sporting rights, often his most valuable source of revenue, by learning the ways of birds, deer and fish and taking care not to molest them or spoil the other fellow's sport.

The appeal, though it may seem sentimental in this phrasing, was effective, especially as backed by the new organisations of the explorers and notably by the code of honour imposed on its members by the Scottish Youth Hostels Association. It is a remarkable fact that this area has suffered very little from the vandal, even the litter-lout, as if the imminence of natural beauty imposed on the children of the cities such a respect for it as they could never give to even the most handsome of municipal parks. Several of what were once the greatest private houses on the shores of Loch Lomond are now Youth Hostels of unusually large size, much used for conferences and such, memorials to the success of a peaceful revolution.

The waters of Loch Lomond provide more than ample space for recreation of the aquatic kind. The sails of yachts were not often to be seen after 1918 ; these fresh waters under high hills are fluky, and the islands in mid-loch not far north of Balloch restrict the playground of vessels under canvas. The motor-boat proved to be the more suitable sort of craft for this inland sea. The place of yachtsmen, however, was taken by eager canoeists, practising with small sail as well as paddle. The angler had his place in the picture.

It is interesting to read in the older gazetteers that the salmon was once regarded as a rarity in Loch Lomond. Possibly they wrote while the River Leven was much polluted by the effluents of the Turkey Red mills of the Vale below, but while the loch is not regarded as one of the great salmon lochs of the North, it yields annually a considerable weight of the noble fish, along with plenty of sea-trout and the ordinary loch-trout. The method, however, is mainly that of trolling, often enough from a power-propelled boat, and this manner of taking fish may not appeal to every taste. Even so, there is good rod-fishing in the shallows, especially at the mouths of the loch's occasional tributaries. These are the pretty Fruin that runs down from the hills behind Helensburgh on the salt-water estuary and, on the western shore, a number of short streams falling from the Lennox heights. At the head of the loch the Falloch pours a volume of peaty waters into the mother-lake, and in the south-eastern corner, near Balloch, the Endrick, rather over-fished but rich enough in salmon and sea-trout, brings in its tribute from the Stirlingshire hills.

Loch Lomond harbours shoals of that odd fish, the powan, sometimes called the " freshwater herring." This is otherwise the Vendace (*Coregonus vandesius*) found in only a few freshwater lakes in Britain. Blue-green above and silvery below in colour, it seldom runs more than nine inches in length. Although esteemed as a delicacy, its numbers are small, and it has virtually no commercial or sporting value. It remains in the lonely class of Curiosities of Nature.

The southern end of the loch has twice within record been so deeply frozen over as to provide the setting of great ice carnivals. During the winter of 1880-81 the ice extended from Balloch to Luss, and on 22nd January, 1881—according to a contemporary record—some 15,000 skaters were reckoned to be enjoying themselves at once. Neil Munro tells in *The Brave Days* of an even more spectacular scene in the cold late winter of 1895 :

" In less than a week the domestic water-taps of Glasgow were frozen solid, and householders had to get their supplies from street wells hastily extemporised by tapping the mains. . . . Loch Lomond was frozen over and bearing by February 16. On that day I skated between Balloch and Inchmurrin. Special trains were run from Queen Street to Balloch and 30,000 people were on the ice. . . . Four days later I made for Balloch again, to find even greater numbers disporting themselves on the ice, which was now much safer. Booths, tents and huxters' barrows lined the shores between the railway and Cameron House ; a roaring business was being done in the hiring and fixing of skates and in hot coffee."

Thirty thousand people and more on the ice at once seems rather a subjective than an objective estimate, but Munro was a trained newspaperman as well as a novelist, and no doubt he consulted the contemporary files and duly checked his references. There would certainly be plenty of room for all on the " diffusion of water " that William Wordsworth found so disappointing.

Loch Lomond : A Sport

A good anthology could be made of writings about Loch Lomond, from Pennant and Tobias Smollett by way of the Wordsworths to Queen Victoria. It is fascinating to discern how the views of the region were coloured by the circumstances of weather and personal convenience, by patriotism and other prejudices. Consider Dr. Samuel Johnson on the islands :

> "Had Loch Lomond been in a happier climate, it would have been the boast of wealth and vanity to own one of the little spots which it encloses, and to have employed upon it all the arts of embellishment. But as it is, the islets, which court the gazer at a distance, disgust him at his approach, when he finds, instead of soft lawns and shady thickets, nothing more than uncultivated ruggedness."

An interesting case of 18th Century taste in uncomprehending contact with the primitive. As for the Wordsworths, jealous for their own Lakes, it is right to record that Dorothy, after a visit to Inchtavannich, wrote a passage that, fairly pulsing with the sense of magic surprisingly encountered, more than atones for her brother's astonishing petulance. The connoisseur of literary velleities may be diverted to discover that, making allowance for italics, Queen Victoria's appreciation of the loch scene in *More Leaves from the Journal of a Life in the Highlands* is surprisingly sensitive as well as characteristically accurate.

The full comprehension of Loch Lomond as a geographical and social entity is beyond the scope of any pen, any paintbrush, any camera. It has to be seen and studied—this remarkable synthesis of geographical interest, natural beauty and the social processes that converted its shores within the space of little more than a century from the stamping-ground of four warlike clans to the playground of the industrial society into which most of the clansmen have now been completely absorbed. " Loch Sloy " was the battle-cry of the Macfarlanes, who ruled over the high grounds along the north-western reaches of the loch. The slogan has since passed to one of the most daring projects of the North of Scotland Hydro-Electric Board.

CHAPTER VIII

Days at the Coast

EVER since the first steamboats appeared on the scene, offering ways of escape from the urban darkness, the industrial folk of the Clyde Basin have made good and full use of the Firth for their pleasures, as we have seen.

The use of the steamers alone met most of the popular needs. There were, and are, many city-dwellers who, armed with a season ticket, thought and think a holiday well spent in merely sailing, day after day, up and down and across an estuary so brilliantly varied in shape and interest. As, however, the seaside communities developed round about the steamboat piers, the urge to use tidal waters for the mere fun of it, the strange human instinct to mess about in boats, led to the development of what may fairly be described as a regional culture in aquatic sport.

It would be very absurd to suggest that every citizen of Glasgow is a powerful swimmer and a dexterous handler of small craft by inheritance. To see the Fair Holiday trippers fooling about in Rothesay Bay is to marvel that the sons and daughters of a great race of shipbuilders should be so handless on the water, so utterly clueless, as the phrase goes, in the dynamics of the business. In fact, these performers reflect Glasgow's remoteness from the sea proper ; they confess its artificiality, akin to Manchester, as a port. Until the buses came to make access to the Ayrshire coast, at least, easy and inexpensive, the masses of the industrial hinterland saw the sea only spasmodically. No Glasgow child could ever learn

203

to feather an oar or tie a couple of half-hitches on the narrow and congested Ship-Channel that so improbably brings the big ships up from the sea into the heart of the city.

The use of the Clyde for pleasure therefore developed on two levels as it were, exactly reflecting the trends of social development on Victorian lines. Given even the cheap facilities of " the boats," the working folk could never be more than day trippers, escaping only occasionally to the shores of the Firth. The energetic man of the employing class could, on the other hand, afford his villa at the Coast and, in these circumstances, came to contribute to the development of the lovely art and science of yachting : this the most decorative use to which the Firth of Clyde was ever put.

Bathing in salt water started as a fashion of the genteel and the privileged. It would appear to have been a late Georgian or Regency vogue in the first place, much favoured by royal patronage of Brighton and other Channel resorts. The fashion was not slow in spreading even to Clydeside in the throes of early industrial expansion. As we have seen, in 1812 Mr. Henry Bell was so eager to attract customers to the Baths Hotel at Helensburgh that he was moved to have the *Comet* built for their convenience, while at an equally early period, if not in fact before it, solid persons travelled by coach to Gourock to get the benefit of " the sea bathing." It must have been long enough before the industrial masses, lacking bathrooms in their own homes, took to salt water in the open. A good measure of the changing of fashion, the improvement of general living conditions and the levelling of incomes both upwards and downwards in recent times is in the fact that the great swimming pools of the Ayrshire coast in particular are playgrounds of the people.

It is odd enough that, naturally endowed with expanses of fine sand, these regions should have to be provided with concreted pools, but that is only a typical expression of the gregariousness of our times, duly exploited by the go-ahead men ; and, to be fair, it is hard to get a proper swim off shores that slope so gradually. There are still many miles of coast on the Clyde from which a man may bathe alone. The bathing is everywhere remarkably safe on the whole, thanks largely to the absence of strong tides and shifting sands, but it is well to remember that these can be stormy seas, and that the average temperature of the water at Tighnabruaich is hardly that of the tides at Torquay. Local advice is always worth taking.

The use of the rowing-boat for pleasure was a natural outcome of the surge outwards towards the coast, and boat-hiring is a considerable industry in the coastal towns and villages. The typical boat used on the Firth of Clyde is a clinker-built, pair-oared craft of about 10 to 12 feet in length on the average. It has the character of regional requirement written all over it, notably in a bluff outward flare of the bows to throw off short and possibly heavy seas ; as an example of naval architecture it has singularly little ostensible affinity with either the Thames skiff or the gondola-shaped craft of the Norwegian fjords.

Not that it really matters much nowadays. For various reasons of universal application that will be discussed later on, the art of rowing is vestigial except as a cultivated sport. Where pleasure is mainly organised on the commercial basis, the holiday-making majority is whizzed about in speed-boats or given small craft with nearly foolproof motors to fool about in. Even the decorous trip from the shore at Dunoon round The Gantocks in a motor-boat, so exciting in 1910, was *vieux jeux* in 1950, tolerantly regarded as highly suitable for grandmothers and their younger grandchildren. All the small aquatic arts, requiring some expenditure of care and skill and physical effort, tended after the Second World War to go into decline.

The Firth of Clyde

It is perhaps worth mentioning that the sport of canoeing, like hiking on the mainland, developed as a minor cult on the Firth of Clyde after the First World War—an odd extension of the instinct of the urban dwellers to reach the far horizons. From time to time during the Victorian era canoeing clubs spasmodically flourished, mainly among the more prosperous sort of people and mainly with headquarters within the sheltered Gareloch. The post-war wave of enthusiasm for the sport came largely out of the escaping instincts of young men and women on the lower income levels, and the cult has made no great mark on the greater affairs of the Firth : if only because its waters are on the whole too tricky for small and fragile craft. Canoeing clubs may occasionally be seen moving in spidery masses across expanses of salt water, but they do so only with the eyes of their leaders on the signs and portents of an eccentric meteorological system. The canoes are thickest on Loch Lomond, and even these sheltered waters are not to be taken casually. A brisk breeze across the southern bight of this inland sea would look on the Serpentine like a catastrophic gale.

Almost everywhere along the shores of the Firth some sort of sea-fishing is to be had. Any enterprising boy using primitive apparatus may at any time catch more than his fill of the abundant saithe off the rocks. Especially above the sandy stretches line-fishing with the conventional paternoster arrangement of hooks should at any time produce a family breakfast of cod, whiting or flounders : usually with a few of the less attractive dogfish creating moments of puzzlement and alarm. The bait is almost invariably the mussel that grows so abundantly on the wooden baulks of the coastal piers ; lines and bait, as well as boats, can be hired almost everywhere, and local advice is apt to be copious.

Where no recognised line-fishing grounds exist there is rather better sport in trolling with artificial lures, from the

sand eel and the minnow down to the penny fly, white, yellow
or red. This exercise always attracts quantities of the voracious
and foolish saithe, but on the right evening in the right place
the angler may encounter a shoal of the darting, barred mackerel
or take a few plump specimens of the coppery lythe : the
pollack of southern waters.

Few of these coarse estuarine fish are of any great
commercial value. (There exists in Scotland, for instance, a
strong and superstitious prejudice against the mackerel in
particular.) They do not, in fact, " travel " well, but they are
good and wholesome eating, even the common saithe, if cooked
by frying when fresh from their natural element. The habits
and distribution of the fishes within the Clyde Sea Area are
described in detail in a following chapter.

Salmon pass up and down the Firth of Clyde in their
mysterious movements from and to the shelves of the Atlantic.
Sea trout hibernate in the sea-lochs and regularly ascend towards their fresh-water spawning grounds in spring. Brown
trout are in all the little streams and in the lochs on the
hillsides.

This sort of fishing is largely controlled. Many of the most
desirable waters are in private ownership. Others are leased
by hotels for the exclusive use of their guests. Angling affairs
in the Loch Lomond area are in the charge of the Loch Lomond
Angling Association. This is not, however, to suggest a
tyrannical exclusiveness. Decent fishing for brown trout is
not hard to come by anywhere ; and it is surprising how a
courteous and *bona fide* application to the landowner or his
agent may more often than not produce a permit for a day
of sport on the best of private waters : not that, within the
economics of the mid-20th Century, permission to take and
kill salmon is lightly granted.

There is a legend, endlessly recurrent as a Silly Season
topic of newspaper correspondence, to the effect that the

indentures of apprentices on Clydeside used to contain a clause against their being fed on salmon more than once or twice in each week. Probably the story is current in other estuarine parts of Britain ; probably nobody elsewhere has succeeded in producing documentary foundation for the pretty fable. It remains true that all the records of monastic and inter-burghal strife on the Clyde right up to Glasgow and beyond stress the importance of the right to take salmon, and it is all the more interesting to note, however roughly, the itineraries of that noble fish within the Firth to-day.

The salmon regularly frequents most of the more sub-stantial rivers of southern Ayrshire. On the other, Highland, side of the estuary it is particularly fond of Loch Fyne and its tributary waters. By the time it has reached the Inner Firth, however, its volition seems to have been largely spent, and we may conclude that nearly two centuries of industrialism with its inevitable effluents have within that period changed the habits of this highly instinctive fish. It is all the more remark-able that the oceanic salmon, not to mention the estuarine sea-trout, still regularly heads for and succeeds in reaching the spawning grounds of Loch Lomond and its tributary rivers. As a glance at the map shows, this involves a journey of some seven miles through industrialised waters from opposite Greenock to Dumbarton and then a traverse of five miles up the River Leven to wholly fresh water at Balloch.

Not a great many salmon are taken in the Leven and on Loch Lomond in any year. That they reach the loch at all is rather the miracle. The Clyde is an infinitely cleaner stream than it was fifty years ago, and the flood tides are large and fresh enough to carry the fish safely over the great sandbanks that lie opposite Greenock and Port Glasgow. The big fish have still, however, to pass through the effluents of the con-siderable town of Dumbarton and then the waters of the Leven itself, heavily impregnated with the sewage of industrial

STORMIER SEAS: A fleet of racing Dragons starting off from Hunter's Quay on a brisk easterly wind.

8-METRE: A yacht in almost the largest class now racing in British waters makes for the finishing line at Hunter's Quay, the wooded point of Strone beyond.

6-METRE: Two famous racers of international class in a breeze off Kirn: *Kyria* leading *Johan*.

townlets and the discharges of industrial establishments up and down its length. The puzzle of this extreme migration was considerably intensified in the summer of 1950, when some untraced source of poison brought to the surface of the Leven in its middle reaches and in one day a much larger number of dead or dying fish than the experts ever imagined likely to venture so far from the sea : a larger number than are easily traceable in Loch Lomond itself.

We are returned by this small episode to the paradox eternally suggested by the Clyde and its Firth : rather the series of paradoxes that arise out of the conflict between the slow forces of Nature and the urgent instincts of exploiting Man. This is a theme with innumerable variations, but surely none of these is more surprising, more enchanting, than the emergence of yachting as the supreme sport of these estuarine waters : the rich providing the poor with a lovely spectacle ; the exploiters, in the Marxian jargon, creating on the Firth the beauty they could not or would not make about the dark, satanic mills or the homes of their workers.

The social and economic elements have already been indicated. The early steamboats opened up the Firth ; the well-to-do built their summer villas along the green shores now so conveniently approached ; they naturally sought to use the rippling waters for pleasure ; yachting under Royal patronage had become a fashion in the South. . . . The theorem is simple, but it should never be forgotten that yacht-owning and yacht-building and yacht-designing on the Firth of Clyde during the earlier years of the cult, at least, stood in close relationship to the regional interest in the design and building of commercial shipping. One craft could always learn from the experience of the other. The shipbuilders and engineers of the Clyde Ship-Channel have always been among the keenest yachtsmen on the open Firth.

The relationship was most curiously illustrated in 1827,

when the Northern Yacht Club (now the Royal Northern), without quite knowing what it did, fostered the development of the steamboat in a decisive fashion.

This was through the offer of a cup for the steamboat that, at the August regatta, could make the fastest passage from Rothesay Bay to the north end of the Great Cumbrae and back. The offer was a challenge to all the eager young engineers of Glasgow and district then experimenting with steam engines. It was of special interest to a man of near-genius, Robert Napier, who entered two vessels powered by his own engines for the race, the *Clarence* and the *Helensburgh*. The first won the cup by a wide margin over all rivals ; the other ran a good second ; and the novelty of the contest having attracted wide and curious attention, Napier's name as the coming man in the new industry was made.

Orders for steamboats came to Napier, even from the conservative South, but the oddest and most significant outcome of his success with steamboats at a yacht regatta was to bring him and his engines to the enthusiastic, powerful notice of T. Assheton Smith, a great English sportsman before the Lord in the hunting field and on the sea. Nothing would do but that Mr. Napier should build Mr. Smith a *steam* yacht (to the considerable annoyance of the Royal Yacht Squadron, to which Assheton Smith belonged) and before the latter was gathered into the shades in the 1850's, Napier in fact built for Assheton Smith nine steam yachts, all experimental in some degree, all fast and in advance of their times.

More than that, much more. Assheton Smith's influence at Westminster was so considerable that, when the Admiralty started slowly to shed its respectable prejudice in favour of wooden walls and square sails, they were directed to heed the advice of the young shipbuilder and engineer on the remote Clyde. It is not an over-simplification of a long and complicated process of industrial history to say that a yacht club, given the enthusiasm and generosity of an Assheton Smith and the capacity for taking pains of a Robert Napier, did much, however accidentally, to help the latter to become in his prime the first steam shipbuilder in the world and to establish through his leadership the Clyde as the world's most productive shipbuilding river.

Meanwhile the shipbuilders of Great Britain were still working in wood. Few of them were building ships of any size ; most were producing fishing vessels, coasting schooners and brigs. The yacht for pleasure was only a specialised application of this craft, a delightful refinement of it for speed : nicely coinciding with the endless search for the ideal lines of craft propelled by sail. The records show that the earliest builders of yachts pure and simple were firms that first built fishing smacks and the like—Scotts of Greenock, Simons of Renfrew, the Steeles of Greenock (who were latterly to build so many fine Clipper ships), Linton of Dumbarton and so on. (It is of historical as well as regional interest that the Simons firm originated in Greenock in 1812, also that Scotts are the oldest shipbuilding firm under continuous family control in the world ; both firms flourished into the mid-20th Century.) The influence of Greenock as, once upon a time, the first port of the Clyde has thus not wholly disappeared into the shadow of the greater and later power of Glasgow.

The Northern Yacht Club was formed in 1824, at Belfast. In the first place, the early enthusiasts of the sport on the Clyde joined the nearest society that happened to organise races and cruises. In due course the Irish section disintegrated while the Scottish branch continued to flourish, no doubt under the industrial impetus. By 1830 it had become the Royal Northern Yacht Club, with headquarters at Rothesay, and it is thus the fifth oldest yacht club in the United Kingdom. After the Second World War the clubhouse was moved to Rhu at the mouth of the Gareloch, as we have already noted.

The Firth of Clyde

The second of the Yacht Clubs in respect of seniority is the Royal Clyde, and it is a nice little irony of social history that it was founded, with headquarters at Largs, rather in reaction to the exclusiveness of the Royal Northern. The latter chose to exclude yachts of under 8 tons from its interest, and the formation of the " Clyde Model Yacht Club " in 1857 was deliberately designed to give the less opulent owners of smaller boats the chance of competing in the new sport on organised lines. By 1871, however, wealth always increasing, the Clyde Model Yacht Club had become the Royal Clyde Yacht Club, since then with headquarters at Hunter's Quay on the Holy Loch and an organisation ranking with the Royal Northern in terms of both dignity and power. The Western Yacht Club, the Royal Largs Yacht Club, the Clyde Corinthian Yacht Club and the Royal Gourock Yacht Club ; the last, the youngest, dating from 1894 : were duly formed. In yachting, by the way, the term " Corinthian," now seldom used, was the equivalent of " amateur " and confessed a reaction against the use of paid hands and professional helmsmen.

Of these early formations the most picturesque was that of the Mudhook Yacht Club in 1873, mainly at the instance of the shipbuilding Scotts of Greenock. Like its name, this sodality is an odd and picturesque one : its membership confined to forty, its Commodore ranking as " Admiral," its exclusiveness such that it has never coveted the " Royal " status, and its secret rites, if legend does not exaggerate, distinctly colourful. This was a typical creation of an almost baronial period, and the old glories of such as the Mudhook have been dimmed by the levelling processes known to us all.

Yachting on the Clyde, however, has never been by any means exclusively the sport of the rich. Two or three artisans, or two or three engineering apprentices for that matter, could and did scrape together enough to buy a tidy cruising sloop. The Royal Yacht Clubs of the Firth were never more enthusiastic than the homelier Sailing Clubs with such names as the Holy Loch and Cardwell Bay ; and it was this less spectacular movement within a cult that produced the Clyde Cruising Club and so its invaluable explorations of the less-frequented places.

It is nevertheless the fact that the pageantry of big yachting at its most spectacular rested on the accumulation of vast industrial wealth towards the end of the 19th Century and into the first decade of the 20th. The early records show that the first enthusiasts formed a fair cross-section of the admittedly more prosperous classes—the shipbuilding men in the first place, a few professional men, and a surprisingly large number of the landed gentry, particularly from Argyllshire. Real enthusiasts they were, sailing their antique craft to regattas in Belfast Lough and at Cork, to Welsh waters, to the Forth and to the Mersey—wherever there was keen competitive sport to be had.

In due course their enthusiasm led, as we have seen, to the formation of the Royal Northern Club and ultimately to " the Fortnight," that period in early July each year when the Clyde clubs are at home to all their friends and white wings of all shapes and sizes shine against the green hills from early morning till evening for days on end. The pioneers at once helped to establish yachting in fashion as an exciting and beautiful sport, to put the Firth of Clyde on the larger map of British yachting, and to give the Clyde clubs a considerable say in the slow and often contentious formation of the accepted rules of the sport. The starting rule now generally observed, for instance—a first warning gun, then five minutes of jockeying towards the line, and then the second and fatal gun—was invented by the early enthusiasts of the Royal Northern.

The cult thus duly established, the social circumstances on the Firth of Clyde so greatly favoured the popularity of the sport in an era of peace and expansion, private wealth duly found an elegant means of expression in the building and sailing of lovely yachts. A few keen aristocrats—the then Earl of Dunraven and the Marquess of Ailsa, for instance—could afford to keep up with the field to the turn of the century and even beyond.

Yacht-racing on the big scale, however, had become so expensive that only industrial wealth and power, supplanting those of the landed aristocracy, could meet the ever-rising costs. Big yachting became competitive in other terms than those of sport. When the Prince of Wales, later Edward VII, became a genuine enthusiast and had his wonderful *Britannia* designed by a man of Clydeside, the late G. L. Watson, and had the ship built on the Clyde by Henderson's of Meadowside ; when the insolent Kaiser of Germany sent his *Meteor* (with a destroyer in attendance) to challenge the Britons in their own waters and at their own game—why, of course, the new industrial aristocracy, approaching nearer and nearer to the Throne, rallied behind the Heir-Apparent.

Those were the fabulous days ; and if we claim to know that the splendour of yachting on the Clyde at the turn of the century rested to a considerable extent on snob values, we should decently remember that the sport was still keen and urgent and dangerous, and above all that few other exercises of the power of wealth have ever created such beauty : the lovely yachts pirouetting against a theatrical backcloth, their crews keyed to their tasks with the fierce intensity that overcomes any jockey, their movements watched through binoculars from the shore by fervently interested men of all classes of society.

Those were the days, indeed ! The Club steamer of the day, usually the *Duchess of Hamilton*, decorously followed the races, her Highland skipper most cautiously threading his course so as not to spoil even a second of the sport ; the coastwise hotels and clubhouses bright with hospitality ; the seaside castles and villas crammed with guests and their numerous body-servants ; bands playing, coloured burgees streaming in the winds, and the bars of pierhead pubs loud with the boastings of deck-hands canvassing the niceties of the day's racing.

All this had the social validity of, say, Epsom. If the Prince himself was not on the scene, the considerable shadow of his patronage lay comfortably across the northern estuary. Those who aspired to approach the Throne closely, perhaps occasionally accommodating an ebullient Heir-Apparent with expensive tastes and a difficult mother, could thus creep within the glow of his eminence.

The old aristocracy was, in that period of historical time, beginning to lose its grip, the new plutocracy to find places among the favourites. In modern social history, with big yachting as one of the most obvious expressions of the power of wealth, there is perhaps nothing more remarkable than the case of a Glasgow messenger-boy called Thomas Lipton, of Irish parentage and almost a waif, who by dint of sheer grit and not a little imagination, made a fortune out of his multiple grocery stores and, through his genuine interest in yacht racing, came to rub shoulders with monarchs and to be almost the ambassador for Britain in his extremely expensive efforts to win back from the United States the legendary *America's* Cup.

There will be more to say later on of the social and historical bearings of yachting on the Firth of Clyde. Now we are interested merely to note that an industry as well as an interest arose out of the cult, vogue, fashion—call it what you please. Men devoted themselves to the building, the refitting and the wintering of yachts up and down the coasts of the Firth from Gourock across to the Gareloch, from the Holy Loch down to Rothesay, from the Ayrshire coast across to Tarbert on Loch Fyne. Tribes of lads skilled in handling sail, and honest fishermen of Argyll and Ayr throughout the winter months, were the happy hirelings of the season. " Skeely skippers," in the phrase of the ballad, might be imported from so far afield as the creeks of Essex. The mere business of catering in terms of food and wine for the festival of the Fortnight was just another way of redistributing the industrial wealth. Tailors made good money out of the clothing in uniform of a smart crew ; shipchandlers flourished ; the river steamers heeled over under the weight of eager sight-seers.

The best effect of the yachting cult on the Firth of Clyde was the emergence of a highly-skilled and highly-critical interest in the designing of ships. Hereabouts the native industry and the native sport merged in an agreeable and useful association. What the designers and builders of yachts could discover about the ways of small vessels at sea must clearly be of interest to the men building big ships in the up-river yards. One of the great designers, the G. L. Watson already mentioned, was found worthy of a place in the *Dictionary of National Biography* after his death in 1904.

A pupil of the Napiers, latterly associated closely with A. & J. Inglis of Pointhouse—one of the old Clyde ship-building firms with a lively interest in yacht design—a specialist in the design of lifeboats, this G. L. Watson was lucky to be born into the golden age. His first great commission was for the legendary *Vanduara* of 1880 ; his most famous, and perhaps successful, was for the Prince of Wales's *Britannia* in 1893. He designed our challengers for the *America's* Cup : *Thistle*, *Valkyrie II* and *III* and Lipton's *Shamrock II*. Ageing men still speak fondly of the loveliness of other creations of his—*Bona*, *Kariad* and the rest.

Watson is mentioned here only as a very prominent member of a highly-specialised profession. His yachts were no more beautiful, no more successful, than those designed and built by the Fifes of Fairlie : at least three generations of a family that, starting modestly as builders of fishing smacks in the early 19th Century, for more than a hundred years enriched their world with the adorable products of an adoring craftsmanship. In another civilisation, Watson and the Fifes, with their rival Alfred Mylne and such loving craftsmen as Robertson of Sandbank and McGruer of Clynder, the Dickies of Tarbert and the rest of them, would have been elected to some such status as that of Royal Academician : so abundant their contribution to beauty.

There is a pleasant story, well-authenticated, of the conflict in the late-middle decades of the 19th Century between the instincts of the craftsman and the conclusions of the scientist in the matter of yacht design.

The great physicist Lord Kelvin, then Sir William Thomson, retired in summer from his duties in the University at Glasgow to a house near Largs on the Ayrshire coast. He was an eager yachtsman, and he was much interested scientifically in the behaviour of wetted, as distinct from dry, surfaces in motion. Out of his profound speculations on the subject there inevitably arose a theory, and on one fine day he took old " Wull " Fife, the founder of the dynasty, down to the sands hard by Fairlie and on the golden surface traced the contour and displacement lines of a yacht that must, theoretically, beat all-comers. At the same time old Wull, working from a pocketful of pebbles, laid out beside the great physicist's plan his own notions of the ideal yacht. Both boats were duly built, and in the issue the old craftsman's *Bluebell* could always show her heels to the embodiment of a theory.

The designers were greatly favoured in their period and the circumstances thereof. They were invited to envisage and to build great yachts at a time when, almost literally, money didn't matter much. Nor was it merely a business of creating vast racing machines. The steam yacht became the fashion, if only to be the floating home and headquarters of a keen yacht-owner.

These were lovely ships, with their fiddle bows, gilded counters, sweeping lines and yellow funnels. Their annual upkeep cost what would nowadays be called a fortune. The crew of a big one might number twenty ; the overheads during long periods of disuse and laying-out were monstrous. Even so, in the early years of this 20th Century, at least a score of these " Sailors' Homes," as they were rather bitterly nick-named, lay in the bays and lochs of the Firth of Clyde : the lovely lilies of an inevitable decadence, maintained out of fortunes acquired from landed property, sewing cotton, whisky, groceries and what-you-will. One authority has hazarded the view that the annual upkeep of a really big steam yacht may have cost as much as £50,000 a year !

There were few of these darlings left after the First World War. Sir Thomas Lipton's famous *Erin* had gone down in the Mediterranean as a result of enemy action while she served as an auxiliary. Many more fine ships of the sort were the casualties of bread-and-butter economics. In the mid-20's of the 20th Century the steam yacht had become vestigial. Of the few sizeable ships of the class remaining afloat in 1936 one remembers Courtauld's *Virginia*, Lord Inchcape's *Rover* and Lady Yule's accidentally notorious *Nahlin*. During the late summer of 1950 the present writer, vaguely wondering where he had seen her before, beheld Miss Barbara Hutton's *Troubadour* tied up at a quay before Oslo's bright new Raadhus and, her fresh paint all agleam and loud-speakers distributing light music, apparently used as a sort of floating hotel.

Even before the First World War, however ; even before heavy taxation had put a check on fantastic expenditure on pleasure, quite another factor came to affect the scene on the Firth of Clyde as on other great estuaries. This was the appearance, in 1912 or thereabouts, of the motor-boat or the motor-cruiser.

Here was a labour-saving device indeed ; here was a way of getting about a lovely Firth without too much servile and tedious dependence on wind and weather. A stout boat capable of sleeping four persons, could be bought new from such a firm as Silvers of Rosneath, powered by a Kelvin engine, for so little as £350. In the nature of things this new attraction, while it no doubt added to the floating population of the Firth of Clyde, seduced many sailing men from the old allegiance to canvas. In particular, the phenomenon announced the doom of the old, expensive, if beautiful steam yacht. When the diesel engine came to lower running costs and raise the margin of safety, a motor yacht of only 150 tons was fit to take the owner and his guests to the Riviera. It was equally competent to serve as tender and tug-boat for the racing craft.

Economics, however, were the decisive factor in revolutionising the spectacular aspects of yachting. In an appendix the curious reader will discover a set of comparative figures that almost sensationally demonstrate the steepness of the curve of rising costs within little more than a generation.

Those who saw them under canvas must think of the gigantic racing machines of the early 1900's as belonging to the order of the fantastic. They would be fully 75 feet in length along the waterline, the best part of 100 feet overall. The towering canvas might be measured in hundreds of square yards ; a new suit of sails cost what would be regarded as a fantastic sum in 1950 ; and it required upwards of a score of highly-skilled seamen to handle the ship with the nimbleness required by the alarming exigencies of yacht racing. Whoever has seen three or four of these great beauties crashing up the Firth under a brisk sou'-wester has witnessed the fabulous, such a vision of dynamic beauty as may never be seen again. It was magnificent. But it was not sound economics.

The Firth of Clyde

It is mere sentimentality to bemoan, as so many do, the passing of these splendours. It is only the onlooker who regrets that the largest yachts racing as a class on the Clyde in 1950 were the old 8-metres, a mere 26 feet or thereabouts along the waterline. Is it a bad thing that the most important international contests are conducted in frail 6-metres, and that the most popular class of all are the still smaller Dragons with, at their tail, a horde of odd little craft, from Scottish Islands to Flying Fifteens, from Loch Longs down to 12-foot dinghies ?

The question is one of scale only. If the cruising sloop has tended to go down before the attractions of the small motor yacht, the number of racing yachts on the Firth of Clyde was not less in 1950 than it was in 1900. The old " Corinthian " tradition was marvellously revived, the rivalry of strangers— American, Norwegian, Irish, Danish—more delightfully menacing than ever before. Yacht racing in a Dragon is in no way less exciting, and is positively rather more dangerous, than in a great *White Heather*, say, of the day before yesterday. The winds and the tides keep on, in their monotonous way, challenging the courage and skill of adventurous men and women.

By mid-Century, indeed, yachting as a racing sport was actually being enjoyed by more people than in the heyday of the wealthy owners. This came largely of the encouragement by the Clubs of young steersmen. The Clyde Cruising Club took to tutoring a Cadet Section in centreboard boats on a freshwater lake near Glasgow. In 1950 the Royal Clyde Yacht Club had four Loch Longs on the Firth for the education of the young in helmsmanship. The number of women owners and steersmen vastly increased during the post-war period, and girl crews from the schools and universities could hold their own with the young men in the annual contests in Dragons— most of these lent by local sportsmen—on the Gareloch.

CHAPTER IX

Aids to Navigation

THROUGHOUT a long period during the Second World War the Firth of Clyde was the very windpipe of embattled Britain. Bombing and blockade had reduced most of the southern ports, and the Clyde's advantageous position in relation to the North American continent conferred on the estuary for a space a remarkable importance in the affairs of a country at war.

Under the peaks of Arran there passed continuously, as regular as the tides, the streams of warlike material from the United States and Canada. Any aged freighter, down to the Plimsoll mark with guns and shells in the hold, could still contrive to carry a deck cargo of aeroplanes in huge wooden crates. It was one of the wonders of those late-middle years of the Second World War to see how, storage space being so short, those crates might lie for weeks on end on the grass verges of Scotland's arterial highways : apparently abandoned to wind, weather and sabotage until the factor of wastage on the Western Front, with a lot of nasty deaths of fine young men involved, cleared the accumulation away for the final air assault upon the tottering defences of the Third Reich.

There was little time for the contemplation of estuarine beauty in those days, but that remained. The skies, the land masses, the islands and the coloured fringes of the Firth remained. The seaweeds were still dull yellow and bright gold along the shores ; the seabirds wheeled against bright blue or cloudy skies, braced their exquisite wings in eddies, and cried like puppies for food. Beauty resided likewise in those vast aggregations of Allied shipping that, within the Boom, which stretched in tidal curves from the Cloch Light to Dunoon, lay at anchor all the way down from the Tail of the Bank to the verges of the Boom area itself : the ancillaries of this international fleet filling every loch and cove within the Safety Area. Whoever saw an Allied convoy pass majestically out to sea in the summer dusk, a procession of great liners packed with troops for North Africa, for instance, beheld something in the nature of the unforgettable.

On the whole, however, these times were very grim, and much ugliness, of which the scars must remain for a long time to come, was imposed upon the estuary. To meet the desperate emergency there were brought round from the South all manner of floating docks and cranes, dumb barges and auxiliary craft, for much of the unloading must be done in the open waters of the anchorage. Destroyers and frigates of the anti-submarine patrols dashed in and out on their mysterious occasions ; ships maimed in sea-battle limped their way to the up-river shipyards and came down again to fight another day. A beastly scum of fuel oil covered the water, and sea birds died, while the rocks and stones of all the shores were befouled by the black greasiness of the stuff.

This episode in the history of the Firth is recalled for two good reasons. It demonstrated the importance of the estuary within any sound scheme of national defence : a consideration to which the Admiralty, with its traditional interest in the Channel Ports, had for long displayed a remarkable indifference. It put the whole of the Clyde Sea Area, the Firth, the anchorage off Greenock and the Ship-Channel up to Glasgow, under one implacable and all-powerful authority, consisting in one part of the Admiralty and, on the other, of a Regional Port Controller. Thus, when the Royal Navy had had its use of the Clyde and returned to the southern bases, and when the

Regional Port Controller had tidied up his affairs and returned the harbour to the local authorities, the government of the Clyde, so to speak, was left where it had been in 1939, with not a few left-over, post-war problems thrown in.

The experiences of the Regional Port Controllers during hostilities had inclined them to think, and recommend, that this great harbour and its resources should be reorganised as a unit under the single control of such a body as the Port of London Authority. There have been official inquiries into the subject, but towards the end of 1950 very little had emerged from the cocoons of bureaucracy. This is indeed a political matter, mainly affecting Glasgow and its Ship-Channel to the sea, but it is not wholly without a bearing on the affairs of the Firth proper.

The control of the Clyde as a harbour is a monstrously complicated business, reflecting the competitive and *ad hoc* circumstances of its development as such.

While Greenock remained the chief port of the region the business of harbour administration was simple enough, but when the magistrates and merchants of Glasgow succeeded in bringing deep tidal water upstream to the very doors of their warehouses the individualism of the early 19th Century inevitably created overlapping and mutually hostile groups.

Glasgow had created its Ship-Channel and naturally claimed, and was duly granted, full responsibility for its control. This was, however, bound to conflict with the interests of the ports on the Firth proper : notably with those of Greenock at the highest point of anchorage. The curious in those matters will discover from the records how both Scottish and English solicitors and the leading pleaders at the Bars of both countries earned among them many thousands of pounds through at least a century of recurrent legislation. It is of historical interest that Parliament has consistently tended to protect the Greenock Harbour Trustees against proposals of the up-river authorities that might damage the older port's installations and reduce its trade.

As matters stood in 1950, the shipping interests of Glasgow still had the largest say (rightly enough) in the navigational affairs of the Clyde, the Firth included. It is all very confused, as we have already noted, but it is well that the organisation should be explained as simply as possible.

Full control of the Clyde Ship-Channel from Glasgow down to a line a few miles upstream from Greenock is vested in a body known, officially, as the Trustees of the Clyde Navigation and, more conveniently, as the Clyde Trust. Its members are elected by public bodies, notably the Corporation of Glasgow, and by Glasgow harbour ratepayers—shipowners, wharfingers and such. In the nature of things, the interests of Glasgow predominate.

This Clyde Trust has some 12 miles of quayage to care for. It handles on the average some 15 million tons of shipping each year and about one-half of that tonnage of goods, thus acquiring an annual revenue of rather more than a million pounds. In return, it provides immediately berthing conveniences, the apparatus of loading and unloading, granaries, cattle lairage and the what-you-will of normal harbour service. No ship of size can proceed up the Ship-Channel from Greenock to Glasgow without attendant tug or tugs, if only to steer the vessel in that narrow waterway, and while the Clyde tugboats, mainly based on Greenock, are in private ownership, the Trustees of the Clyde Navigation dictate their manners and the rates at which they may be properly rewarded.

This may seem to have little to do with the Firth of our immediate interest. On the maps and charts of the region you will see a line drawn across the sandbanks between Port Glasgow and Cardross on the northern shore and marked "Limit of the Clyde Trust authority" or words to that effect. This is

BIG STUFF: A ketch of 70-tons, *Fiumara*, drives into short seas towards the Cowal coast.

SPINNAKERS: A clutch of 6-metres making the best of a south-west wind off Gourock. *Circe*, nearest camera, won the Seawanakha Cup in 1938.

HIGHLAND COUNTRY: A typical stretch of bracken-infested, sheep-farming land above lonely Loch Striven.

BLUE DAYS AT SEA: A motor-yacht of modern design turns out of dark Loch Goil into its parent, Loch Long.

only a symbol of the confusion in the management of the Clyde as a whole. In one of its functions the Clyde Trust operates far below Greenock and well out into the Firth.

The arbitrary line, Port Glasgow to Cardross, is marked by an ominous row of black beacons, but it indicates merely the frontier at which the Clyde Trust surrenders only a part of its authority to the Clyde Lighthouses Trust : like itself an elected and representative body and so similarly constituted that the two are hardly recognisable apart. . . . It is all very difficult ; but the fine distinction is that, while the Clyde Trust is responsible for the lighting, as well as the dredging, of the Ship-Channel above the Port Glasgow-Cardross line, the lighting and buoying thereafter is the affair of these Clyde Lighthouses Trustees. The Clyde Trust proper remains in the meantime the Clyde Pilotage Authority, so that, in important ways, its writ runs far down the Firth below Greenock.

Apart from vessels in a few exempted classes, all ships proceeding inwards to Glasgow or outwards from that port must be in charge of a licensed pilot, who boards the inward-bound craft off Gourock Pier. Theoretically, at least, vessels carrying passengers should be piloted to and from the light-house on the Lesser Cumbrae, some 18 miles below Greenock. Meanwhile (if only to iron out the last wrinkle in this over-lapping pattern) the authority of the Clyde Lighthouses Trust also ends at that point—on an imaginary line due East and West from Ayrshire to Kintyre and passing through the southernmost point of the Lesser Cumbrae. Thereafter, in the wide spaces of the Outer Firth, the navigational beacons are the charge of the national body, the Commissioners of Northern Lighthouses, the Scottish equivalent of Trinity House and controlled through the Scottish Office.

If the intricacies of this pattern are understood, it is clear that the merchants and shippers of Glasgow have kept a firm grip on the affairs of the harbour they did so much to create, and it is not difficult to understand why some powerful groups favour unification under a single Authority, while the majority of regional authorities concerned approach the prospect with certain reservations. Greenock's position in this conflict of interests has always been peculiarly delicate and difficult. Would this town, under unified control and against the natural rivalry of Glasgow, get the deep-water berths for Atlantic liners and the graving dock for the largest vessels that have been discussed as national projects on the highest level and are on the highest of local priorities ? . . . We leave these nice considerations to the politicians and return to the actual scene.

The navigation of the Firth of Clyde from its stormy approaches right up to the Tail of the Bank presents few difficulties. The fairway is wide and the water deep all the way. The estuary has its share of gales, but fogs are infrequent and, as we have seen, the tides move with reliable dignity in the main channels. Big shipping comes in from the Atlantic or up from the Irish Sea, keeping the lights of Ailsa Craig to the port hand and passing between Arran and the Ayrshire coast. It makes its signals to the lighthouse at the southern tip of the Lesser Cumbrae and passes between the twin islands and the low-lying mass of Bute. Ahead then is the tall white pillar of Toward Lighthouse, and course is changed for a swing eastwards on a bearing to pass the stubby tower of the Cloch Lighthouse on the Renfrewshire coast. Hereabouts the big ships slacken speed, whether to pick up the pilot off Gourock or to come to anchor off Greenock a mile or so beyond. There is no bar to cross ; there are no shoals to be feared ; the few hazards are all close inshore, beyond the care of a big ship's master.

The buoyage system of the Firth of Clyde, especially within the responsibility of the Clyde Lighthouses Trust, is inevitably as complicated as the tortuous lochs and kyles of the Sea Area, but there is no need to describe here in detail how this complex system of these seamarks, red and black, flat-topped and conical cans, beacons and perches is laid out. The details are there for all to see in the charts and the nautical almanacs. Those who may think of cruising the Clyde waters in small craft are however advised, nay implored, to take detailed advice from the admirable Sailing Directions for the West Coast of Scotland of the Clyde Cruising Club : a bible of small-ship navigation compiled with loving care and not without hazard by devoted amateurs.

The three lighthouses maintained on the Inner Firth by the Clyde Lighthouses Trust are, as we have seen and taking the outwards order, the Cloch on the Renfrewshire shore, Toward on the Argyllshire shore, and Cumbrae on the smaller isle of that name. A tall but unattended pillar marks The Gantocks, a reef hard against the Cowal coast off Dunoon. Another light, raised high on piles and carrying a fog-gun, marks a shallow patch against the Rosneath peninsula opposite Greenock. Over a sandy shoal by Skelmorlie off the Ayrshire coast a bell-buoy tolls mournfully but musically in the swell. None of these inner lights, save perhaps that on the Lesser Cumbrae, has the glamour of remoteness we look for in coastwise beacons.

The Cloch Light in particular seems a sort of cosy seaside residence, the turning-point of a pleasant walk along the shore-road from Gourock. Its white light flashes every five seconds regularly, and its foghorn makes noises remarkably like those of a cow in intestinal agony. Toward on the other side of the Firth seems more remote, being situated near the end of a *cul de sac* : all the more remote since a steamboat pier was demolished not long after the First World War. Its white light flashes every ten seconds over a range of 14 miles, and its horn in fog has a steadier and less dismal note than the siren of the Cloch. The Cumbrae Light, situated on a small and rough island, fits more neatly into the proper romantic pattern.

All three lighthouses were built, in their original forms at least, during the second half of the 18th Century, when Glasgow was shaping to become one of the first ports of Britain. That on the Lesser Cumbrae, given the island's strategic situation, was naturally the first. In 1755 or thereabouts an Act of Parliament empowered " the Earl of Eglintown to feu out two acres of land in the south-west end of Little Cumray as a site for a lighthouse and a wharf at which to land coals to be burned in it," and this was the historical beginning of the Clyde Lighthouses Trust. This was the lighthouse which, as we have noted already, was first set up on the highest point of the islet. The coal fire seems to have been succeeded by a battery of candles, and in 1793 the present lighthouse, with 32 oil lamps and reflectors of silvered glass, was set up just above the shore on the island's south-western extremity.

The Cumbrae Light remains the most important within the Firth system : the milestone marking the significant point of distinction between Inner and Outer Firth. With its tower of light abeam the vessel inward-bound has reached harbour home, while that voyaging outwards here counts the long journey just fairly begun. Here the pilotage and supervision of a regular harbour overcome traffic in one direction, while that in the other is released from these disciplines. In another way of putting it, the Cumbrae Light marks the end of a purely local authority. It gives two quick flashes every 30 seconds ; it is elaborately equipped with echo-sounding and all the other devices proper to a lighthouse in a key position.

The mariner then faces the expanses of the Outer Firth, his ship perhaps beginning to lift to the swell coming in from the Atlantic, his seamarks spaced on the oceanic scale. Within this stretch of the Outer Firth of Clyde are eight attended lighthouses, with that on the Mull of Kintyre and that on Corsewall Point at the mouth of Loch Ryan marking the extreme outer limits of the estuary.

Of these lights three—Turnberry, Corsewall and the Mull —are more or less cosily situated on mainland territory. The remaining five stand on islands—the Holy Isle, Pladda, Ailsa Craig, Davaar and Sanda. As we have seen, Holy Isle and Pladda are mere calves of Arran, clinging close to the mother isle, and Davaar lies securely enough within the arms of Campbeltown Loch. But Ailsa Craig is a lonely chunk of rock, and Sanda, though the island itself is farmed for grazing at least, is ringed by skerries of the most tempestuous and dangerous kind.

The siting of some of these lighthouses may puzzle the layman. On Ailsa Craig and the Holy Isle in particular the white towers appear to be tucked away in folds of the surrounding rocks, in quite the wrong positions in relation to a proper command of the fairway, while only their auxiliary towers, fed from the main houses, seem to command the channel properly. This is an optical illusion. The engineers who sited those lights—mainly of the family that incidentally produced Robert Louis Stevenson—knew exactly what they were doing.

While the main light of Ailsa Craig is at the northern and eastern tip of the rock, with a subsidiary light on the north-western corner ; and while the main light of the Holy Isle seems to look towards Arran across a narrow strait, with only the auxiliary light apparently staring towards the Ayrshire coast, the man on the bridge of the ship at sea, whether inward- or outward-bound, has them all continuously and clearly in sight. It was for his guidance that they were sited as they are, and for his alone. The layman can rest content with the romantic thought that several of these lighthouses of the Outer Firth flash red as well as white beams across the tumultuous waters.

The Firth of Clyde

These outer waters of the Firth of Clyde can be extremely dangerous, and the Royal National Life-Boat Institution maintains four stations on these reaches—at Campbeltown, at Girvan and Troon on the Ayrshire coast, and at Portpatrick against the Galloway cliffs. At one time seven other stations existed, but these were all closed during the early years of the 20th Century : the last, that at Ayr, in 1932.

This does not at all argue penury on the part of the admirable Institution ; it reflects rather the increasing efficiency and range of the modern, motor-powered lifeboat. It is of interest that the late G. L. Watson of Glasgow, of whom something has already been learned, was the prime mover in the evolution of the new type of boat, and that the yacht-building firm of Robertsons of Sandbank, Holy Loch, are among the few British firms approved for the construction of this very highly-specialised sort of craft. Eleven Robertson-built boats of the latest pattern were, in 1950, in service at Life-Boat Stations all round the British Isles, from Wick near John o' Groat's to Selsey in Sussex, and from Peterhead in Aberdeenshire to Baltimore in County Cork.

In a brief Appendix the reader may discover some interesting facts and figures concerning the regional service. It will be noted that the two stations on either side of the entrance gate, so to speak—Campbeltown and Portpatrick—are most frequently called upon for help.

In the eye of the visitor the navigational aid most characteristic of the Firth of Clyde is probably the signalling apparatus that stands high above most of the piers used by the river steamers. This device is nothing but a triangular box, its base to the shore and the sides facing the sea each pierced to carry three black discs, for all the world like a row of musketry targets. Each disc has a bull's-eye, so to speak, through which a light may shine in the darkness. On the approach of a steamer, or even of two or three, or again of vessels making

230

for the pier in opposite directions, it is the function of the piermaster, with the factor of safety uppermost in his mind, to decide which should have priority of approach. The decision made, he pulls a chain which changes one of the black discs to white, with a white bull's-eye at night, thus indicating which ship—out of a possible maximum of six—is favoured in the scramble for place.

The device is vestigial and nearly obsolescent. It dates from the days when competition among privately-owned steamboats ran high, wide and handsome. Rival skippers, proud of a mere capacity for speed and manœuvrability of their craft, so ruthlessly barged, butted and bored for first place at the piers that even the majestic *Glasgow Herald* was moved at one period to devote a leading article to their dangerous cantrips. Public opinion was, as they say, aroused, and an open competition for the best system of signalling to promote the interests of safety on the Firth was instituted.

Those black and white bull's-eyes above most of the Clyde piers are of the winning design by Mr. Charles Allan, of the shipowning family that created the Allan Line, latterly absorbed in the Canadian Pacific Railway concern. They served a useful purpose for many years, even into the more temperate era of railway competition, but the reduction of the pleasure fleet and the wiping-out of competition through nationalisation have largely reduced them to the status of monuments to a glory, riotous and even murderous but picturesque, departed.

The two Measured Miles of the Firth of Clyde are equally likely to arouse the curiosity of the intelligent stranger, not that the apparatus is in any way spectacular. These were laid out for the obvious purpose of scientifically checking the speeds of the innumerable vessels built in the up-river yards and proving to owners that the ship's speed is according to contract.

The Firth of Clyde

The first of these, and the most frequently used, is off Skelmorlie on the Ayrshire coast and within the Inner Firth. Its limits are marked unmistakably by two pairs of tall masts set one behind the other and adorned with angled crosstrees. The observers on the bridge of the vessel on trial touch off their stop-watches as the first pair of poles come exactly in line and stop them when the second pair similarly converge. Several runs up and down this green coast, a simple calculation, and the speed of any new vessel is established to the second point of decimals at least.

The Measured Mile off Skelmorlie was laid out in 1866 at the instance of John Napier, son of the great Robert Napier. He quickly got the agreement of the then Earl of Eglinton to the free use of the small patches of land required for the poles, and then that of the Admiralty to have the knot remeasured and tested by competent naval hydrographers. Mr. Napier's fellow-shipbuilders supported the scheme with enthusiasm, and there duly appeared the following official announcement :

NOTICE TO MARINERS
No. 36
Scotland—West Coast

Measured Mile in Firth of Clyde

Notice is hereby given that beacons to indicate the length of a nautical mile (6080 feet) have been erected on the eastern shore of the Firth of Clyde.

Each beacon consists of a single pole 45 feet high with arms 10 feet long forming a broad angle 15 feet from the base, the whole being painted white.

The two northern beacons are erected near Skelmorlie Pier, the outer one being close to the high-water shore on the south side, and from it the inner one (in the recess of a cliff) is 83 yards distant, bearing S.E. by E.¾E.

Aids to Navigation

The two southern beacons stand on level ground near Skelmorlie Castle, the inner one being 100 yards from the outer one, in a S.E. by E.¾E. direction.

The courses parallel with the measured mile at right angles to the line of transit of the beacons are N.N.E.¼E. and S.S.W.¼W. The shore may be approached to the distance of a third of a mile.

GEORGE HENRY RICHARDS,
Hydrographer.

Hydrographic Office,
Admiralty,
London, 4th July, 1866.

This is rather more than a fragment of local lore. The Measured Mile off Skelmorlie was the first set up in British coastal waters at the instance of civilian interests : a portent of the dominance of the Clyde as a shipbuilding river.

As ships were designed ever bigger and faster—and the two considerations are largely interdependent—it was found necessary to lay out another measured mile in deeper waters and along less populous shores than those in the region of Skelmorlie. A big ship travelling very fast can set up a wash that may smash everything on the neighbouring beaches and even flood the shore roads. So in the 1930's, a new measured distance was laid out along the north-eastern coast of the Isle of Arran where the water is deep and the shores thinly inhabited. Over this course the *Queen Mary* and then H.M.S. *Vanguard* first showed their paces. (It will be recalled that the *Queen Elizabeth* slipped out of the Clyde in time of war, untried.) The seamarks of the course are easily spotted by the voyager in the steamer to Arran. Along this stretch the course is much longer than the Skelmorlie mile : 12,160 feet to be exact, divided by a centre line of beacons.

A big-ship trial in these waters can be spectacular. There

233

exists somewhere a sensational picture taken by that great
photographer of shipping, the late Stewart Bale. It shows the
Queen Mary apparently in the act of sinking. It was in fact
taken from the deck of a tugboat that had momentarily
dropped into a trough of the big ship's monumental wash, so
that only her funnels, masts and upper parts remained visible
in the eye of the camera.

CHAPTER X

Fishes and Fisheries

So FAR, we have considered mainly what *homo sapiens* has made of his inheritance along the shores of a northern estuary, and now we look at what Nature has made of the same opportunities in the slow and fantastic processes of evolution. These notes on the fishes and fisheries of the Clyde Sea Area are contributed by Dr. David J. Gauld of the Marine Station at Millport.

The herring of Loch Fyne and the Clyde have long been famous for their fatness and their flavour, and the herring fishery is much the most important and valuable fishery in the Sea Area. Before the introduction of the internal combustion engine, just before the First World War, the fishing was carried out by small sailing boats, nearly all less than thirty feet in length, from a large number of harbours all along the coast. Since then there has been a rapid decline in the number of boats, and many harbours, such as Lochgilphead and Inveraray, which used to be the headquarters of considerable fleets of herring skiffs, now have no fleets at all. But motor power has enabled the fisherman to use larger boats, most of which to-day are fifty or more feet long, and the total catching-power of the Clyde herring fleet is to-day as great as, or greater than, it has ever been.

The herring is one of the fishes classified in the Fishery Statistics as a pelagic fish : that is, a fish which is caught close to the surface of the sea, unlike demersal fish such as cod, or

235

flat fish, which are caught by nets set on or dragged along the bottom of the sea. Of the other pelagic fish, sprats are not uncommon in the Clyde, but are not fished ; mackerel are fairly abundant, but are fished only on a very small scale.

The herring, unlike all other commercial fish, deposits its eggs on the bottom of the sea. Even its close relatives, the sprat and the pilchard, lay eggs, which like those of the vast majority of marine fishes, float near the surface of the sea.

The most important spawning grounds of the herring in the Clyde are the Ballantrae Banks, close to the Ayrshire coast and the Iron Rock ledges off the south-west coast of Arran. There, in six or seven fathoms of water, the eggs are laid in February and March and stick to stones and seaweed on the bottom, by means of their sticky outer coats. In about two to three weeks, usually about the middle of March, they hatch out, and the herring larva, a slender transparent creature about a quarter of an inch long, begins to drift northwards at the mercy of tides and currents.

Within a week the yolk which distended the stomach of the newly-hatched larva is used up, and the young herring begins to feed, at first on eggs and minute larvae of planktonic creatures. The herring hatched at Ballantrae for the most part drift up the east coast of Arran, those from the Iron Rock up Kilbrennan Sound ; and at the end of June they reach the mouth of Loch Fyne. By this time they are nearly two inches long and have reached the whitebait stage, when the body deepens, the silver scales first appear and the little fish are recognisably herring.

They can swim strongly now and are no longer carried by current and tides. They continue their migration northwards into Loch Fyne and the other lochs, feeding steadily. Little is known of their movements for the next three years, but they may migrate southwards in winter, following the older spawning fish, and northwards again every summer. Certainly some of them follow the spawning fish in their third year, when they are about eight inches long and still not yet mature. They spawn first at four years old, and from the onset of maturity, growth is much slower, about one-quarter of an inch each year. Each year the adult fish migrate from Loch Fyne to the spawning grounds in winter, and after a period of recuperation in deep water, migrate northwards in summer, to feed and grow fat in the lochs. Most herring are at least four years, and many eight or nine years, old when they reach the breakfast table.

Throughout its life the herring feeds on plankton, the small animals which swim and float freely in the open waters of the sea, although young herring and sand eels are also eaten. The food is caught in two ways ; small fish and larger crustaceans are caught individually in the herring's mouth. The smaller planktonic creatures are filtered from the water as it passes through the gills, by the gill-rakers, rows of long bristles set on the gill-arches.

The most important of these planktonic creatures are two groups of small crustaceans, Copepods and Euphausids. (The latter are the "krill," which forms the bulk of the food of the great whales.) It is the abundance of copepods in the Clyde Sea Area that gives the Loch Fyne herring the fine flavour and fatness to which it owes its fame. Copepods and euphausids are so numerous because their food, the microscopic plants of the plankton, flourish in the Clyde where the water is comparatively rich in the essential mineral salts, nitrate and phosphate, of which there is half as much again as there is in the English Channel.

Like most animals, the herring is prey as well as predator. Apart from man, who may not be the most destructive of its enemies, the herring is eaten by seals, whales, porpoises, gannets and other sea birds, and many kinds of fish ; even the eggs—one might almost say, especially the eggs—are greedily sought by haddock and cod, who eat them in such numbers that the capture of " spawny " haddock or cod is much the easiest way of locating the banks on which herring spawn. Young herring are again the principal food of many fishes, such as hake and haddock, and of many sea birds, flocks of which can be seen following a shoal as it moves from place to place. Dogfish are also important destroyers of herring, especially the black " Piked Dogfish " or " Spurdog " which hunts the shoals, often in huge packs. Gannets and whales so consistently feed on herring that their presence in an area is another of the " signs " by which herring fishermen choose their fishing grounds.

The Clyde herring fisherman of 1950 continued to use the " signs " his forebears used to mark the general position of the herring shoals, but he had more modern and more exact means of locating the fish. Once on his chosen ground, he cruised slowly over the area, waiting for the appearance on the record of his Echometer of the marks which tell when a shoal is below.

The Echometer, originally designed as a rapid and accurate means of obtaining soundings, detects the herring by means of the sound-echo returning to the instrument from the fish, just as Radar detects the approaching aircraft or ship by means of its radio echo. It has proved so valuable that few herring fishermen go out without it. When the tell-tale marks appear, the skipper criss-crosses the shoal to locate it more exactly and to estimate its size. Then the net is shot round the shoal to encircle or " ring " it. As soon as the skipper of the neighbour boat—for ring-netters work in pairs—sees the net being shot, he hurries to the spot to assist with the hauling and landing of the fish. The fish is taken aboard by the second boat, which then, if the catch is large enough, takes it to the nearest port, while the first makes its way to a convenient anchorage at which to lie until evening comes and fishing can start again.

Fishes and Fisheries

The herring fishing season in the Firth of Clyde starts in May or June, when the fish are making their way north towards Loch Fyne and beginning to recover from the exhaustion that follows spawning. As the season advances the fish improve in condition, and for most of the season Loch Fyne herring are prime fish and very fat. Later in the year the roes begin to develop and the fish become " full " fish and move southwards to the spawning grounds, where the fishing starts again in January and February on the Ballantrae Banks.

Apart from the herring, the fish caught for sale in the Clyde nearly all belong to two groups, the cod family and the plaice, or flatfish, family, although a few fish like skate and dogfish which don't belong to either of these groups are caught to a lesser extent. It is convenient in describing the fisheries of the Clyde to treat these important fish in their families.

The Cod family contains seven or eight common species which are all found in the Clyde. They are all round fish, as distinct from flatfish, usually grey or brownish on the back, shading to white or silvery on the underside, and they all have more than one fin on the back. They are fish which live near the bottom and feed largely on invertebrate animals, like worms, crustacea and molluscs, living on or in the bottom. In the Clyde they are fished commercially for the most part by small seine net boats, less than forty feet long, which mostly come down to the Clyde for winter fishing from their home ports in the Moray Firth and on the Aberdeenshire coast. These East coast fishers find it easier and often more profitable to work the sheltered waters of the Clyde than their own stormy coast ; they land most of their catches at Tarbert and Ayr.

All the members of the Cod family lay enormous numbers of eggs ; a large cod may lay two million, usually in winter or early spring. They are very small, perhaps one-twentieth of an inch in diameter, and float at the surface of the sea. (For this reason, any talk of seine nets or trawls destroying spawn or spawning banks is unrealistic. As for herring spawn, it is laid on the bottom, but on ground where no fisherman would shoot a trawl or seine.) As the eggs drift with the wind and currents the little fish develops within the transparent egg, and in about ten days it hatches to a minute larva barely half an inch long, which, like that of the herring, lives in the upper parts of the water and feeds on plankton. At the age of six weeks it undergoes a transformation and acquires the form of the adult fish. A young cod, for instance, has the comparatively large head and mouth and the barbel which characterise it for the rest of its life, although at this age it is more brightly and more attractively coloured than its sober and even dingy elders. Cod grow rapidly to a length of four or five inches in their first year, and about ten inches at the end of two years. By the time they are four or five years old, cod are fair-sized fish and ready to spawn, and they may live for many years. Cod of up to fifteen years old and nearly five feet long have been caught.

The food of the Cod family is very varied—fish, especially herring and other smaller members of the cod family, shellfish of many kinds, crabs, shrimps and prawns, etc. The cod is a catholic feeder, and nothing seems to come amiss.

What has been said above applies broadly to all the members of the family, but each of the different species has its own peculiarities.

(1) *Cod.*—This is the largest and the commonest member of the family ; it can be distinguished from its relatives by the grey-brown colour and the long barbel on its chin. It is a fairly important commercial fish in the Clyde, although the numbers caught are insignificant compared with the enormous catches of the cod fisheries of Iceland, Bear Isle, etc. Young cod in their first and second year are commonly caught by

shore anglers, when they are often spoken of as codling or rock cod.

(2) *Haddock.*—The haddock can easily be recognised by its grey back, black lateral line and "St Peter's thumb mark" above the pectoral fin. It used to be much more abundant in the Clyde than it is now, and was commonly caught by line fishermen. It declined greatly in numbers in the early years of this century. This decline is said to be due to the destruction of enormous numbers of "aichens" (*Spisula subtruncata*), its favourite food, when most of the shores of the Clyde were snowbound in the winter of 1904-5. It is certainly a more fastidious feeder than the cod, which largely replaced it.

(3) *Saithe or Coalfish.*—The saithe has many names, such as cuddy, podley, etc., varying with the locality and the age of the fish. In its first two years, *Gadus virens*, the green cod, is a beautiful fish, green and gold in colour, but its back darkens to nearly black as it grows older. It has no barbel. It is not important in commercial catches but is quite common, especially close to rocky shores, and young saithe are easily caught on handlines from the shore or small boats.

(4) *Lythe or Pollack.*—The lythe has similar habits to the saithe but is much less common. It is a southern form, more common off the south and south-west coasts of Britain than in the Clyde. It is lighter in colour than a saithe of the same size, has a conspicuous lateral line and a protruding lower jaw.

(5) *Whiting.*—This is a smaller fish than its cousins. It is light in colour, with a black lateral line and a black spot at the base of the pectoral fin. It is abundant in deep water and well represented in commercial landings.

(6) *Poor Cod or Bib.*—The poor cod is a small fish, growing to seven or eight inches long, with a short body, fawny-brown on the back and a long barbel. It is quite common in commercial catches, and it is usually sold as whiting, or lightly smoked and sold as "crumbs."

(7) *Hake.*—The hake can readily be recognised by its long, rather slender body and silvery colour. It is sometimes abundant in the deeper parts of the Firth and is usually caught on long lines. It is a first-class eating fish, but for some mysterious reason it is unpopular in Scotland.

(8) *Ling.*—Another long-bodied fish, frequenting deep water, is occasionally taken on lines set for hake.

The fishes of the plaice family are the most remarkable for the marked changes in form which accompany the progress of the pelagic larva to its adult habitat on the bottom. Like the cod, flat fishes lay planktonic eggs that float at the surface of the water and are carried hither and thither by the currents. After some days—in the plaice itself usually about a fortnight—the young " flatfish " hatches as a larva, about quarter of an inch long, very similar in appearance to the larvæ of a round fish like the cod and with no trace of the asymmetry of the adult fish.

In the plaice the first sign of asymmetry appears when the little fish is about a month old ; the left eye begins to move upwards and forwards, and about ten days later appears on the upper margin of the head, just in front of the right eye. The adult form is finally achieved a few days later, when the left eye reaches a position above and in front of the right eye on the right side of the head. During the migration of the left eye and the accompanying deformation of the head, the young flatfish has been growing deeper in the body and has gradually acquired the habit of swimming with its right side uppermost. Finally, when it leaves the plankton and takes to life on the bottom of the sea, it settles on its left side, for although the head has been profoundly modified by the metamorphosis into the adult flatfish, the body retains its essential symmetry almost unchanged.

The flatfish live on the bottom, and feed on invertebrate

animals from the bottom, and because their mouths are nearly all much smaller than those of the cod family they must feed on smaller prey. Small shellfish, such as young cockles, marine worms, such as lugworm, and small crustaceans (Amphipods) related to the sand hoppers of the shore, are the most important food.

Of the flatfish caught and landed by fishing boats in the Clyde the plaice itself, which can easily be recognised by its smooth grey back marked with clear red spots, and the witch, are the most common and most abundant. The witch has reddish-brown, rough-looking skin and prefers deeper water and muddier ground than the plaice. Witches are usually sold in the shops as sole, but the true sole is rare in the Clyde. Young plaice, as well as dabs and flounders, may be caught with bait and line or by spearing in most of the sandy bays of the area. Of these the flounder is most often found at the heads of the sea lochs and at the mouths of streams, for it prefers slightly brackish water.

These, then, are the fish which are most important commercially in the Clyde. There are of course many other kinds of fish of little or no value. Most of these are of interest only to the naturalist, but some which occur close to the shore, where they may be caught or seen by holiday-makers, may be mentioned in passing.

Such are the Wrasses, deep-bodied fishes, often of beautiful iridescent colours, which are not uncommonly landed by sea-anglers. The Bullhead or Sea Scorpion is another common inshore fish which may be caught off a rocky shore. At first sight it is an ugly creature, with a large head and mouth and a short body, its gill-cover armed with strong spines, but it is admirably adapted to its life, and the rather irregular shape and mottled colour enable it to look like just another stone among the seaweed until a small fish or prawn strays within reach of its wide ugly mouth.

All the fish mentioned so far have a skeleton of true bone, but there is a large group of fish which have no bone in their skeleton, only cartilage, a tough gristle-like substance. These are the skates, dogfish and sharks.

In the Clyde there are two common kinds of dogfish, the Spotted Dogfish and the Black Dogfish. The spotted variety is light grey in colour, marked with many small dark spots and grows up to nearly three feet in length ; its food consists largely of crabs, crayfish and other crustaceans, as well as some fish. It lays large eggs, in the horny cases known as "mermaids' purses," in shallow water among weeds. The black species, on the other hand, is viviparous, the female bearing four to six young in spring.

Black dogfish, which reach lengths of over four feet, move in enormous packs, pursuing the shoals of herring and other smaller fish and destroying large numbers of them. Oddly enough, these large shoals, occasionally of a thousand or more fish, contain in the Clyde very few females. They take their name from the very dark grey colour, and from the strong spines placed just in front of each of the dorsal fins, spines which can inflict ugly wounds on a careless fisherman. But the fishermen have other, more important reasons for disliking dogfish ; a large shoal of dogfish may cause serious damage to a seine net, because, while a net full of cod or haddock will float—because the air in the swim-bladder of these fish expands as they are lifted from the bottom and makes them buoyant—dogfish, which have no air-bladder, may burst the net from sheer dead-weight. Moreover, a large catch of dogfish usually means few if any of the other more valuable kinds of fish.

Dogfish are always skinned before sale and usually marketed under a pseudonym, such as " rock turbot," so that much more of it is eaten than the public realises. The flesh is not of very high quality, but its flavour is better than much of the cod that is marketed to-day, and it does not deserve its unpopularity.

Fishes and Fisheries

The cartilaginous fishes include the Sharks, one of which, the notorious basking shark, is a regular and sometimes abundant visitor to the Clyde. It is an inhabitant of the Atlantic Ocean and migrates northwards along the west coast of Europe every summer, appearing first off the coast of South-western Ireland in June. It reaches the Firth of Clyde in July in varying numbers each year, and usually leaves before the end of September. It is the largest fish occurring in British waters—specimens of thirty feet in length are not uncommon —but, in spite of reports to the contrary, it is probably one of the least offensive, and feeds on plankton. A basking shark surfacing just below a small boat or jumping, as it occasionally does, near it, can very easily capsize it, and a man sitting in such a boat has every excuse to be frightened by the sight of a thirty-foot shark swimming straight towards him, whatever the shark's intentions may be. It is doubtful, however, if unprovoked attacks have ever occurred.

There remain the whales and their smaller cousins, the dolphins and porpoises. The bottle-nosed whale and the white-sided dolphin are fairly regular visitors to the Clyde, especially in the autumn. Their food consists largely of cuttlefish and squids. The common porpoise is resident throughout the year and is much the most abundant cetacean in the Clyde Sea Area. Small schools of half a dozen to a dozen individuals can be seen almost any day, rolling and blowing as they follow the herring on which they feed.

CHAPTER XI

Seabirds, Shellfish and Seaweed

WITHIN the economy of any tidal Estuary or Firth, the fishes that man can catch for the table and sell through the markets are naturally the most important denizens. Economics are not all of life, however. In this chapter, the work of Dr. R. H. Millar of the Marine Station at Millport, our concern is largely with the innumerable seabirds of the Firth of Clyde and their riparian associates ; and it will be seen that the birds of the Firth do, in fact, impinge to a considerable extent on the economics of the fishing industry. Dr. Millar is also responsible for the brief notes on the Shellfish of the area, and his colleague, Mr. H. T. Powell, B.Sc., has provided the useful passage on the Seaweeds.

Any area that can present a variety of distinct types of country, coastline, or sea, may be expected to possess a corresponding diversity of birds, and in the Clyde Sea Area we have just such a variety of habitats. Rocky shores, high cliffs, sandy tidal flats, and the many small islands—all have their characteristic species ; and, of course, we are especially fortunate on the Firth of Clyde in having Ailsa Craig, one of the most interesting breeding places of sea birds in Britain.

The region being thus so rich in bird life, it is necessary to select certain species for mention and to omit others ; and the task of selection has not been easy ! Most of the common birds of the sea and shore are included. Some less common ones have been mentioned, but only where of special interest.

A few not generally associated with the sea, but which often wander from the adjacent land, are included in the catalogue, which may be found a useful guide, however rough from the scientific point of view.

Raven.—On a few wild coastal cliffs the Raven, our largest crow, still nests in South Ayrshire, Ailsa, Arran and Bute. It feeds largely on carrion but takes small birds and mammals, and also eggs, and only occasionally weak lambs and sheep.

Chough.—Red legs and a red bill distinguish this rare crow. Up to a few years ago the Chough was still a breeding species in the Clyde Area, although in very small numbers, and it is to be hoped that it may again spread to suitable sea cliffs.

Peregrine Falcon.—This powerful falcon, slate-coloured above and barred below, inhabits the same kind of country as the Raven, and is restricted to much the same districts. A special order was made during the Second War, authorising the destruction of Peregrines, because they kill carrier pigeons.

Common Buzzard.—The brown plumage and slow, wheeling flight of the Buzzard are easily recognised. A few Buzzards still remain on the wilder coasts of the Clyde, but the species has been much and unjustly persecuted ; it rarely takes game birds.

Golden Eagle.—The Eagle, which is like a large edition of the Buzzard, nests in very small numbers in our area, but is commoner in the mountains north of the Clyde.

Heron.—The grey Heron is quite a common bird along our coasts. It wades in shallow water to capture small fish, but little in the way of food comes amiss to it. Its long legs are adapted for wading and its long spear-like bill for stabbing at its prey. Many people are surprised that the Heron nests in trees. Scattered colonies exist in all the counties bordering the Firth.

Mute Swan.—This is the common swan, which breeds throughout the Clyde area by inland waters, and may often be seen on the coast. In England swans have a royal history. For centuries they were owned by the Crown and were semi-domestic, but when this system lapsed they reverted to a wild state. In Scotland, however, swans were not Crown property, and we do not know their history ; they may possibly be a mixture of semi-domestic stock and immigrant wild birds from the Continent.

Whooper Swan.—The Whooper visits our coastal waters in winter, when it is not uncommon. The rather straight neck and repeated trumpeting call help to distinguish it from the Mute Swan.

Geese.—Geese are of two kinds ; grey geese, large brownish-grey birds which feed on grassland ; and black geese, which resort to tidal flats. The identification of the different geese is not easy, because they are all rather alike at a distance and are very difficult to approach.

Grey Lag-Goose.—This is our largest grey goose and is very like the farmyard bird, which was derived from it. As a winter visitor from Northern Europe it is sometimes seen in fair numbers on coastal flats in Ayrshire and Kintyre.

Pink-footed Goose and the *White-fronted Goose* are both uncommon birds in the Clyde area, the latter being seen mainly during migration.

Bean Goose.—The exact status of this, and of the other geese, is doubtful, both in the Clyde area and in Scotland as a whole. In any case it cannot be called common, although it does occur in Ayrshire, but mainly on inland moors.

Barnacle Goose.—This and the Brent Goose are our two black geese. The Barnacle Goose is known by its white face, which the Brent lacks. It seems that formerly this bird was a tolerably common winter visitor, but it is not so now.

Brent Goose.—The Brent Goose regularly visits our area in

winter, especially the North Ayrshire coast, but it has been subject to persecution, which may diminish its numbers.

Ducks.—The drake of most species is fairly easy to identify, but the duck, being dressed in brown, is more difficult. The notes on colour given here refer to the drake, unless otherwise stated.

Sheld-Duck.—Both male and female of this large, rather goose-like duck are boldly marked with white, black, and chestnut. The Sheld-Duck may be seen at all seasons in the Clyde, and nests commonly in suitable places, such as the west coast of Arran.

Mallard or Wild Duck.—The best-known of all our ducks. Although not everywhere the commonest, the Mallard is seen inland and along the coast. It favours the mouths of river estuaries, to which many resort in winter. Large numbers of Mallard arrive in this country from the Continent in autumn. The domestic duck was bred from the Mallard.

Widgeon.—This chestnut-headed duck is mainly a winter visitor to Britain, but for over a hundred years it has bred in Scotland in increasing numbers. Colonisation has spread southwards from the North of Scotland and has reached the Clyde area, although breeding here is still very rare. On parts of the Ayrshire coast it is sometimes the commonest duck in winter. The abundance of Widgeon seems to depend to some extent on the existence of eel-grass. This is a grass-like plant of the shore, which some twenty years ago mysteriously died out in many districts. With its disappearance the Widgeon often went too.

Scaup.—The Scaup has a black head, grey back, and white sides. In winter, the only season when it is likely to be seen on the Firth, the Scaup frequents coastal waters in flocks of varying size.

Common Eider.—The Eider drake, with its bold white and black plumage and large wedge-shaped bill, is now a familiar sight round rocky shores of the Firth of Clyde. It is, nevertheless, only during the last 25 years that it has become so. The Clyde area was probably populated by Eiders from Colonsay, where the birds multiplied rapidly, largely as the result of protection by Lord Colonsay towards the end of last century. It has also been suggested that its spread in the Clyde is connected with an increase in mussels on the shores, for Eiders feed largely on that mollusc.

Common Scoter.—The plumage is uniformly black. This is a winter visitor to the Clyde, and is now much more common than it used to be. It has been seen off the mouth of the River Doon, Ayrshire, in flocks of hundreds.

Red-breasted Merganser.—The dark, crested head, chestnut breast, and slender red bill make this a very handsome bird. We may be pleased that it is increasing in the Clyde area, where it has made remarkable progress in the present century. It eats a good deal of fish, and around the coast dives for small cod, coal-fish, and plaice ; but in fresh water, which it commonly frequents in the Highlands, it takes trout and young salmon, and the angler is not its friend.

Cormorant.—The dark, ungainly figure of the Cormorant standing motionless on a rock must be well known to many. On the sea it looks more at home, as it dives from the surface to swim under water in pursuit of its food, much of which is marketable fish. It does not breed commonly in the Clyde but quite often resorts to inland fresh-water lochs for this purpose.

Shag.—Often confused with the Cormorant, the Shag is rather smaller and more slender. Its habits are similar, but it takes few sea fish of economic importance. The Shag appears to be attached to one district, and even in winter it seldom wanders far. It nests on isolated rocky coasts along the Firth. Both the Cormorant and the Shag can often be seen standing with half-open wings, apparently drying them after a spell of fishing.

Seabirds, Shellfish and Seaweed

Gannet.—The Gannet is recognised by its large size, gleaming white plumage with black-tipped wings, and above all by its spectacular dives for fish. It nests on Ailsa, which it has been known to frequent since the 16th Century. The numbers there fluctuate between three and seven thousand breeding pairs. This is one of the few birds of which the world-population has been estimated ; in 1932 it was about 166,000 breeding birds. Throughout the summer Gannets wander over the Firth in search of shoals of fish, and for these they dive from heights up to a hundred feet or more. In winter the adults disperse to the South and West, many leaving the Clyde ; and young birds migrate southwards to African coastal waters.

Storm-Petrel.—This small dark sea-bird formerly bred on Ailsa and may still breed within the Clyde area as it is sometimes seen off-shore.

Manx Shearwater.—The Shearwater is black above and white below and flies low over the sea with a graceful skimming motion. Although it does not nest anywhere in the Clyde area, the Shearwater often gathers in large numbers on the calm evenings of late summer and autumn. These are birds which have finished breeding farther north, probably in the Hebrides, and are on their leisurely way southwards for the winter. Birds seen in the Clyde during the summer may be on feeding flights from their breeding quarters, for these flights are known to take them a hundred miles or more from the nest. Shearwaters seem to feed mainly on small fish, such as young herring.

Fulmar Petrel.—At first sight the Fulmar might be taken for one of the grey-backed gulls, but the thick-set head and neck and the gliding flight are typical. The Fulmar has spread from St Kilda, once its only British breeding ground, and by 1939 had nested on Ailsa. This colonisation is part of a spread round many parts of the British coast and results from a marked increase in numbers in its previous quarters. The tendency to colonise will probably continue, and we may look for new

251

breeding stations in the Firth where there are suitable cliffs. The Fulmar is one of the few birds to feed on plankton (the small floating organisms of the sea), and it also takes small molluscs, fish offal and oily matter floating on the surface.

Divers.—The slender body, neatly patterned black and white plumage, pointed bill, and diving habits are typical of this family.

Great Northern Diver.—This, the largest of our divers, is present in the Clyde during the autumn, winter and spring. Until early spring it is a rather undistinguished brown and whitish bird, but after moulting is very handsome in chequered black and white. It dives from the surface and swims expertly under water in pursuit of fish which constitute its common food.

Black-throated Diver.—In winter, when it visits the Clyde estuary in uncertain numbers, this bird is somewhat similar to the last species but is smaller.

Red-throated Diver.—This diver breeds in small numbers within the Clyde area, and is widely distributed on the Firth during the winter. In breeding plumage the brown upper parts and chestnut throat are characteristic, but in winter it is hard to distinguish it from the Black-throated Diver.

Rock Dove.—This dove, the stock from which our domestic birds were bred, frequents caves in rocky parts of the Clyde estuary.

Waders.—This is a very large group of birds generally associated with water, but not true sea-birds.

Oyster-catcher.—The bold, pied plumage, long orange-red bill, and red legs serve to distinguish this familiar bird of the shore. It nests in the Clyde area and is common within it at all seasons. Mussels, cockles, limpets and worms form a large part of its diet, and although, as its name suggests, it is able to open small oysters, it rarely takes them.

Ringed Plover.—In spite of its black collar and white neck and underparts, the Ringed Plover is inconspicuous on the shore, for its back is sand-coloured, and it is a small bird. It is quite common on sandy and pebbly beaches, and nests along our coasts. It runs quickly about the shore in search of its food, and it often flies in small flocks, each bird rising, turning, and banking in unison with its companions.

Lapwing.—Most people associate the crested Peewit with farm land, but it is also a visitor to the shores, especially in severe winter weather. The numbers of Lapwings are swollen in autumn by migrants from the Continent, and at this time many of our own birds pass across to Ireland for the winter.

Golden Plover.—In build this bird resembles a Lapwing. It lacks the crest, however, and is mottled golden brown above and whitish beneath in its winter plumage. It is in winter that it is found on the shore.

Grey Plover.—This is a winter visitor to our tidal flats, and is at that season very like the Golden Plover.

Turnstone.—The Turnstone is mottled brown, white and black, with orange legs. During the winter months it frequents the rocky shores of the Clyde but is never very common, and in spring all but a few stragglers desert us for their breeding quarters in Northern Europe.

Sanderling.—The Sanderling, out of its breeding plumage, is a small pale grey and white wader of the sandy beaches. It passes through our area on migration between its Siberian summer quarters and its southern winter quarters.

Knot.—This is another bird that comes to Britain for the winter, and it then looks like a large, heavy Sanderling. It can sometimes be seen in considerable flocks on the sands of the Ayrshire coast.

Dunlin.—In summer the chestnut back and black patch underneath distinguish this, the commonest of our waders, on the shore ; in winter the plumage is duller. As a breeding species the Dunlin resorts mainly to inland moors, but it is common on the shore at other seasons, either as a winter visitor or passage migrant.

Purple Sandpiper.—This wader frequents our rocky shores in winter, but is not very common. It is a small, sturdy, dark bird not easily confused with other shore birds.

Common Sandpiper.—The Sandpiper is quite a small bird, brown above and whitish below ; when disturbed it flies low over the water with wings alternately beating rapidly, and gliding. It is more familiar inland, by lochs and the banks of streams, than on the coast, but can be seen by the sea also, and in autumn it may come down to the estuaries and rocky shores as a first stage of its southward journey.

Redshank.—A very familiar shore bird at all seasons, the Redshank has mainly brownish plumage and long red legs. It appears to have a nervous nature, and when approached starts bobbing up and down, then flies off with a ringing flute-like cry.

Greenshank.—The Greenshank is a near relative of the Redshank, but is rather larger and has greenish legs. It is not a resident in the Clyde area but may spend some time on our coasts, for instance on the Ayrshire sands, during migration to and from its breeding places in the Highlands.

Bar-tailed Godwit.—The Godwit is one of our largest waders and has long legs and a long straight bill. It is a bird of passage over the Firth of Clyde, but is also seen in the winter.

Curlew.—The Curlew, with its long legs, brown plumage, and long, curved bill, is a well-known bird round the Clyde coast, and its musical call is no less familiar. At all seasons birds are found on the sands, rocks and estuaries, feeding at low water and retiring to nearby fields as the tide rises.

Whimbrel.—This bird looks like a small Curlew. It passes through the Clyde area only in migration and is never common.

Terns and Gulls.—The Gulls are too well known to need any introduction. The Terns can be distinguished from them by their slender graceful form, long, pointed wings, and forked tail, features which have earned them the name of " Sea Swallows."

Sandwich Tern.—The black bill and legs of this tern distinguish it from all others likely to be seen. It nests in small numbers in the Firth.

Roseate Tern.—The name refers to the delicate pink of the breast during the nesting season. The Roseate Tern, which is one of the rare British birds, was first recorded on the Eilans, Millport, in 1812. It disappeared as a nesting species in the Clyde in the second half of the 19th Century, but has quite recently nested again on an island in the Firth, and steps have been taken to protect it.

Common Tern.—This is one of our common sea birds in summer, particularly by low rocky shores and islands, where it nests in colonies. It is a beautiful bird in white plumage, black cap, and red legs. The terns are gregarious and noisy and, when fishing, flutter and hover over the sea and dive lightly into it for sand eels and other food.

Arctic Tern.—This species, scarcely distinguishable from the last, is a rather more northern bird, but it also breeds in the Clyde area, although in smaller numbers. Abroad it ranges as far as Siberia and Alaska in the nesting season and spans the globe in its great southward migration to reach the shores of the Antarctic Continent.

Little Tern.—The yellow bill and legs, and the smaller size, serve to identify this tern. It breeds within the area, but is not abundant.

Black-headed Gull.—This is a gull both of the shore and inland waters, and it has several large breeding colonies by fresh water lochs and reservoirs in the Clyde counties. It is, strictly, misnamed, as the head is chocolate coloured in summer and almost white in winter.

Common Gull.—This bird is about the same size as the last, but lacks the dark head and has greenish, instead of red, bill and legs. It also frequents inland as well as coastal waters, but as a nesting bird it is commonest in the Clyde on rocky shores and islets.

Herring Gull.—The Herring and the Lesser Black-backed Gulls are about the same size, the former being distinguished by its grey back and wings. Both gulls are great scavengers and also take many eggs of other birds.

Lesser Black-backed Gull.—Unlike the Herring Gull, which is present all the year round, the Lesser Black-backed Gull is only a summer visitor and is to be found nesting on several of our islands.

Great Black-backed Gull.—This resembles the previous bird, but is much larger and more powerful, and also much less common. It will eat almost any kind of animal matter that it can find or kill. It nests in a few places on the Clyde, and is present all the year round.

Kittiwake.—The Kittiwake is more truly marine than our other gulls. It cannot be called common, except in summer at Ailsa, where it nests on the cliffs. The adult is like a small, graceful Common Gull with dark legs, and the young have a dark half-collar and wing-bar. After breeding, the birds disperse in autumn, and only a few appear to remain in the Clyde area during the winter. The name is a good imitation of the call which can be heard from the nesting birds.

Skuas.—The Skuas are like the Gulls, but are either all brown or have a great deal of brown in the plumage. They are pirates by nature, and get much of their food by chasing other sea birds until they disgorge their catch, which the Skuas then promptly retrieve.

Great Skua.—This is a large bird, brown in colour. It is not common in the Firth, but perhaps it is often overlooked.

Arctic Skua.—This Skua has two colour patterns, some birds being all brown, and others brown above and whitish below.

FISHERMEN IN ACTION: Ring-net boats heading out of Campbeltown Loch against the morning sun. Davaar Island in background, left.

FISHERMEN AT REST: Ring-net boats of the Clyde herring fleet tied up in the inner harbour of Tarbert, Loch Fyne.

WAR AND PEACE: The Gareloch, looking south-west from Rhu, cluttered with surplus naval and merchant shipping after the Second World War.

PEACE: The outer Firth of Clyde from the Ayrshire coast near Skelmorlie. All the islands—Bute, the Cumbraes and Arran—rest immemorially in the sunset.

Seabirds, Shellfish and Seaweed

They do not nest here but pass through the area during migration.

Auks.—The Auks, to which the extinct Great Auk belonged, are birds of the open sea and wild rocky coasts. They never frequent sandy shores except when oiled and helpless, a condition too often their fate in the past.

Guillemot.—The dark brown upper and white under-parts and dark slender bill distinguish the Guillemot. It is rarely seen in flight, but often swimming or resting on the sea well off-shore. When alarmed it will often dive instead of flying off.

It is expert in diving for fish, in pursuit of which it swims under water, using its wings for propulsion. During the spring and summer great numbers of nesting Guillemots are found around the narrow ledges of Ailsa, and at other seasons it is more generally distributed in the Clyde area.

Black Guillemot.—This striking bird—in summer all black, with white wing patch and red legs—nests in small numbers in the Clyde area, and although not common it is worth looking out for.

Razorbill.—The name refers to the deep, compressed bill which, along with the black upper-parts, suffices to distinguish the Razorbill from its relative, the Guillemot. It also nests on Ailsa and frequents the Firth all the year round.

Little Auk.—The Little Auk, the smallest of its family, is a stumpy black-and-white bird, which properly belongs to the Arctic but visits us in variable numbers during the winter.

Puffin.—The Puffin is a strange-looking bird in the summer, with a huge red, blue, and yellow sheath on its bill. In winter this sheath is partly shed and the bill is duller. Formerly the Puffin nested abundantly on Ailsa, but it is thought that rats were responsible for the great reduction in numbers in recent years.

The Firth of Clyde

A NOTE ON SHELLFISH

The term Shellfish includes two very different kinds of animal-molluscs like the Oyster, Cockle and Mussel; and crustaceans such as the Lobster and Crab. Among the molluscs only the Clam and the Oyster have been of much economic importance in the Clyde area.

Clam.—More commonly known in the South as the Scallop, it is a large mollusc whose strongly-ribbed shells are sometimes found cast up on the shore. The *Queen* is a relative of the Clam, but is much smaller. Both kinds, which live in off-shore waters, can swim actively by vigorous flapping movements of the shells, and the Queen, at least, may migrate from place to place in this way.

The flesh of Clams is highly esteemed because of its delicate flavour, and fishing for Queens is an old-established occupation on the East coast of Scotland. In the Clyde an irregular fishery exists for the large Clams, and has greatly increased since the beginning of the century. It originated as a stop-gap occupation for fishermen whose principal trade had temporarily failed them, but as the value of the Clams became more apparent the fishery intensified.

Oyster.—The main Scottish oyster beds once lay along the East coast, and although very rich in their period, they are now almost extinct. On the West coast the only remaining fishery is that in Loch Ryan. The oysters of Loch Ryan are the remnants of imported French stock, and the annual yield is steadily decreasing.

Lobster.—This crustacean lives in waters where the bottom is rocky, and moves off-shore in winter and in-shore in summer, but only occasionally as far up the shore as the ebb line of spring tides. They are fished in many parts of the Firth of

258

Clyde and are landed chiefly at Campbeltown, Ballantrae, Inveraray and Rothesay.

A NOTE ON SEAWEEDS

In most parts of the comparatively sheltered Firth of Clyde seaweeds grow luxuriantly. There are three main groups of these plants, either green, brown or red in colour, but some of the last group may be difficult to distinguish from the brown seeweeds by colour alone. Plants of all three groups have long been used by Man for a variety of purposes in different parts of the world.

In parts of Scotland, crofters and farmers living near the coast often use the large brown seaweeds as cattle food and as manure, and their wives have long used the extract of small quantities of the red seaweeds, Carrageen and Dulse, to set milk-jellies. In former times the coast-dwellers burned the large brown seaweeds and extracted from the solidified ash, known as " kelp," at first soda and potash, and later iodine. The remains of the simple kilns in which the weeds were burned can still be seen in some places in the West of Scotland.

Nowadays, however, seaweeds are becoming increasingly important commercially, being used mainly as the source of two valuable jelly-like extracts ; one from the large brown seaweeds, known as Alginic acid, the other from certain red seaweeds, known as Agar.

Alginic acid is widely used in industry in the manufacture of fibres, thickeners, protective colloids and insulating material. The sodium and calcium salts of this acid find outlets in the production of textiles, plastics, transparent paper, cosmetics, films, ice-cream, salad-creams, custards, sauces and jellies ; they are also used as an emulsifier and binding material in pharmaceutical, medical and surgical preparations, and in the brewing industry.

The Firth of Clyde

The brown seaweeds, which are the raw material of this rapidly expanding industry, are especially well developed along the coasts of Scotland, and it has been estimated that Scottish seaweeds could support a chemical industry worth £15,000,000 a year. A recent survey carried out by the Scottish Seaweed Research Association has shown that at least 180,000 tons of the common brown shore weeds are available on the rocks between high-water and low-tide levels alone, some 70 per cent of this quantity occurring in the Outer Hebrides. In addition, from another survey it is estimated that over one million tons of "Tangles" grow around the Orkney Islands alone of the extensive Scottish beds of the large brown "Tangles," which grow from low-tide level down to a depth of six fathoms or more.

The Clyde Sea Area has good growths of these various brown seaweeds, especially along the coasts of Arran, the northern parts of Bute and the south-eastern coast of Kintyre, and at least one private firm has begun to harvest the Tangles growing in this area.

Agar is manufactured from the extract of two common red seaweeds, known collectively as Carrageen. One of the most important uses of this product is in medical and bacteriological work, but it is also widely used in the canning of meats and fish, in the preparation of table-jellies, as a thickening agent in creams and puddings, in greaseless cosmetics and in films as a constituent of various high-grade adhesives, and in many other products. The large-scale manufacture of Agar from British seaweeds is a comparatively new enterprise, for before 1939 the manufacture of best quality bacteriological Agar was almost entirely a monopoly of the Japanese. When this source of supply was cut off during the Second War, search was made for a British substitute, and from a survey of the whole coast of Great Britain it was found that the only suitable red seaweed available in sufficient quantity was Carrageen.

This weed had not been used before to make Agar, but scientists working at the Marine Station at Millport developed a technique for the extraction and refinement of a very good Agar from this source.

Some of the richest beds of Carrageen in Britain occur on the coasts of the islands and mainland of the Firth of Clyde, the seaweed growing as a dense reddish-brown mat on the lower half of the shore exposed by the receding tide. During and since the Second War, considerable quantities of Carrageen have been collected in this area.

Epilogue by way
of Farewell to the Firth

Any man's love of the Firth of Clyde is almost always nostalgic, a harking back to the best days of his life, as one has recalled the ecstasies of those Twins in our Introduction. The existence in Glasgow of the Clyde River Steamer Club, numerous and enthusiastic, witnesses to the existence of a regional cult : one had almost said of a regional poetry. The literature of the cult, ever since Captain Williamson produced his classic, had so grown by mid-Century that an enthusiast could line a shelf of his bookcase with works of specialised devotion. No newspaper on Clydeside need look far for a Silly Season topic of the most fruitful sort. Minor bards, some of them not wholly negligible, have recollected in tranquillity the raptures of evening cruises long ago and the pretty landfalls of youth ; even the German Band has been celebrated in song.

The nostalgia of the middle-aged apart, this mass sentimentality confesses a regret for glories departed beyond recall ; and it is the fact that, during the third, fourth and fifth decades of the 20th Century, much of the old gaiety and colour of the scene disappeared from the Firth of Clyde. Most of the causes of the change have already been explained and discussed, and we have seen that they arose mainly out of evolutionary tendencies in the economic and political fields. No doubt the Marxian economist would see the process as possessing an almost charming inevitability : from the scramble of private ownership to the still competitive efforts of railway companies ; from the workings of large railway groups largely directed from London to the logical but somewhat null conclusion of complete State control of all means of public transport. . . . It may be added that the Scottish Nationalist might reasonably be allowed his views on the subject.

We are not here, however, concerned with politics ; rather with the humanities which that bleak science is so often apt to ignore. We see merely that standardisation robbed the Firth of much colour, if only of those of the funnels and hulls of the three competing railway companies' fleets and those of their still-independent competitors. The layman sticks to the facts, and is incensed by them, that travel on the Firth of Clyde was infinitely cheaper (even relatively) in 1910 than it was in 1950, and that the traveller's range was vastly wider. There were more piers to call at, and therefore more happy landfalls to be enjoyed. In 1908 or thereabouts a young boy could have a monthly season ticket, entitling him to travel where he liked and as often as he liked in one railway company's vessels, for eleven shillings or thereabouts.

This convenience did, in fact, contribute its own coloured web to the pattern of social life in a large industrial area. Those Twins of 1908 and their parents were conforming exactly to the convention of the period. As school holidays were then devised in Scotland, the more substantial folk of the middle-classes took their " house at the Coast " for the month of July, the average furnished rent for a solid villa of up to even eight rooms, with the use of a rowing-boat thrown in, being about £20 for the month. For the month of August, when Papa had returned to business and Mama wished to have them off her hands, a great many boys of that class of society were given " a Season for the Boats " and daily dispatched, with a packet of sandwiches, to roam the Firth as they pleased.

The Firth of Clyde

. . . It is a pleasant memory that the ambition of every right-minded boy was to use as many steamers as possible in the course of a long summer's day. Thus a lad living in Greenock, for instance, could sail across the Firth to Kirn in the early morning and disembark. Waiting on the pier there with the golden patience of mechanically-minded boyhood— and he never had to wait very long—he took the next steamer to Dunoon, less than a couple of miles away. At this point he disembarked again to await the next boat for Innellan, another mere step westwards. From Innellan in due course he boarded still another vessel for Rothesay ; and so on and so on until, such being the facilities of the period, a tired boy, drugged with sea-air, could just find his way home in the late evening to boast of his so-many ships used during the day, of so-many miles of water covered.

There was keen competition among the youthful seafarers ; and one seems to remember the creation of a recognised record. This involved a split-second connection from Whiting Bay in Arran to Ardrossan on the Ayrshire coast and back while the Arran steamer from Greenock lay for an hour or two at the island pier. There was but a small margin of minutes either way, and many gallant attempts failed : the bad boys duly returned to their homes by rail from the mainland port, in disgrace before both stern parents and their coevals in the sport. . . .

In such ways, then, did the proportionately large if nominally *petite bourgeoisie* of a vast industrial concentration become so sentimentally and deeply attached to the estuarine playground beyond the gates of their suburban villas. In due course most of the young holders of Season Tickets would grow up to be small yachtsmen in early manhood. The tradition seemed to be founded on rock.

Even so, a regional cult could never depend only on such as the Twins and their parents. Up till the outbreak of the

Farewell to the Firth

First World War in 1914 the well-to-do, even the very rich, maintained their mansions and villas at the Coast, their fine yachts snubbing at moorings before the private slips ; while the poorest people of all looked no farther afield than Gourock or Dunoon or Rothesay, than Largs or Millport or Saltcoats, for their precious week of escape at the time of the Fair. A whole, large section of a given economic grouping was content to find its relaxation in places near home and within no more than a couple of hours' journey from Glasgow.

This accounts fairly enough for the cult of the river steamers of the day before yesterday. Many men not yet old were boys when the Firth of Clyde bubbled with action and colour, and they have seen during that brief space of historical time a vast number of levelling changes. They are in the same boat (the pun is accidental) with those who regret the passing of the Clippers on the high seas or the horse-drawn buses along the Strand. They are but nearly voiceless poets, almost inarticulately protesting against the ineluctable.

Among the appendices, in sets of facts and figures compiled by the Rev. William C. Galbraith (himself a native of Rothesay), the reader sufficiently interested in the statistics of such matters will discover a set of tables that clearly show the considerable decline in the tonnage and carrying capacity of the Firth of Clyde pleasure fleet during the first half of the 20th Century. These can be summarised briefly, thus :

In 1900 there were 42 paddle-steamers and four screw vessels at work on the Firth of Clyde during the summer months. In round figures, these were capable of carrying more than 52,000 passengers.

In 1910 the number of paddle-steamers in service had come down from 42 to 33, while the number of screw vessels had risen from four to eight : the latter including some sizeable turbine steamers of the new sort. The passenger-carrying capacity remained about the figure for 1900—just about 52,000.

By 1950, however, the number of steamers plying on the Firth of Clyde under the flag of British Railways was only 18 : 7 surviving paddlers and 11 screw-vessels, 3 of the latter being glorified launches, useful only over short distances, such as from Largs to Millport. Passenger-carrying capacity had fallen to 24,000 plus.

It will be noticed that the extended tables show that 1906 was the peak year of the Clyde Fleet, when it had a daily carrying capacity of 60,000 passengers—that is, on every working day of the season.

These figures seem to indicate something like the collapse of an old trade, but it is merely romantic to interpret them in political terms. We may very well agree that, say, 16 vessels in 1950 could not do the work done by 40 in 1910. We may even agree that the nationalised service was, in 1950, rather less gracious and intimate than the service of even the railway groups in 1939. We make every allowance for the fact that improved living and working conditions for crews in terms of Mr. Attlee's mandate reduced the passenger-carrying capacity of the few ships remaining in the Firth of Clyde trade. The difference between a daily potential of 52,000 passengers in 1910 and of only 24,000 in 1950, however, has still to be explained ; and it is explicable rather in terms of mechanics —or logistics, if you please—than in those of the —ologies.

It is instructive next to take the passenger piers of the estuary and observe how many of them have been demolished or closed since 1914. No pleasure steamer is ever likely to ply again on the Gareloch, and of six piers along those gentle coasts only one or two were being used in 1950 for occasional naval purposes. Two out of five piers within the short Holy Loch disappeared during the Wars. Within the Kyles of Bute only the pier at Tighnabruaich remained in use. Roughly, of rather more than 50 piers that were all more or less busy in 1910, rather less than one-half remained open by mid-Century, and that with a much-reduced volume of traffic in most cases. The last of the old ship-to-shore ferries, were among the first casualties of Hitler's War.

Here is the master key to the problem. The internal combustion engine arrived to compete with the steam-driven ship.

Just as the development of railways out of Glasgow affected many mainland piers during the second half of the 19th Century, so did the motor-bus in particular completely remove any economic justification for the existence of so many closely spaced piers even on one of the islands. The mere stopping and starting of a steamer at and from a pier costs money ; and if we complain that once upon a time any honest man could get from Glasgow to Arran through Ardrossan in 85 minutes, we must see that the motor-coaches waiting at any terminal pierhead can distribute the steamboat passengers to their nearby destinations with a swiftness and cheapness beyond " the Boats."

In another way the development of the private motor-car affected the Firth of Clyde trade. This vastly widened the holiday range of those solid citizens who, with their seaside villas, owned or rented, had been the props and stays of many resorts along miles of coast. When it became more convenient to drive from Glasgow to your seaside home at, say, Cove, and that in your own private conveyance, then the pier at Cove was obviously doomed. When buses waited at the railway terminus of Helensburgh to carry humbler folks round the shores of the Gareloch, then the small piers at Rhu, Shandon, Garelochhead, Mambeg, Clynder and Rosneath must put up the shutters against the economic blizzard. It is, however, one of the nice little ironies of the situation that such communities as Cove and Kilcreggan, their development encouraged in the first place by the steamboat, were lifted out of the doldrums of near-stagnation when the cheap and reliable motor-car came to give the city workers easier access to those peninsular settlements than the steamboats could ever contrive.

Geography plays another trick on the traveller in these regions. It is difficult to transport a motor-car from one side of the Firth to the other, almost impossible to carry a motor-bus. This is due in part to the considerable rise and fall of the tides, and to the fact that neither the piers nor the pleasure steamers were designed (as they are on the Norwegian fjords) for vehicular traffic. A great many holidaymakers were still eager in mid-Century to take their cars to Arran, for instance, and that could be contrived, but the operation depended on tidal conditions at Ardrossan and Brodick respectively, and the allotted time of embarkation of the vehicle usually failed to coincide with that of the family party.

As we have noted, the establishment of a vehicular ferry across the Kyles of Bute at Colintraive in 1950 seemed likely to affect the island's economy in a considerable degree, but a fantastic and picturesque paradox remained.

Any man may halt his car beside the Cloch Lighthouse on the Renfrewshire coast and look across the widening Firth to Dunoon in Argyllshire. The distance is little more than two miles. But if the motorist aims to reach Dunoon he must, short of an elaborate arrangement with British Railways, make a detour of more than 100 miles by way of the vehicular ferry at Erskine on the Ship-Channel and over roads that are largely narrow and tortuous, rising at one point to a height of nearly 900 feet above sea-level !

The internal combustion engine still more subtly affected the ways of people and pleasure steamers. It had the large and immeasurable effect of widening the human horizons.

Farewell to the Firth

The devotion of the industrial folk of Lowland Scotland to the Firth of Clyde during the 19th Century came mainly of a static—or shall we call it "modest"?—condition of mind, deriving in part from limited social experience, in part from the religious inhibitions of the race, and in part from the absence of what are nowadays called "tourist facilities." It is no exaggeration to say that in any small community in Scotland about the turn of the century a person who had visited Paris, for instance, was by way of being a landmark, duly pointed out as such : even if a retired shipmaster, rolling along the same promenade with a weatherly eye on the behaviour of the Firth, had been in every considerable port of the wide world. Retired sea-captains and chief-engineers were two-a-penny in every town and hamlet on the Clyde Coast from Gourock down to Campbeltown, but the independent traveller for pleasure abroad was almost a monstrosity.

This comfortable and unadventurous attitude began to change during the First World War. It is perhaps not too fanciful to suggest that the conflict brought the Continent nearer than it ever had been before ; a grave in Flanders could set up a new and sharp, if bitter, sense of the smallness of the world. Meanwhile the motor-car of the well-to-do led to adventure far afield, just as the motor-bus of the less well-to-do took them far beyond Dunoon and Rothesay, as we have observed in another context, to Blackpool and Scarborough. If they still must travel by sea, they made for the Isle of Man and the Channel Islands.

Given a second War with its fantastic ramifications, and it was nothing for a party of lads from Clydeside to hitch-hike their way from Glasgow to Switzerland and back. Meanwhile, the reduction of middle-class incomes, along with Service experience during that Second War, swept away many of the old social barriers, so that the managing director's son, for example, became perfectly happy along the road in the company of a dock labourer in the strange, new *camaraderie* of adventure shared outdoors.

The issues hereabouts are subtle and, in 1950, it was hardly possible to discern how the structure of British society was likely to shape itself under so many new and often disconcerting pressures. It is much more to our point now that the various forces indicated above explain adequately enough the decline of the smaller Clyde Coast resorts and of the steamboat services that once so abundantly enriched them.

It is well also to make a small note to the effect that the middle-class family, occupying a seaside villa for a month on end *circa* 1906, could do so only with the help of cheap female labour. That was no longer available in 1950, and the economic fact hastened the collapse of a social convention. The well-to-do drifted towards the hotels ; the furnished villas became boarding-houses. Already the great seaside houses of the prosperous were largely given over to the shelter of the aged or the sick, of the convalescent or the mentally deficient.

One last twist of the economic screw hurt the natives of the Firth of Clyde region rather more in their pride than through their pockets. This was the virtual desertion of the harbour by transatlantic liners during the second, third and fourth decades of the 20th Century.

Until the outbreak of the First War regular services from the Clyde to New York on the one hand and the St Lawrence ports on the other were run by two great shipping concerns based on Glasgow, the Anchor Line and the Allan Line. On any Saturday of those distant days the big ships would be lying at the Tail of the Bank, waiting for the boat trains to rocket down the hill from Glasgow ; while, every Sunday, one of the Anchor Liners, the *Columbia*, the *Caledonia* or the *Cameronia*, the black funnels and white upperworks gleaming in the sun, would come up from the sea as regular as the clock. This trade, prosperous in its day, depended largely on mass-emigration from Central Europe and the Baltic countries as well as from Scotland itself, however, and it declined with the slackening of the popular impulse towards the Promised Lands of North America.

The Allan Line was ultimately merged in the Canadian Pacific group, and while the Anchor Line faithfully maintained its New York service until the outbreak of the Second War, the drifts of trade latterly directed its sailings towards India and the East and mainly from southern ports. The post-war shortage of shipping, and the high costs of any diversion, along with the ever-increasing flexibility of internal communications, finally robbed the Clyde of its status as a transatlantic port. This fate was also determined in part by the lack of deep-water berthage and dry-docking facilities for very large ships in the neighbourhood of Greenock.

In 1950 such issues remained mere matters of debate, and we leave the topical subject with a bald record of the fact that, in that middle year of the century, and in strict relation to the demands of the tourist industry, a liner of the Canadian Pacific Railway, only once a fortnight and only during the summer months, cruised up the Firth under the peaks of Arran to lie for a brief space of time at the Tail of the Bank and then to go its ways.

The Firth remains ; and beauty remains even in the vestigial and decaying relics of industrial man's endeavour to create pleasure domes of his own along those lovely shores. The phenomena we have considered at such length have been largely social and concerned mainly with the events of 150 restless years ; we have looked at this northern estuary mainly as a cockpit of the human frenzies during a period of expansion.

Short of another geological cataclysm, the physical entity remains much as it was when Haco of Norway sailed his longboats with their carven prows up Loch Long and down Loch Lomond itself. We cannot guess how human restlessness may have shaped the Clyde and its Firth by 2050, but we may be reasonably sure that Ailsa Craig will still be there, the sea-birds overcrowding its cliffs and rising in fleecy, fluttering clouds at any alarm. The waters of the lochs and the kyles will still be moving in their priestlike task, assuming on a quiet evening their low-toned but vibrant and powerful colours. It is hard to think that a hopeful boy, with a crude fly at the end of a bit of string tied to a bough of hazel, will not somewhere be fishing from the rocks.

THE END

APPENDIX I

Comparative Cost of Yachts

YEAR	COST TO BUILD	2ND HAND PRICE	COST OF SUIT OF SAILS	NO. OF PAID HANDS	WAGES WEEKLY	LAYING UP AND OVERHAUL	INSURANCE
1912							
60 ton Schooner or Ketch - - -	£4,500	£3,000	£200	Six	£11 10/-	£280	£50
20 ton Racing Yacht - - -	£1,600	£700	£100	Five	£10	£120	£35
22 ft. Cruising Yacht, 3 berths, no engine	£150	£110	£15	None	—	£12	Nil
1936							
60 ton Auxiliary Cruising Ketch, -	£8,400	£6,500	£400	Four	£14 15/-	£500	£140
8 Metre, - - - - -	£2,500	£1,000	£180	Three	£12	—	£70
6 ton Auxiliary Cruiser, 3 berths, -	£750	£650	—	—	—	£25	£18
1946							
60 ton Cruising Ketch, - - -	£15,600	—	£850	Three	£20 10/-	£800	£450
6 Metre, - - - - -	£2,200	—	£280	One	£8 10/:	£160	£50
6 ton Auxiliary, 3 berth, - - -	£1,600	£1,600	£70	—	—	£50	£25
Dragon Racing Yacht, - - -	£1,000	£950 Average	—	—	—	—	—

POWER YACHTING

1912, - - Steam Yachts from 25 to 1500 tons. Annual Expenditure could be anything from £500 to £50,000 per annum.

1912, - - First 30-ft. Motor Cruisers appear on Clyde. Total cost, new, £350 to £450.

1936, - - Steam Yachts disappearing. The Diesel Motor Yacht had now come into the picture.

COMPARATIVE COST OF YACHTS

YEAR	NEW COST	2ND HAND PRICE	NO. OF CREW	WAGES WEEKLY	LAYING UP AND OVERHAUL	INSURANCE
1936						
80 ton Diesel Motor Yacht, - - -	£9,600	—	Four	£23 10/-	£250	£180
25 ton Motor Yacht, - - -	£3,200	£2,500	One	£3 10/-	£110	£60
15 ton Motor Yacht - - -	£2,000	£1,500	—	Owner-driven Family boats	£60	£35
9 ton Four berth - - - -	£850	£650	—	Owner-driven Family boats	£32	£50
1946						
70 ton Motor Yacht, - - -	£20,000	—	Three	£23 10/-	£550	£500
34 ton Motor Yacht - - -	£8,500	—	One	£8 10/-	£180	£130
15 ton Motor Yacht, - - -	£4,000	£4,000	—	—	£85	£80
1950†						
34 ton Motor Yacht, - - -	£10,000	£750 Max.*		Sailing Yachts: Now practically only two classes being built.		
Dragon, - - - -	£950					
Loch Long Class, - - -	£380					

* A marked drop here in 2nd-hand prices, due to the large Clyde class of well over 40 boats, and a consequent larger number changing hands each winter.

† The effects of devaluation and increasing cost of wages and materials making themselves felt.

Lifeboat Stations and Services

In amplification of the material contained in Chapter VIII The Royal National Life-Boat Institution has kindly provided the following statistical record :

EXISTING STATIONS	YEAR ESTAB-LISHED	LAUNCHES ON SERVICE	LIVES RESCUED
CAMPBELTOWN - - -	1861	133	341
GIRVAN - - - - -	1865	88	73
PORTPATRICK - - - -	1877	113	129
TROON - - - - -	1871	73	97
		407	640

CLOSED STATIONS	YEAR ESTAB-LISHED	YEAR CLOSED	LAUNCHES ON SERVICE	LIVES RESCUED
ARDROSSAN - - -	1869	1930	32	132
AYR - - - -	1802	1932	20	71
ISLE OF ARRAN - -	1870	1901	17	27
BALLANTRAE - -	1871	1919	9	14
IRVINE - - -	1834	1914	21	70
MACHRIHANISH - -	1911	1931	—	—
SOUTHEND - - -	1869	1930	15	4
			114	318

The life-boats on active service in 1950 were :

CAMPBELTOWN   Motor Barnett Stromness, type 51 ft. by 13 ft. 6 ins. " City of Glasgow." Provided by the Institution's Funds and named in recognition of support given by Glasgow.

GIRVAN   Motor Self-Righting type, 35 ft. 6 ins. by 8 ft. 10 ins. " Lily Glen—Glasgow." Gift of Mrs. Lawrence Glen of Glasgow.

PORTPATRICK   Motor Watson Cabin type, 46 ft. by 12 ft. 9 ins. " Jeanie Speirs." Gift of the late Miss E. S. Paterson, of Paisley.

TROON   Motor Watson type, 40 ft. 6 ins. by 11 ft. 8 ins. " Sir David Richmond of Glasgow." Provided by Legacy of Lady Richmond of Glasgow and gift of Mrs. A. J. J. R. Fairlie, of Glasgow.

Clyde Passenger Vessels, 1900-1950

In the following tables, compiled by the Rev. William C. Galbraith, the symbols used are :

GT—Gross Tonnage at the time. This is apt to be a variable factor.

UDT—Under Deck Tonnage, the best basis of comparison between one hull and another, but not the basis of passenger counting.

PASS—Number of Passengers carried on Steam 5 Certificate of the Board of Trade i.e. to Rothesay.

P—Paddle steamers ; S—Screw steamers.

The phrase " Winter and Occasions " refers to the practice of using relatively small West Highland vessels on the curtailed services of the winter months and for emergencies. The purpose of including these seasonal visitants in the count is that of arriving at the maximum figure of carrying capacity within the Firth in any one year.

TABLES

A—The Fleet in 1900
B—Profit and Loss—1900-1906
C—The Fleet in 1910
D—The Fleet in 1950

TABLE A : 1900—46 Vessels plus 4 Winter & Occasions

PADDLE 42

BUILT	Vessel	GT	UDT	PASS
1878	Columba	543·29	543	2,116
1864	Iona	395·89	387	1,400
1891	Lord of the Isles	465·89	421	1,624
1879	Edinburgh Castle	260·98	224	1,028
1875	Windsor Castle	223	195	978
1891	Carrick Castle	592	456	1,300
1891	Isle of Arran	312·53	254	1,350
1877	Isle of Bute	248·05	225	1,017
1864	Vivid	163·99	164	890
1884	Duchess of York	258	234	998
1871	Heather Bell	271	261	1,000
1897	Strathmore	315·53	261	1,113
1876	Benmore	235·01	198	954
1899	Waverley	448·52	354	1,467
1898	Kenilworth	332·99	262	1,230
1896	Talisman	278·88	252	1,233
1895	Redgauntlet	276·56	255	1,114
1891	Lady Rowena	362·36	220	938
1895	Dandie Dinmont	218·05	204	961
1898	Lucy Ashton	271·27	205	903
1891	Lady Clare	257	166	709
1885	Diana Vernon	192·78	159	732
1892	Glen Sannox	609·65	486	1,701
1898	Juno	591·63	437	1,497
1896	Jupiter	394·33	359	1,406
1892	Mercury	378·02	340	1,267
1892	Neptune	378·02	340	1,267
1875	Viceroy	236	201	1,140
1893	Minerva	306·45	269	1,035
1893	Glen Rosa	306·45	269	1,035
1868	Marquis of Bute	196	163	781
1880	Chancellor	272	214	881
1890	Duc. of Hamilton	552·71	472	1,780
1889	Galatea	330·96	303	1,307
1895	Duc. of Rothesay	384·85	309	1,376
1883	Meg Merrilees	279	226	1,004
1891	Mar. of Lorne	294·84	262	1,159
1880	Ivanhoe	281·87	272	1,198
1890	Mar. of Bute	246·22	223	1,119
1890	Mar. of Breadalbane	246·22	223	1,119
1889	Caledonia	244·44	222	1,093
1886	Madge Wildfire	210·41	196	983

WINTER & OCCS. 4

BUILT	Vessel	GT	UDT	PASS
1885	Grenadier	357	300	[1,150
1866	Chevalier	334·46	287	1,074
1888	Fusilier	280	242	1,078
1858	Mountaineer	178	157	753

SCREW 4

BUILT	Vessel	GT	UDT	PASS
1885	Davaar	568	422	1,175
1878	Kinloch	427	343	887
1868	Kintyre	314	280	701
1882	Minard Castle	246	180	403

		GT	UDT	PASS
	Total Screw	1,482	1,225	3,066
	Total Paddle	13,693·65	1,626	49,183
	Grand Total	15,175·65	2,851	52,249
	Winter & Occasions	1,149·46	986	4,055
	Total Plus	16,325·11	3,837	56,304

TABLE B : 1900-1906—when also 46 vessels plus 4 Winter & Occasions
(MAXIMA occurred in both 1900 and 1906)
In this table the names italicized are those of vessels broken up or sold out of the Firth

BUILT		GT	UDT	PASS		GT	UDT	PASS
1875	P Windsor Castle	223	195	978	Total in 1900 1st Max.	15,175·65	12,851	52,249
1891	P Carrick Castle	592	456	1,300	Loss in 1900	1,086	912	3,278
1871	P Heather Bell	271	261	1,000	Balance to 1901	14,089·65	11,939	48,971
1901	S King Edward	562·37	456	1,994				
1880	P Chancellor	272	214	881				
1885	P Diana Vernon	192·78	159	732	Loss in 1901	181·41	143	623
1883	P Meg Merrilees	279	226	1,004	Balance to 1902	13,908·24	11,796	48,348
1902	S Queen Alexandra	665	558	2,077				
1902	P Duc. of Montrose	322	293	1,221				
1902	P Mars	317	289	1,291	Gain in 1902	777·65	746	2,761
1891	P Lady Rowena	362·36	220	938	Balance to 1903	14,685·89	12,442	51,109
1864	P Vivid	163·99	164	890				
1877	P Lady of the Isles	451	369	1,450	Gain in 1903	787	660	2,656
1903	P Duch. of Fife	336	291	1,206	Balance to 1904	15,472·89	13,102	53,765
1897	P Vulcan	318	261	1,113				
1904	S Cygnet	191	150	200	Loss in 1904	138	121	574
1877	P Lady of the Isles	451	369	1,450	Balance to 1905 and on to 1906	15,334·89	12,981	53,191
1868	P Marquis of Bute	196	163	781				
1906	S Duc. of Argyll	593	445	1,713				
1906	S Atalanta	486	358	1,414	Gain to July, 1906	1,225	923	3,633
1906	P Marmion	403	286	1,215	Balance to August 2nd Max.	16,559·89	13,804	56,824
1891	P Lady Clare	257	166	709				
	MAXIMUM Paddle 37 : Screw 9							
1889	P Galatea	330·96	303	1,307	Loss in August	330·96	303	1,307
					Balance to 1907	16,228·93	13,501	55,517
						17,709·25	14,790	60,879

MAXIMUM in July, 1906, plus Winter & Occasions 4

TABLE C: 1910—41 Vessels plus 4 Winter & Occasions

PADDLE 33

BUILT		GT	UDT	PASS
1878	Columba -	602·24	538	2,116
1864	Iona -	395·89	387	1,400
1891	Lord of the Isles -	465·89	421	1,624
1879	Edinburgh Castle -	260·98	224	1,028
1910	Eagle III -	392	317	1,315
1891	Isle of Arran -	312·53	254	1,350
1877	Isle of Bute -	248·05	225	1,017
1884	Isle of Cumbrae -	258	234	998
1897	Kylemore -	318	261	1,113
1876	Benmore -	235·01	198	934
1899	Waverley -	448·52	354	1,457
1906	Marmion -	403	286	1,215
1898	Kenilworth -	332·99	262	1,230
1896	Talisman -	278·88	252	1,233
1895	Dandie Dinmont -	218·05	204	1,008
1898	Lucy Ashton -	271·27	205	903
1892	Glen Sannox -	609·65	486	1,701
1888	Juno -	591·63	437	1,447
1896	Jupiter -	394·33	359	1,406
1892	Mercury -	378·02	340	1,267
1892	Neptune -	378·02	340	1,267
1902	Mars -	317	289	1,291
1893	Minerva -	306·45	269	1,035
1893	Glen Rosa -	306·45	269	1,035
1890	Duc. of Hamilton	552·71	472	1,780
1895	Duc. of Rothesay -	384·85	309	1,376
1903	Duc. of Fife -	336	291	1,206
1902	Duc. of Montrose	322	293	1,221
1891	Mar. of Lorne -	294·84	262	1,159
1880	Ivanhoe -	281·87	272	1,198

BUILT		GT	UDT	PASS
1890	Mar. of Breadalbane -	246·22	223	1,119
1889	Caledonia -	244·44	222	1,093
1886	Madge Wildfire -	210·41	196	983
	WINTER & OCCASIONS 4			
1886	Grenadier -	357	300	1,150
1866	Chevalier -	334·46	287	1,074
1888	Fusilier -	280	242	1,078
1910	Mountaineer -	235	182	851
	SCREW 8			
1902	Queen Alexandra	665	558	2,077
1901	King Edward -	551	456	1,994
1906	Duc. of Argyll -	593	445	1,713
1906	Atalanta -	486	358	1,414
1885	Davaar -	495	422	1,294
1878	Kinloch -	427	433	887
1904	Cygnet -	191	150	544
1882	Minard Castle -	246	180	403
	Total Screw -	654	2,912	10,326
	Total Paddle -	14,596·11	9,951	41,585
	Grand Total -	15,250·11	12,863	51,911
	Winter & Occasions -	1,206·46	1,011	4,153
	Total Plus	16,456·57	13,874	56,064

TABLE D : 1950—15 vessels plus 3 small plus 4 Winter & Occasions

BUILT			GT	UDT	PASS
PADDLE 7					
	1931 Jeanie Deans	-	813·59	418	1,480
	1946 Waverley	- -	693·13	391	1,350
	1937 Jupiter -	- -	641·91	432	1,509
	1934 Caledonia	- -	623·36	437	1,766
	1935 Talisman	- -	544·01	327	1,259
	1935 Mar. of Lorne	-	427·47	259	1,233
	1903 Duc. of Fife	- -	329·18	291	1,101
SCREW 11					
(8 plus 3 small)					
	1912 St. Columba -	-	827	557	1,800
	1933 Q. Mary II -	-	870·50	572	1,928
	1932 Duc. of Hamilton	-	785·92	542	1,918
	1930 Duc. of Montrose	-	806·27	537	1,937
	1925 Glen Sannox -	-	689·92	465	1,622
	1906 Duc. of Argyll	-	583	445	1,514
	1901 K. Edward -	-	562·37	456	1,966
	1936 Mar. of Graham	-	585·13	442	1,300
	1938 Leven - -	-	38·26	38	112
	1938 Ashton - -	-	38·26	38	112
	1935 Wee Cumbrae	-	37·16	37	65
WINTER &					
OCCASIONS 4					
	1926 King George V	-	791	528	1,905
	1931 Lochfyne	- -	754	355	1,202
	1934 Lochnevis	- -	568	313	723
	1939 Lochiel -	- -	580	299	817
in 1950	Total Screw -	- -	5,833·79	4,129	14,598
,,	Total Paddle -	- -	4,082·65	2,555	9,698
,,	*Grand Total* -	- -	9,916·44	6,684	23,970
	Winter & Occs. -	-	2,693	1,495	4,447
,,	*Total Plus* -	- -	12,609·44	8,179	28,417

A Short Bibliography

GENERAL

The River Clyde and the Clyde Burghs. By Sir James D. Marwick. (Maclehose, 1909.)
Ordnance Gazeteer of Scotland. 6 vols. (Jack, 1882-85.)
The History of Greenock. By Robert Murray Smith. (Orr, Pollock, 1921.)
The History of Port Glasgow. By William Forrest Macarthur. (Jackson, Wylie, 1932.)
Days at the Coast. By Hugh Macdonald. (Murray, Glasgow, 1857.)
Down to the Sea. By George Blake. (Collins, 1937.)
The Book of Arran. 2 vols. (Hugh Hopkins for the Arran Society of Glasgow, 1910 and 1914.)

SHIPPING AND NAVIGATION

The Clyde Passenger Steamer. By Captain James Williamson. (Maclehose, 1904.)
Brown's Nautical Almanac, current issue.
Reports of the Royal National Life-Boat Institution.
Sailing Directions—West Coast of Scotland. (Clyde Cruising Club.)
British Yachts and Yachtsmen. By C. Bateman. (Yachtsman Publishing Co., 1907.)

NATURAL HISTORY, ETC.

British Sea Fishermen. By Peter F. Anson. (Collins, 1944.)
The Fish Gate. By Michael Graham. (Faber, 1949.)
The Fishes of the British Isles. By J. Travis Jenkins. (Warne, 1925.)
Men and Herring. By Naomi Mitchison and Denis Macintosh. (Serif Books, 1949.)
The Birds of the Firth of Clyde. By J. M. McWilliam. (Witherby, 1936.)
Bird Recognition, Vol. I: Sea-Birds and Waders. By James Fisher. (Penguin Books.)
A Study of Certain British Seaweeds, etc. By Marshall, Newton and Orr. (H.M.S.O., 1949.)
Annual Reports, Scottish Seaweed Research Association, Musselburgh.
The Sea Shore. By C. M. Yonge. (Collins, 1949.)
The Geology of Arran. By G. W. Tyrrell. (H.M.S.O., 1928.)
Fauna, Flora and Geology of the Clyde Area. Various Contributors. (British Association, 1901).

Index

Index

history, 146-48; its distilleries, 146, 147; its colliery workings, 147; its fishing industry, 147, 148
Campbeltown lifeboat, 230
Campbeltown Loch, 71, 148
Canals, 129, 130
Canoeing Clubs, 206
Carradale, 146
Carrageen seaweed, 260, 261
Carrick, 142
Carrick Highlands, 142
Catacol, 177
Cavendish-Bentincks, The, 134
Chemical resources, 260
Clarence, The, 210
Climbing Clubs for unemployed, 197
Cloch Lighthouse, 101, 227
Cloy glen, 172
Clyde, Firth of, its course and history, 51, 52; its tides, 52, 66, 74; its upward extension, 55; its depth, 58-60, 62, 63, 65, 66, 69, 70, 160, 189; its underwater configurations, 58; its fitness as one of the world's greatest harbours, 59; tidal race, 60; defence needs and public amenities, 64; war uses, 60, 61, 62, 64, 70, 72; its industries, 71, 72, 75, 77, 78, 99-101, 103, 127, 128, 130, 132, 136, 139, 141-43, 145-48, 152, 153, 162, 170, 171, 184, 185; its proportion of ocean water, 73; the measured miles, 112, 231-34; land-holding curb on exploitation, 157; navigation, 226; signalling apparatus, 230, 231; transatlantic shipping, 270, 271
Clyde Lighthouse Trust, 225, 226, 228.
Clyde Passenger Steamers, by Captain James Williamson, 79
Clyde Passenger Steamers, 125, 150, 151, 162, 163, 171, 183, 203, 262, 263; Henry Bell's *Comet* the pioneer, 75; its first successor, the *Elizabeth*, 76; sailings to Ireland and London, 77; their creation of a tourist industry, 78; James Williamson's history of the steamers, 79; cut-throat private enterprise, 80; development of coast resorts, 80, 81; cheap and extensive journeys, 82; rise of new type of passenger, 83; Captain Williamson's *Ivanhoe*, 84; railway companies and the steamboat business, 85-88; the R.M.S.

Columba, 89, 90; the cult of the Clyde steamer, 90; racing between rival vessels, 90; competition between three railway companies, 91, 130; creation of the turbine steamer, 91-93; the "Sunday-breakers," 94, 97; railway rivalry ended by amalgamations, 95, 96; decline of the services, 96, 265, 266; steamers' influence on social life, 263, 264; the Clyde piers, 266, 267
Clyde Pilotage Authority, 225
Clyde river: its source, tributaries, course and history, 52, 53; its fish, 52
Clyde River Steamer Club, 90
Clyde Sea Area, 57-59, 73
Clyde Sea Area: fishes and fisheries, 235-45; (*see also* Fish); birds, 246-57 (*see also* Sea Birds); shell fish, 258
Clyde Ship Channel, 55, 56, 74, 100, 107, 224
Clyde Trust, 224, 225
Clydesdale horses, 152
Clydeside as a playground, 203-206; pleasure resorts and a new social set-up, 78, 80, 81, 183, 184
Coal mining, 71, 147
Cobbler, The, 63
Colintraive, 66, 67, 125, 268
Colquhouns of Luss, 196
Colquhoun, Sir Iain, 198
Colquhoun of Luss, Sir James, 94, 95, 107, 108, 134, 157
Columba, R.M.S., 89, 90
Columban missionaries, 179
Columbia, S.S., 270
Comet, The, 75, 76, 103, 204
Commissioners of Northern Lighthouses, 225
Corra Linn, 53
Corrie, 180
Corrie, High, 180
Corsewall Point Lighthouse, 229.
Coulport, 121
Courtauld, 218
Cove, 81, 110, 111
Cowal, 60, 62, 66, 73
Cowal coast, 59
Cowal narrows, 67
Cowal peninsula, 65
Craigendoran, 86
Crichton-Stuarts, The, 158
Cross of Lorraine, 97
Culdee recluse, The, 186

283

Index

Index

Glasgow *Journal*, 107

Glasgow & South-Western Railway, 85, 86, 141

Glasgow & South-Western Railway Steamboats, 88, 95

Glenashadale, 176

Glen Caladh, 68

Glendaruel valley, 67

Gleneagles, 141

Glen Sannox, 180

Goatfell, 170, 172

Goil, Loch, 59, 62-64, 122

Golborne, John, 54

Golf courses, 128, 129, 132, 135, 146, 160, 167

Gourock, 86, 102, 104-106, 112

"Granny Kempock," 104, 105

Great Bank, 56

Greenock, 52-54, 56, 86; its loss of sovereignty, 55; its physical aspects, 97, 98; its war casualties, 99; its early history, 99, 100; its golden age during Napoleonic wars, 100; its sugar refining industry, 100; decline of shipowning business, 101; its shipbuilding and engineering, 101; plans for a new town, 101

Greenock Harbour Trustees, 223

Hambrough, Windsor Dudley Cecil, 68

Hamilton family, The, 182

Harmony, The Brig, 54, 55

Helensburgh, 60, 61, 75, 76, 107-110, 112, 204

Helensburgh, The, 210

Henderson's of Meadowside, 214

Herring curing, 104

Herring fisheries, 71, 99, 104, 136, 145, 162, 235-39

Herrings, freshwater, 199

"Highland Mary," 115

Hikers, landowners attitude towards, 198

Hiking by unemployed, 197

Holiday camps, 73, 139, 172

Holiday habits, Clydeside, 131

Holy Isle, 169, 173, 185, 186

Holy Isle Lighthouse, 229

Holy Loch, 64, 65, 122, 212

Houston, 101

Humphrey Clinker, by Smollett, 191

Hunter, Leslie, 195

Hunter's Quay, 122

Hutton, Miss Barbara, 218

Hydro-electric development, 194

Inchcape, Lord, 218

Inchlonaig, 191

Inchtavannich, 201

Industrial Revolution, The, 56

Inglis, A. & J., 216

Innellan, 123, 124

Inveraray, 70, 82, 144, 145

Inversnaid, 193, 194

Irvine, 72, 129, 131, 132

Irvine Bay, 127

Ivanhoe, The, 84, 85, 87

James IV of Scotland, 104

James Watt, The, 77

Johnson, Dr. Samuel, 201

Kames, 125, 126

Kames Bay, 160, 166

Kames Castle, 158

Kean, Edmund, 159

Kean's cottage, 159

Kelvin, Lord, 217

Keppel, 167

Kidnapped, by R. L. Stevenson, 144

Kilbrennan Sound, 58, 69, 177

Kilchattan Bay, 155

Kilcreggan, 81, 110, 111

Kildonan, 176

Kilmun, 64, 122, 123

Kintyre, 58

King Edward, The, 92, 93

King's Cross, 174

Kipling, Rudyard, 82

Kip Valley, 101

Knowles, Sheridan, 160

Kyles of Bute, 59, 65, 66, 68-70, 74, 124, 125, 151

Lady Isle, 134

Lagg, 177

Lamlash, 150, 173, 174, 185

Lamlash Bay, 74, 172

Lamont, Mary, 104

Lanark, 53

Lanarkshire, 52

Land-holding in Scotland, 157

Largs, 81, 118-21

Largs, Battle of, 120

Lendalfoot, 142

Leven, River, 195, 199

Leven, Vale of, 195

Lifeboats, 230

Lighthouses, 101, 182, 227-229

285

Index

Index

Index

Smollett, Tobias, 191, 201
Souter Johnny, 139
Spens family, 158
Steam shipbuilding, 75-77, 79, 80, 84, 89, 91, 92
Steele's of Greenock, 101, 211
Stevenson, Robert Louis, 142
Stewart, James, of Appin, 144
Stewarts of Scotland, Royal, 160, 179
Strachur, 70
Stranraer, 71, 72, 143
Stranraer, coast road to, 140
Strathnaver, Lord, 107
" String," The, 181
Striven, Loch, 65, 66
Strone, 122
Strone Point, 65
Submarine base, 71
Sugar refining, 100
" Sunday-breakers," 94, 95, 157

Tam o' Shanter, 139
Tannahill, Robert, 129
Tarbet, 193
Tarbert, 71, 145
Tarbert, East Loch, 71
Telford, Thomas, 54
Thomson, J. & G., 89
Thomson, Sir William, 217
Tighnabruaich, 125
Tiree Island, 158
Toward Point, 124
Trespass, Scottish law of, 198
Troon, 72, 128, 129, 132-134, 141
Troon Lifeboat, 230
Turbine engine, The, 91, 92
Turbine Syndicate, The, 91
Turnberry, 141
Turnberry Castle, 141
Turnberry Lighthouse, 141, 182, 229
Tyrrell, Dr. G. W., 182

Vanguard, H.M.S., 233
Victoria, Queen, 191, 201

Watson, G. L., 214, 216, 230
Watt, James, 76
Wemyss Bay, 86, 112, 113
Wester Kames, 158
Western Yacht Club, The, 212
West Highland Railway, 63
West Kilbride, 97, 128
Whistlefield, 62
Whiting Bay, 172, 174-176
Williamson, Alexander, 87
Williamson, Captain James, 78-80, 82-84, 87, 91, 262
Williamson, Captain John, 87, 91, 93
Windsor, Duke of, 160
Wood, Messrs., boatbuilders, 76
Wordsworth, Dorothy, 196, 201
Wordsworth, William, 190, 194

Yacht building, 209, 216, 217, 210, 211
Yachting, 122, 165, 204, 209, 212, 213
Yachting Clubs: Clyde Corinthian Yacht Club, 212; Clyde Cruising Club, 213, 220; Clyde Model Yacht Club, 212; Mudhook Yacht Club, 212; Northern Yacht Club, 211; Royal Clyde Yacht Club, 212; Royal Gourock Yacht Club, 212; Royal Largs Yacht Club, 212; Royal Northern Yacht Club, 165, 211, 213; Western Yacht Club, 212
Yacht racing, 213-217
Yachts: The Bluebell, 217; The Bona, 216; The Britannia, 214, 216; The Erin, 218; the Kariad, 216; The Meteor, 214; The Nahlin, 218; The Rover, 218; Shamrock II, 216; The Thistle, 216; The Troubadour, 218; The Valkyrie II and III, 216; The Vanduara, 216; The Virginia, 218
Yachts, steam, 210, 217, 218
Youth Hostels, 199
Youth Hostels Association, 197
Yule, Lady, 218